Spectral Feature Selection
for Data Mining

Chapman & Hall/CRC
Data Mining and Knowledge Discovery Series

SERIES EDITOR
Vipin Kumar
University of Minnesota
Department of Computer Science and Engineering
Minneapolis, Minnesota, U.S.A

AIMS AND SCOPE

This series aims to capture new developments and applications in data mining and knowledge discovery, while summarizing the computational tools and techniques useful in data analysis. This series encourages the integration of mathematical, statistical, and computational methods and techniques through the publication of a broad range of textbooks, reference works, and handbooks. The inclusion of concrete examples and applications is highly encouraged. The scope of the series includes, but is not limited to, titles in the areas of data mining and knowledge discovery methods and applications, modeling, algorithms, theory and foundations, data and knowledge visualization, data mining systems and tools, and privacy and security issues.

PUBLISHED TITLES

UNDERSTANDING COMPLEX DATASETS:
DATA MINING WITH MATRIX DECOMPOSITIONS
David Skillicorn

COMPUTATIONAL METHODS OF FEATURE SELECTION
Huan Liu and Hiroshi Motoda

CONSTRAINED CLUSTERING: ADVANCES IN
ALGORITHMS, THEORY, AND APPLICATIONS
Sugato Basu, Ian Davidson, and Kiri L. Wagstaff

KNOWLEDGE DISCOVERY FOR COUNTERTERRORISM
AND LAW ENFORCEMENT
David Skillicorn

MULTIMEDIA DATA MINING: A SYSTEMATIC
INTRODUCTION TO CONCEPTS AND THEORY
Zhongfei Zhang and Ruofei Zhang

NEXT GENERATION OF DATA MINING
Hillol Kargupta, Jiawei Han, Philip S. Yu,
Rajeev Motwani, and Vipin Kumar

DATA MINING FOR DESIGN AND MARKETING
Yukio Ohsawa and Katsutoshi Yada

THE TOP TEN ALGORITHMS IN DATA MINING
Xindong Wu and Vipin Kumar

GEOGRAPHIC DATA MINING AND
KNOWLEDGE DISCOVERY, SECOND EDITION
Harvey J. Miller and Jiawei Han

TEXT MINING: CLASSIFICATION, CLUSTERING, AND
APPLICATIONS
Ashok N. Srivastava and Mehran Sahami

BIOLOGICAL DATA MINING
Jake Y. Chen and Stefano Lonardi

INFORMATION DISCOVERY ON ELECTRONIC HEALTH
RECORDS
Vagelis Hristidis

TEMPORAL DATA MINING
Theophano Mitsa

RELATIONAL DATA CLUSTERING: MODELS,
ALGORITHMS, AND APPLICATIONS
Bo Long, Zhongfei Zhang, and Philip S. Yu

KNOWLEDGE DISCOVERY FROM DATA STREAMS
João Gama

STATISTICAL DATA MINING USING SAS APPLICATIONS,
SECOND EDITION
George Fernandez

INTRODUCTION TO PRIVACY-PRESERVING DATA
PUBLISHING: CONCEPTS AND TECHNIQUES
Benjamin C. M. Fung, Ke Wang, Ada Wai-Chee Fu, and
Philip S. Yu

HANDBOOK OF EDUCATIONAL DATA MINING
Cristóbal Romero, Sebastian Ventura,
Mykola Pechenizkiy, and Ryan S.J.d. Baker

DATA MINING WITH R: LEARNING WITH
CASE STUDIES
Luís Torgo

MINING SOFTWARE SPECIFICATIONS: METHODOLOGIES
AND APPLICATIONS
David Lo, Siau-Cheng Khoo, Jiawei Han, and Chao Liu

DATA CLUSTERING IN C++: AN OBJECT-ORIENTED
APPROACH
Guojun Gan

MUSIC DATA MINING
Tao Li, Mitsunori Ogihara, and George Tzanetakis

MACHINE LEARNING AND KNOWLEDGE DISCOVERY FOR
ENGINEERING SYSTEMS HEALTH MANAGEMENT
Ashok N. Srivastava and Jiawei Han

SPECTRAL FEATURE SELECTION FOR DATA MINING
Zheng Alan Zhao and Huan Liu

Spectral Feature Selection
for Data Mining

Zheng Alan Zhao
Huan Liu

CRC Press
Taylor & Francis Group
Boca Raton London New York

CRC Press is an imprint of the
Taylor & Francis Group, an **informa** business

A CHAPMAN & HALL BOOK

CRC Press
Taylor & Francis Group
6000 Broken Sound Parkway NW, Suite 300
Boca Raton, FL 33487-2742

© 2012 by Taylor & Francis Group, LLC
CRC Press is an imprint of Taylor & Francis Group, an Informa business

No claim to original U.S. Government works

Printed in the United States of America on acid-free paper
Version Date: 20111028

International Standard Book Number: 978-1-4398-6209-4 (Hardback)

Visit the Taylor & Francis Web site at
http://www.taylorandfrancis.com

and the CRC Press Web site at
http://www.crcpress.com

To our parents:

HB Zhao and GX Xie
— ZZ
BY Liu and LH Chen
— HL

and to our families:

Guanghui and Emma
— ZZ
Lan, Thomas, Gavin, and Denis
— HL

Contents

Preface

This book is for people interested in feature selection research. Feature selection is an essential technique for dimensionality reduction and relevance detection. In advanced data mining software packages, such as SAS Enterpriser Miner, SPSS Modeler, Weka, Spider, Orange, and scikits.learn, feature selection procedures are indispensable components for successful data mining applications. The rapid advance of computer-based high-throughput techniques provides unparalleled opportunities for humans to expand capabilities in production, services, communications, and research. Meanwhile, immense quantities of high-dimensional data keep on accumulating, thus challenging and stimulating the development of feature selection research in two major directions. One trend is to improve and expand the existing techniques to meet new challenges, and the other is to develop brand new techniques directly targeting the arising challenges.

In this book, we introduce a novel feature selection technique, *spectral feature selection*, which forms a general platform for studying existing feature selection algorithms as well as developing novel algorithms for new problems arising from real-world applications. Spectral feature selection is a unified framework for supervised, unsupervised and semi-supervised feature selection. With its great generalizability, it includes many existing successful feature selection algorithms as its special cases, allowing the joint study of these algorithms to achieve better understanding and gain interesting insights. Based on spectral feature selection, families of novel feature selection algorithms can also be designed to address new challenges, such as handling feature redundancy, processing very large-scale data sets, and utilizing various types of knowledge to achieve multi-source feature selection.

With the steady and speedy development of feature selection research, we sincerely hope that this book presents a distinctive contribution to feature selection research, and inspires new developments in feature selection. We have no doubt what feature selection can impact on the processing of massive, high-dimensional data with complex structure in the near future. We are truly optimistic that in another 10 years when we look back, we will be humbled by the accreted power of feature selection, and by its indelible contributions to machine learning, data mining, and many real-world applications.

The Audience

This book is written for students, researchers, instructors, scientists, and engineers who use or want to apply feature selection technique in their research or real-world applications. It can be used by practitioners in data mining, exploratory data analysis, bioinformatics, statistics, and computer sciences, and researchers, software engineers, and product managers in the information and analytics industries.

The only background required of the reader is some basic knowledge of linear algebra, probability theory, and convex optimization. A reader can acquire the essential ideas and important concepts with limited knowledge of probability and convex optimization. Prior experience with feature selection techniques is not required as a reader can find all needed material in the text. Any exposure to data mining challenges can help the reader appreciate the power and impact of feature selection in real-world applications.

Additional Resource

The material in the book is complemented by an online resource at http://dmml.asu.edu/sfs.

Acknowledgments

We are indebted and grateful to the following colleagues for their input and feedback on various sections of this work: Jiepying Ye, Lei Wang, Jiangxin Wang, Subbarao Kambhampati, Guoliang, Xue, Hiroshi Motoda, Yung Chang, Jun Liu, Shashvata Sharma, Nitin Agarwal, Sai Moturu, Lei Tang, Liang Sun, Kewei Chen, Teresa Wu, Kari Torkkola, and members of DMML. We also thank Randi Cohen for providing help in making the book preparation a smooth process. Some material in this book is based upon work supported by the National Science Foundation under Grant No. 812551. Any opinions, findings, and conclusions or recommendations expressed in this material are those of the authors and do not necessarily reflect the views of the National Science Foundation.

Zheng Alan Zhao Huan Liu
Cary, NC Tempe, AZ

Authors

Dr. Zheng Alan Zhao is a research statistician at the SAS Institute, Inc. He obtained his Ph.D. in Computer Science and Engineering from Arizona State University (ASU), and his M.Eng. and B.Eng. in Computer Science and Engineering from Harbin Institute of Technology (HIT). His research interests are in high-performance data mining and machine learning. In recent years, he has focused on designing and developing novel analytic approaches for handling very large-scale data sets of extremely high dimensionality and huge sample size. He has published more than 30 research papers in the top conferences and journals. Many of these papers present pioneering work in the research area. He has served as a reviewer for over 10 journals and conferences. He was a co-chair for the PAKDD Workshop on Feature Selection in Data Mining 2010. More information is available at http://www.public.asu.edu/~zzhao15.

Dr. Huan Liu is a professor of Computer Science and Engineering at Arizona State University. He obtained his Ph.D. in Computer Science from the University of Southern California and his B.Eng. in Computer Science and Electrical Engineering from Shanghai Jiaotong University. He was recognized for excellence in teaching and research in Computer Science and Engineering at Arizona State University. His research interests are in data mining, machine learning, social computing, and artificial intelligence, investigating problems that arise in many real-world applications with high-dimensional data of disparate forms such as social media, group interaction and modeling, data preprocessing (feature selection), and text/web mining. His well-cited publications include books, book chapters, and encyclopedia entries as well as conference and journal papers. He serves on journal editorial boards and numerous conference program committees, and is a founding organizer of the International Conference Series on Social Computing, Behavioral-Cultural Modeling, and Prediction (`http://sbp.asu.edu/`). More information is available at `http://www.publi.asu.edu/~huanliu`.

Symbol Description

n	Number of instances	$\mathbf{C}$	Covariance matrix
m	Number of features	$\mathbf{I}$	Identity matrix
C	Number of classes	$\mathbf{1}$	$\mathbf{1} = [1, \ldots, 1]^{\top}$
l	Number of selected features	λ	A regularization parameter
$\mathbb{F}$	A set of features	$\mathcal{K}^{FEA}$	Knowledge sources related to features
F_i	The i-th feature		
$\mathbf{X}$	Data matrix	$\mathcal{K}^{SAM}$	Knowledge sources related to instances
$\mathbf{f}_i$	The i-th feature vector, $\mathbf{X} = [\mathbf{f}_1, \ldots, \mathbf{f}_m]$	$\mathcal{K}^{int}$	Internal knowledge
$\mathbf{x}_i$	The i-th instance, $\mathbf{X} = [\mathbf{x}_1, \ldots, \mathbf{x}_n]^{\top}$	$\mathcal{K}^{ext}$	External knowledge
		$\exp(\cdot)$	Exponential function
$\mathbf{y}$	Target vector	$\log(\cdot)$	Logarithm function
$\mathbf{Y}$	Target matrix	$\|\cdot\|$	A norm
$\mathbf{W}$	Weight matrix	$\|\mathbf{a}\|_2$	L_2 norm of vector $\mathbf{a}$
$\mathbf{w}^i$	The i-th row of the weight matrix $\mathbf{W}$	$\|\mathbf{a}\|_1$	L_1 norm of vector $\mathbf{a}$
		$\|\mathbf{a}\|_0$	L_0 norm of vector $\mathbf{a}$
$\mathbf{R}$	Residual matrix	$\|\mathbf{A}\|_2$	L_2 norm of matrix $\mathbf{A}$
$\mathcal{A}$	Active set	$\|\mathbf{A}\|_{2,1}$	$L_{2,1}$ norm of matrix $\mathbf{A}$
$\mathbb{G}$	A graph	$\|\mathbf{A}\|_F$	Frobenius norm of matrix $\mathbf{A}$
$\mathbf{S}$	Similarity matrix	$\mathcal{M}(\cdot)$	Model function
$\mathbf{A}$	Adjacency matrix	$\text{Trace}(\cdot)$	Trace of a matrix
$\mathbf{L}$	Laplacian matrix	$Card(\cdot)$	Cardinality of a set
$\mathbf{D}$	Degree matrix	$\varphi(\cdot)$	Feature ranking function
$\mathcal{L}$	Normalized Laplacian matrix, $\mathcal{L} = \mathbf{D}^{-1/2}\mathbf{L}\mathbf{D}^{-1/2}$	$Q(\cdot)$	Q function
		$\mathbb{R}$	Real numbers
ξ_i	The i-th eigenvector	$\mathbb{R}^n$	Real n-vectors ($n \times 1$ matrices)
λ_i	The i-th eigenvalue		
$\mathbf{K}$	Kernel matrix	$\mathbb{R}^{n \times m}$	Real $n \times m$ matrices

Chapter 1

Data of High Dimensionality and Challenges

Data mining is a multidisciplinary methodology for extracting nuggets of knowledge from data. It is an iterative process that generates predictive and descriptive models for uncovering previously unknown trends and patterns via analyzing vast amounts of data from various sources. As a powerful tool, the data mining technology has been used in a wide range of profiling practices, such as marketing, decision-making support, fraud detection, and scientific discovery, etc. In the past 20 years, the dimensionality of the data sets involved in data mining applications has increased dramatically. Figure 1.1 plots the dimensionality of the data sets posted in the UC Irvine Machine Learning Repository [53] from 1987 to 2010. We can observe that in the 1980s, the maximal dimensionality of the data is only about 100; in the 1990s, this number increases to more than 1500; and in the 2000s, it further increases to about 3 millon. The trend line in the figure is obtained by fitting an exponential function on the data. Since the y-axis is in logarithm, it shows the increasing trend of the dimensionality of the data sets is exponential.

Data sets with very high (>10,000) dimensionality are quite common nowadays in data mining applications. Figure 1.2 shows three types of data that are usually of very high dimensionality. With a large text corpus, using the bag-of-words representation [49], the extracted text data may contain tens of thousands of terms. In genetic analysis, a cDNA-microarray data [88] may contain the expression of over 30,000 DNA oligonucleotide probes. And in medical image processing, a 3D magnetic resonance imaging (MRI) [23] data may contain the gray level of several million pixels. In certain data mining applications, involved data sets are usually of high dimensionality, for instance, text analysis, image analysis, signal processing, genomics and proteomics analysis, and sensor data processing, to name a few.

The proliferation of high-dimensional data within many domains poses unprecedented challenges to data mining [71]. First, with over thousands of features, the hypothesis space becomes huge, which allows learning algorithms to create complex models and overfit the data [72]. In this situation, the performance of learning algorithms likely degenerates. Second, with a large number of features in the learning model, it will be very difficult for us to understand the model and extract useful knowledge from it. In this case, the interpretability of a learning model decreases. Third, with a huge number of

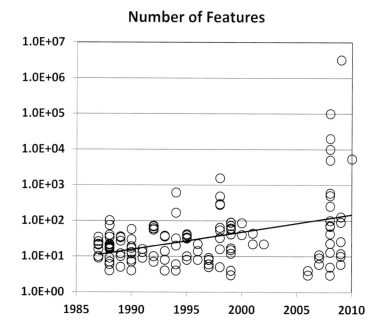

FIGURE 1.1: The dimensionality of the data sets in the UC Irvine Machine Learning Repository. The x-axis is for time in year and the y-axis is for dimensionality. The y-axis is logarithmic. It shows an exponentially increasing trend of data dimensionality over time.

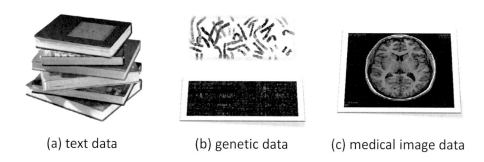

(a) text data   (b) genetic data   (c) medical image data

FIGURE 1.2: Text data, genetic data, and image data are usually of high dimensionality.

features, the speed of a learning algorithm slows down and their computational efficiency declines. Below is an example that shows the impact of the data dimensionality on learning performance.

Example 1 *Impact of data dimensionality on learning performance*

When data dimensionality is high, many of the features can be irrelevant or redundant. These features can have negative effect on learning models, and decrease the performance of learning models significantly.

To show this effect, we generate a two-dimensional data set with three classes, whose distribution is shown in Figure 1.3. We also generate different numbers of irrelevant features and add these features to the data set. We then apply a k nearest neighbor classifier (k-nn, k=3) with 10-fold cross-validation on the original data set as well as the data sets with irrelevant features. The obtained accuracy rates are reported in Figure 1.4(a). We can observe that on the original data set, the k-nn classifier is able to achieve an accuracy rate of 0.99. When more irrelevant feature are added to the original data set, its accuracy decreases. When 500 irrelevant features are added, the accuracy of k-nn declines to 0.52. Figure 1.4(b) shows the computation time used by k-nn when different numbers of irrelevant features are added to the original data. We can see when more features present in the data, both the accuracy and the efficiency of the k-nn decrease. This phenomenon is also known as the curse of dimensionality, which refers to the fact that many learning problems become less tractable as feature number increases [72].

1.1 Dimensionality Reduction Techniques

In data mining applications with high-dimensional data, dimensionality reduction techniques [107] can be applied to reduce the dimensionality of the original data and improve learning performance. By removing the irrelevant and redundant features in the data, or by effectively combining original features to generate a smaller set of features with more discriminant power, dimensionality reduction techniques bring the immediate effects of speeding up data mining algorithms, improving performance, and enhancing model comprehensibility. Different types of dimensionality reduction techniques generally fall into two categories: *feature selection* and *feature extraction*.

Figure 1.5 shows the general idea of how feature selection and feature extraction work. Given a large number of features, many of these features may be irrelevant or redundant. Feature selection achieves dimensionality reduc-

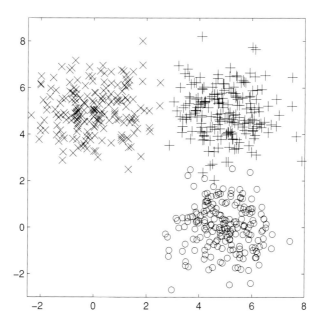

FIGURE 1.3: A two-dimensional data set of three different classes.

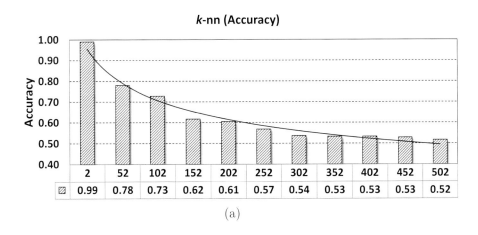

(a)

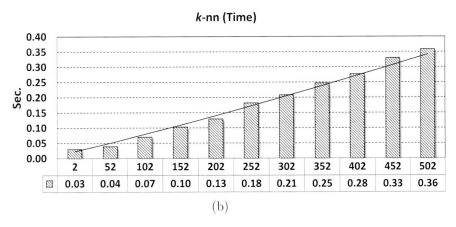

(b)

FIGURE 1.4: Accuracy (a) and computation time (b) of k nearest neighbor classifier ($k = 3$), when different numbers of irrelevant features are added to the data.

tion by removing these irrelevant and redundant features. To achieve this, a feature evaluation criterion is used with a search strategy to identify the relevant features. And a selection matrix $\mathbf{W}$ is used to filter the original data set and generate a reduced data set containing only the relevant features.[1] Unlike feature selection, feature extraction achieves dimensionality reduction by combining the original features with a weight matrix $\mathbf{W}'$ to generate a smaller set of new features.[2] In the combination process, the irrelevant and redundant features usually receive zero or very small coefficients, therefore have less influence on the newly generated features. One key difference between feature selection and feature extraction is that the data set generated by feature selection contains the *original features*, while the data set generated by feature extraction contains a set of *newly generated features*.

Feature selection and feature extraction each have their own merits. Feature selection is able to remove irrelevant features and is widely used in data mining applications, such as text mining, genetics analysis, and sensor data processing. Since feature selection keeps the original features, it is especially applicable in applications where the original features are important for model interpreting and knowledge extraction. For instance, in genetic analysis for cancer study, our purpose is not only to distinguish the cancerous tissues from the normal ones, but also to identify the genes that induce cancerogenesis. Identifying these genes helps us acquire a better understanding on the biological process of cancerogenesis, and allows us to develop better treatments to cure the disease.

By combining the original features, feature extraction techniques are able to generate a set of new features, which is usually more compact and of stronger discriminating power. It is preferable in applications such as image analysis, signal processing, and information retrieval, where model accuracy is more important than model interpretability.

The two types of dimensionality reduction techniques have different strengths and are complementary. In data mining applications, it is often beneficial to combine the two types of techniques. For example, in text mining, we usually apply feature selection as the first step to remove irrelevant features, and then use feature extraction techniques, such as Latent Semantic Indexing (LSI) [100], to further reduce dimensionality by generating a small set of new features via combining original features.

In this book, we will present a unique feature selection technique called *spectral feature selection*. The technique measures feature relevance by conducting spectral analysis. Spectral feature selection forms a very general framework that unifies existing feature selection algorithms, as well as various feature extraction techniques. It provides a platform that allows for the joint study of a variety of dimensionality reduction techniques, and helps us achieve a better understanding on them. Based on the spectral feature se-

---

[1]The element of a selection matrix is either 0 or 1. More details about the selection matrix will be discussed in Section 1.2.1.

[2]The element of a weight matrix can be any real number.

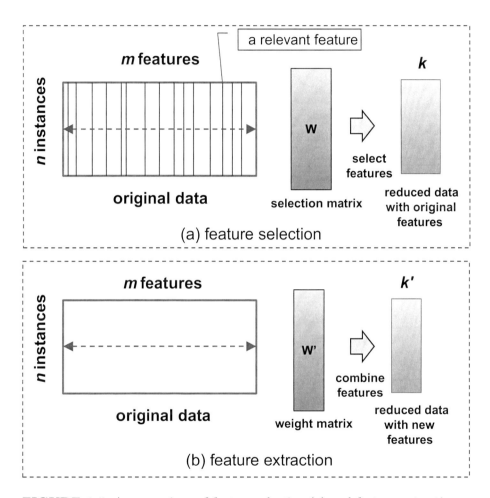

FIGURE 1.5: A comparison of feature selection (a) and feature extraction (b).

lection framework, we can also design novel feature selection algorithms to address new problems, such as handling large-scale data and incorporating multiple types of knowledge in feature selection, which cannot be effectively addressed by using existing techniques. Below, we start with a brief introduction to the basic concepts of feature selection.

1.2 Feature Selection for Data Mining

Feature selection [108, 109] in data mining has been an active research area for decades. The technique has been applied in a variety of fields, including genomic analysis [80], text mining [52], image retrieval [60, 180], and intrusion detection [102] to name a few. Recently, there have been several good surveys published that systematically summarize and compare existing works on feature selection to facilitate the research and the application of the technique. A comprehensive survey of existing feature selection techniques and a general framework for their categorization can be found in [113]. In [67], the authors review feature selection algorithms from a statistical learning point of view. In [147], the authors provide a good survey for applying feature selection techniques in bioinformatics. In [80], the authors review and compare the filter with the wrapper model for feature selection. And in [121], the authors explore the representative feature selection approaches based on sparse regularization, which is a branch of embedded feature selection techniques. Representative feature selection algorithms are also empirically evaluated in [114, 106, 177, 98, 120, 179, 125] under different problem settings and from different perspectives to provide insight into existing feature selection algorithms.

1.2.1 A General Formulation for Feature Selection

Assume we have a data set $\mathbf{X} \in \mathbb{R}^{n \times m}$, with m features and n samples (or instances, data points). The problem of feature selection can be formulated as

$$\max_{\mathbf{W}} \; r\left(\widehat{\mathbf{X}}\right)$$
$$s.t. \quad \widehat{\mathbf{X}} = \mathbf{XW}, \; \mathbf{W} \in \{0,1\}^{m \times l},$$
$$\mathbf{W}^{\top} \mathbf{1}_{m \times 1} = \mathbf{1}_{l \times 1}, \; \| \mathbf{W} \mathbf{1}_{l \times 1} \|_0 = l. \qquad (1.1)$$

In the above equation, $r\left(\cdot\right)$ is a score function to evaluate the relevance of the features in $\widehat{\mathbf{X}}$: the more relevant the features, the greater the value. $\mathbf{W}$ is the selection matrix, whose element is either 0 or 1. And $\| \cdot \|_0$ is the vector zero norm [59], which counts the number of nonzero elements in the vector. The constraints in the formulation ensure that: (1) $\mathbf{W}^{\top} \mathbf{1}_{m \times 1} = \mathbf{1}_{l \times 1}$: each column of $\mathbf{W}$ has one and only one "1." This ensures the original features rather than a linear combination of them to be selected; (2) $\| \mathbf{W1}_{l\times 1} \|_0 = l$: among the m rows of $\mathbf{W}$, only l rows contain one "1," and the remaining $m - l$ rows are zero vectors; (3) $\widehat{\mathbf{X}} = \mathbf{XW}$: $\widehat{\mathbf{X}}$ contains l different columns of $\mathbf{X}$. This guarantees that l of the m features are selected, and no feature is repeatedly selected. Altogether, the three constraints ensure that $\widehat{\mathbf{X}}$ contains l different original features of $\mathbf{X}$. The selected l features can be expressed as $\widehat{\mathbf{X}} = \mathbf{XW} = (\mathbf{f}_{i_1}, \ldots, \mathbf{f}_{i_l})$, where $\{i_1, \ldots, i_l\} \subseteq \{1, \ldots, m\}$, and usually, $l \ll m$. Clearly, if $r(\cdot)$ does not evaluate features independently, this problem is non-deterministic polynomial-time (NP) hard. Therefore, to make the problem solvable, we usually assume features are independent or their interaction order is low [220].

Example 2 *Filtering a data set with a selection matrix*

Figure 1.6 shows how a selection matrix can be used to filter a data set with the selected features. The data set $\mathbf{X}$ contains three features, and we want to select the first and the third features (corresponding to the first and the third columns of $\mathbf{X}$). To achieve this, we create a matrix $\mathbf{W}$ that has two columns. The first element of the first column and the third element of the second column are set to 1, and all the other elements of $\mathbf{W}$ are set to 0. $\mathbf{X} \times \mathbf{W}$ results in a data set $\widehat{\mathbf{X}}$ containing the first and the third columns of $\mathbf{X}$.

$$\begin{bmatrix} 1 & 7 & 3 \\ 5 & 6 & 4 \\ 10 & 9 & 8 \end{bmatrix} \times \begin{bmatrix} 1 & 0 \\ 0 & 0 \\ 0 & 1 \end{bmatrix} = \begin{bmatrix} 1 & 3 \\ 5 & 4 \\ 10 & 8 \end{bmatrix}$$

$$X \quad \times \quad W \quad = \quad \widehat{X}$$

FIGURE 1.6: A selection matrix for filtering data with the selected features.

1.2.2 Feature Selection in a Learning Process

Figure 1.7 shows a typical learning process with feature selection in two phases: (1) feature selection, and (2) model fitting and performance evaluation. The feature selection phase has three steps: (a) generating a candidate set containing a subset of the original features via a certain research strategy; (b) evaluating the candidate set and estimating the utility of the features in the candidate set. Based on the evaluation, some features in the candidate set may be discarded or added to the selected feature set according to their relevance; and (c) determining whether the current set of selected features are good enough using a certain stopping criterion. If so, the feature selection algorithm returns the set of selected features, otherwise it iterates until the stopping criterion is met. In the process of generating the candidate set and evaluation, a feature selection algorithm may use the information obtained from the training data, the current selected features, the target learning model, and some given prior knowledge [76] to guide their search and evaluation. Once a set of features is selected, it can be used to filter the training and the test data for model fitting and prediction. The performance achieved by a particular learning model on the test data can also be used as an indicator for evaluating the effectiveness of the feature selection algorithm for that learning model.

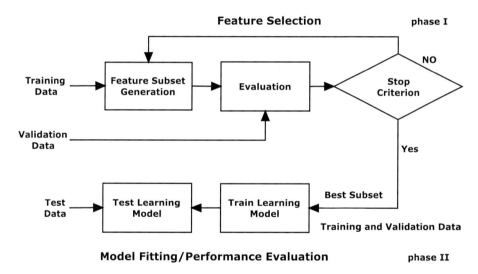

FIGURE 1.7: A learning process with feature selection.

1.2.3   Categories of Feature Selection Algorithms

Feature selection algorithms can be classified into various categories from different perspectives. Below we show five different ways for categorizing feature selection algorithms.

1.2.3.1   Degrees of Supervision

In the process of feature selection, the training data can be either labeled, unlabeled, or partially labeled, leading to the development of *supervised*, *unsupervised*, and *semi-supervised* feature selection algorithms. In the evaluation process, a supervised feature selection algorithm [158, 192] determines feature relevance by evaluating their correlation with the class or their utility for creating accurate models. And without labels, an unsupervised feature selection algorithm may exploit feature variance or data distribution to evaluate the feature relevance [47, 74]. A semi-supervised feature selection algorithm [221, 197] can use both labeled and unlabeled data. The idea is to use a small amount of labeled data as additional information to improve the performance of unsupervised feature selection.

1.2.3.2 Relevance Evaluation Strategies

Different strategies have been used in feature selection to design feature evaluation criteria $r\,(\cdot)$ in Equation (1.1). These strategies broadly fall into three different categories: the *filter*, the *wrapper*, and the *embedded* models.

To evaluate the utility of features in the evaluation step, feature selection algorithms with a filter model [80, 147, 37, 158, 74, 112, 98, 222, 161] rely on analyzing the general characteristics of features, for example, the features' correlations to the class variable. In this case, features are evaluated without involving any learning algorithm. The evaluation criteria $r\,(\cdot)$ used in the algorithms of a filter model usually assume that features are independent. Therefore, they evaluate features independently, $r\left(\widehat{\mathbf{X}}\right) = r\left(\mathbf{f}_{i_1}\right) + \ldots + r\left(\mathbf{f}_{i_k}\right)$. Based on this assumption, the problem specified in Equation (1.1) can be solved by simply picking the top k features with the largest $r\,(\mathbf{f})$ value. Some feature selection algorithms with a filter model also consider low-order feature interactions [70, 40, 212]. In this case, heuristic search strategies, such as greedy search, best first search, and genetic-algorithmic search can be used in a backward elimination or a forward selection process for obtaining a suboptimal solution.

Feature selection algorithms with a wrapper model [80, 91, 92, 93, 111, 183, 110] require a predetermined learning algorithm and use its performance achieved on the selected features as $r\,(\cdot)$ to estimate feature relevance. Since the predetermined learning algorithm is used as a black box for evaluating features, the behavior of the corresponding feature evaluation function $r\,(\cdot)$ is usually highly nonlinear. In this case, to obtain a global optimal solution is infeasible for high-dimensional data. To address the problem, heuristic search strategies, such as greedy search and genetic-algorithmic search can be used for identifying a feature subset.

Feature selection algorithms with an embedded model, e.g., C4.5 [141], LARS [48], 1-norm support vector machine [229], and sparse logistic regression [26], also require a predetermined learning algorithm. But unlike an algorithm with the wrapper model, they incorporate feature selection as a part of the training process by attaching a regularization term to the original objective function of the learning algorithm. In the training process, the features' relevance is evaluated by analyzing their utility for optimizing the adjusted objective function, which forms $r\,(\cdot)$ for feature evaluation. In recent years, the embedded model has gained increasing interest in feature selection research due to its superior performance. Currently, most embedded feature selection algorithms are designed by applying an L_0 norm [192, 79] or an L_1 norm [115, 229, 227] constraint to an existing learning model, such as the support vector machine, the logistic regression, and the principal component analysis to achieve a sparse solution. When the constraint is derived from the L_1 norm, and the original problem is convex, $r(\cdot)$ (the adjusted objective function) is also convex and a global optimal solution exists. In this case, various existing convex optimization techniques can be applied to obtain a global optimal solution efficiently [115].

Compared with the wrapper and the embedded models, feature selection algorithms with the filter model are independent of any learning model, and therefore, are not biased toward a specific learner model. This forms one advantage of the filter model. Feature selection algorithms of a filter model are usually very fast, and their structures are often simple. Algorithms of a filter model are easy to design, and after being implemented, they can be easily understood by other researchers. This explains why most existing feature selection algorithms are of the filter model. On the other hand, researchers also recognize that feature selection algorithms of the wrapper and embedded models can select features that result in higher learning performance for the predetermined learning algorithm. Compared with the wrapper model, feature selection algorithms of the embedded model are usually more efficient, since they look into the structure of the predetermined learning algorithm and use its properties to guide feature evaluation and feature subset searching.

1.2.3.3   Output Formats

Feature selection algorithms with filter and embedded models may return either a subset of selected features or the weights (measuring the feature relevance) of all features. According to the type of the output, feature selection algorithms can be divided into either *feature weighting* algorithms or *subset selection* algorithms. Feature selection algorithms of the wrapper model usually return feature subsets, and therefore are subset selection algorithms.

1.2.3.4   Number of Data Sources

To the best of the authors' knowledge, most existing feature selection algorithms are designed to handle learning tasks with only one data source, therefore they are *single-source feature selection* algorithms. In many real data mining applications, for the same set of features and samples, we may have multiple data sources. They depict the characters of features and samples from multiple perspectives. *Multi-source feature selection* [223] studies how to integrate multiple information sources in feature selection to improve the reliability of relevance estimation. Figure 1.8 demonstrates how multi-source feature selection works. Recent study shows that the capability of using multiple data and knowledge sources in feature selection may effectively enrich our information and enhance the reliability of relevance estimation [118, 225, 226].

Different information sources about features and samples may have very different representations. One of the key challenges in multi-source feature selection is how to effectively handle the heterogenous representation of multiple information sources.

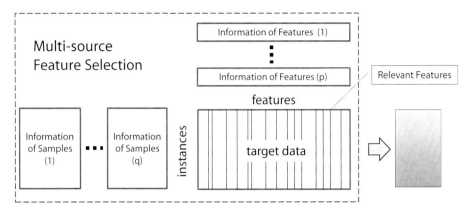

FIGURE 1.8: Feature selection with multiple data and knowledge sources.

1.2.3.5 Computation Schemes

Different computation schemes roughly fall into two categories: serial computation and parallel computation. Most existing feature selection techniques are designed for serial computation in a centralized computing environment. An advantage of this computing scheme is its simplicity. However, in recent years, the size of data sets in data mining applications has increased rapidly. It is common to have a data set of several terabytes (TB, 2^{12} bytes). A data set of this size poses scalability challenges to existing feature selection algorithms. To improve the efficiency and scalability of existing algorithms, parallel computation techniques, such as such as Message Passing Interface (MPI) [163, 63] and Google's MapReduce [1], can be applied [160]. By utilizing more computing (CPU) and storage (RAM) resources, a parallel feature selection algorithm is capable of handling very large data sets efficiently.

1.2.4 Challenges in Feature Selection Research

Although much work has been done on research of feature selection and a large number of algorithms have been developed, as new applications emerge, many challenges have arisen, requiring novel theories and methods to address high-dimensional and complex data. Below, we consider some of the most challenging problems in feature selection research.

1.2.4.1 Redundant Features

A redundant feature refers to a feature that is relevant to the learning problem, but its removal from the data has no negative effect.[3] Redundant features unnecessarily increase dimensionality [89], and may worsen learning performance. It has been empirically shown that removing redundant features can result in significant performance improvement [69]. Some algorithms have been developed to handle redundancy in feature selection [69, 40, 56, 210, 6, 43]. However, there is still not much systematical work that studies how to adapt the large number of existing algorithms (especially the algorithms based on the filter model) to handle redundant features.

1.2.4.2 Large-Scale Data

Advances in computer-based technologies have enabled researchers and engineers to collect data at an ever-increasing pace [1, 215, 50]. Data were measured in megabytes (MB, 2^6 bytes) and gigabytes (GB, 2^9 bytes), then terabytes (TB, 2^{12} bytes), and now in petabyte (PB, 2^{15} bytes). A large-scale data set may contain a huge number of samples and features. Most existing feature selection algorithms are designed for handling data with a size under several gigabytes. Their efficiency may significantly deteriorate, if not become totally unapplicable, when data size exceeds hundreds of gigabytes. Efficient distributed computing frameworks, such as MPI [163, 63] and Google's MapReduce [1], have been developed to facilitate applications on cloud infrastructure, enabling people to handle problems of very large scale. Most existing feature selection techniques are designed for traditional centralized computing environments and cannot readily utilize these advanced distributed computing techniques to enhance their efficiency and scalability.

1.2.4.3 Structured Data

Not only are data sets getting larger, but new types of data are emerging. Examples include data streams from sensor networks [2], sequences in proteinic or genetic studies [174], hierarchial data with complex taxonomies in text mining [49], and data in social network analysis [152] and system biology [5]. Existing feature selection algorithms cannot handle these complex data types effectively. For instance, in many text mining applications, documents are organized under a complex hierarchy. However, most existing feature selection algorithms can only handle class labels with a flat structure. Also, in the cancer study, feature selection techniques are applied on microarray data for identifying genes (features) that are related to carcinogenesis. Genetic interaction networks can be used to improve the precision of carcinogenic gene detection [224]. For instance, recent studies show that most carcinogenic genes are the core of the genetic interaction network [134, 189]. However, to the best of the authors' knowledge, most existing algorithms can-

---

[3]Mainly due to the existence of other features which is more relevant.

not integrat the information contained in a genetic interaction network (a network of feature interaction) in feature selection to improve the reliability of relevance estimation.

1.2.4.4 Data of Small Sample Size

Opposite to the problem discussed in Section 1.2.4.2, in which sample size is tremendous, another extreme is a terribly small sample size. The small sample problem is one of the most challenging problem in many feature selection applications [143]: the dimensionality of data is extremely high, while the sample size is very small. For instance, a typical cDNA microarray data set [88] used in modern genetic analysis usually contain more than 30000 features (the oligonucleotide probes), yet the sample size is usually less than 100. With so few samples, many irrelevant features can easily gain their statistical relevance due to sheer randomness [159]. With a data set of this kind, most existing feature selection algorithms become unreliable by selecting many irrelevant features. For example, in a cancer study based on cDNA microarray, fold differences identified via statistical analysis often offer limited or inaccurate selection of biological features [118, 159]. In real applications, the number of samples usually do not increase considerably, since the process of acquiring additional samples is costly. One way to address this problem is to include additional information to enhance our understanding of the data at hand. For instance, recent developments in bioinformatics have made various knowledge sources available, including the KEEG pathway repository [87], the Gene Ontology database [25], and the NCI Gene-Cancer database [151]. Recent work has also revealed the existence of a class of small noncoding RNA (ribonucleic acid) species known as microRNAs, which are surprisingly informative for identifying cancerous tissues [118]. The availability of these various information sources presents promising opportunities to advance research in solving previously unsolvable problems. However, as we pointed out in Sections 1.2.3.4 and 1.2.4.3, most feature selection algorithms are designed to handle learning tasks with a single data source, and therefore cannot benefit from any additional information sources.

1.3 Spectral Feature Selection

A good feature should not have random values associated with samples. Instead, it should support the target concept embedded in the data. In supervised learning, the target concept is the class affiliation of the samples. In unsupervised learning, the target concept is the cluster affiliation of the samples. Therefore, to develop effective algorithms for selecting features, we need to find effective ways to measure features' consistency with the target concept. More specifically, we need effective mechanisms to identify features that associate similar values with the samples that are of the same affiliation.

Sample similarity is widely used in both supervised and unsupervised learning to describe the relationships among samples. It forms an effective way to depict either sample cluster affiliation or sample class affiliation. *Spectral feature selection* is a newly developed feature selection technique. It evaluates features' relevance via measuring their capability of preserving the pre-specified sample similarity. More specifically, assuming the similarities among every pair of samples are stored in a similarity matrix **S**, spectral feature selection estimates the feature relevance by measuring features' consistency with the spectrum of a matrix derived from **S**, for instance, the Laplacian matrix [33].[4]

Example 3 *The top eigenvectors of a Laplacian matrix*

Figure 1.9 shows the contour of the second and third eigenvectors of a Laplacian matrix derived from a similarity matrix **S**. The color of the samples denotes their class or cluster affiliations. The gray level of the background shows how eigenvectors assign values to the samples. The darker the color, the smaller the value.

The figure shows that the second and third eigenvectors assign similar values to the samples that are of the same affiliations. So, if a feature is consistent with either of the two eigenvectors, it will have a strong capability of supporting the target concept, which defines the affiliation of samples.

Spectral feature selection is a general feature selection framework. Its advantages include:

- A unified framework: Spectral feature selection forms a general framework that enables the joint study of supervised, unsupervised, and semi-supervised feature selection. With this framework, families of novel feature selection algorithms can be designed to handle data with different characteristics.

- A solid theoretical foundation: Spectral feature selection has a solid theoretical foundation, which is supported by spectral graph theory [33], numerical linear algebra [38], and convex optimization [131, 18]. Its properties and behaviors can be effectively analyzed for us to gain insight for improving performance.

- Great generability: Spectral feature selection includes many existing successful feature selection algorithms as its special cases. This allows us to

---

[4]The concepts of similarity matrix and Laplacian matrix will be introduced in Chapter 2.

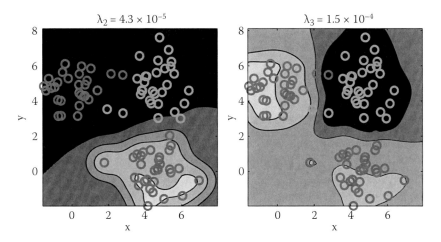

FIGURE 1.9: (**SEE COLOR INSERT**) The contour of the second and third eigenvectors of a Laplacian matrix derived from a similarity matrix **S**. The numbers on the top are the corresponding eigenvalues.

study them together to achieve better understanding on these algorithms and gain interesting insights.

- Handling redundant features: Any algorithm that fits the framework of spectral feature selection can be adapted to effectively handle redundant features. This helps many existing feature selection algorithms to overcome their common drawback of handling feature redundancy.

- Processing large-scale data: Spectral feature selection can be conveniently extended to handle large-scale data by applying mature commercialized distributed parallel computing techniques.

- The support of multi-source feature selection: Spectral feature selection can integrate multiple data and knowledge sources to effectively improve the reliability of feature relevance estimation.

1.4 Organization of the Book

The book consists of six chapters. Figure 1.10 depicts the organization of the book.

Chapter 1. We introduce the basic concepts in feature selection, present the challenges for feature selection research, and offer the basic idea of spectral feature selection.

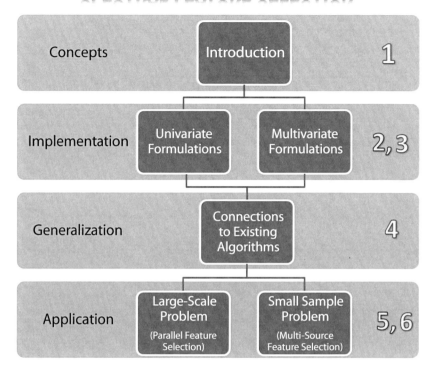

FIGURE 1.10: The organization of the book.

Chapters 2 and 3. Features can be evaluated either individually or jointly, which leads to univariate and multivariate formulations for spectral feature selection, respectively. We present a spectral feature selection framework based on univariate formulations in Chapter 2. This general framework covers supervised, unsupervised, and semi-supervised feature selection. We study the properties of the univariate formulations for spectral feature selection and illustrate how to derive new algorithms with good performance based on these formulations. One problem of the univariate formulation is that features are evaluated independently. Therefore redundant features cannot be handled properly. In Chapter 3, we present several multivariate formulations for spectral feature selection to handle redundant features in effective and efficient ways.

Chapter 4. Although spectral feature selection is a relatively new technique for feature selection, it is closely related to many existing feature selection and feature extraction algorithms. In Chapter 4, we show that many existing successful feature selection and feature extraction algorithms can be considered special cases of the proposed spectral feature selection frameworks.

The unification allows us to achieve a better understanding of these algorithms as well as the spectral feature selection technique.

Chapters 5 and 6. Spectral feature selection can be applied to address difficult feature selection problems. The large-scale data problem and the small sample problem are two of the most challenging problems in feature selection research. In Chapter 5, we study *parallel spectral feature selection* and show how to handle a large-scale data set via efficient parallel implementations for spectral feature selection in a distributed computing environment. In Chapter 6 we illustrate how to address the small sample problem by incorporating multiple knowledge sources in spectral feature selection, which leads to the novel concept of *multi-source feature selection*.

Although readers are encouraged to read the entire book to obtain a comprehensive understanding of the spectral feature selection technique, readers can choose the chapters according to their interests based on Figure 1.10. Chapters 1, 2, and 3 introduce the basic concept of feature selection, and show how spectral feature selection works. For the readers who are already familiar with feature selection and want to learn the theoretical perspectives of spectral feature selection in depth, we recommend they read Chapters 2, 3, and 4. Chapters 2, 3, 5, and 6 provide implementation details of spectral feature selection algorithms, and can be useful for the readers, who want to apply spectral feature selection technique to solve their own real-world problems.

To read the book, a reader may need some knowledge of linear algebra. Some basic convex optimization techniques are used in Chapter 3. Some concepts from biology and bioinformatics are mentioned in Chapter 6. These concepts and techniques are all basic and relatively simple to understand. We refer readers not familiar with these concepts and technique to the literature provided as references in the book.

Chapter 2

Univariate Formulations for Spectral Feature Selection

Spectral feature selection tries to select features that are consistent with the target concept via conducting [171]. In this chapter, we present several univariate formulations for spectral feature selection, and analyze the properties of the presented formulations based on the perturbation theory developed for symmetric linear systems [38]. We also show how to derive novel feature selection algorithms based on these formulations and study their performance. Spectral feature selection is a general framework for both supervised and unsupervised feature selection. The key for the technique to achieve this is that it uses a uniform way to depict the target concept in both learning contexts, which is the sample similarity matrix. Below, we start by showing how a sample similarity matrix can be used to depict a target concept.

2.1 Modeling Target Concept via Similarity Matrix

Pairwise sample similarity is widely used in both supervised and unsupervised learning to describe the relationships among samples. It can effectively depict either the cluster affiliations or the class affiliations of samples. For example, assume s_{ij} is the similarity between the i-th and the j-th samples. Without class label information, a popular similarity measurement is the Gaussian radial basis function (RBF) kernel function [21], defined as

$$s_{ij} = \exp\left(-\frac{\|\mathbf{x}_i - \mathbf{x}_j\|^2}{2\delta^2}\right),$$

where $\exp(\cdot)$ is the exponential function and δ is the parameter for controlling the width of the "bell." This function ensures samples from the same cluster have *large* similarity and samples from different clusters have *small* similarity. On the other hand, when class label information is available, the sample similarity can be measured by

$$s_{ij} = \begin{cases} \frac{1}{n_l}, & y_i = y_j = l \\ 0, & otherwise, \end{cases}$$

where n_l denotes the number of samples in class l. This measurement ensures that samples from the same class have a nonnegative similarity, while samples from different classes have a zero similarity. Given n samples, the $n \times n$ matrix $\mathbf{S}$ containing the sample similarity of all sample pairs, $\mathbf{S}(i,j) = s_{ij}$, $i,j = 1,\ldots,n$, is called a *sample similarity matrix*. $\mathbf{S}$ is also called a *kernel matrix* [150], if any of its submatrices is positive semi-definite. A matrix $\mathbf{A} \in \mathbb{R}^{n \times n}$ is called semi-positive definite [150] ($\mathbf{A} \succeq 0$), if and only if

$$\mathbf{x}^\top \mathbf{A} \mathbf{x} \geq 0, \forall \mathbf{x} \in \mathbb{R}^n.$$

Example 4 *The consistency of a feature reveals its relevance*

In Figure 2.1, the target concept specifies two categories indicated by the two ellipses: C1 and C2. Different shapes correspond to the feature values of the samples. As we can see, feature F assigns similar values to the samples that are of the same category, while F' does not. Compared to F', by using F to cluster or classify samples, we have a better chance of obtaining correct results. Therefore, F is more relevant compared with F'.

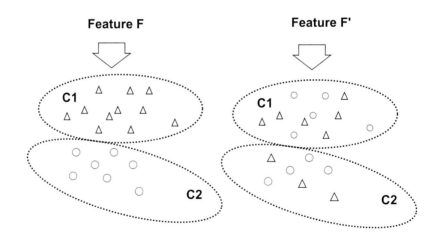

FIGURE 2.1: Consistency of two different features.

Given a sample similarity matrix $\mathbf{S}$, a graph $\mathbf{G}$ can be constructed to represent it. The target concept is reflected by the structure of $\mathbf{G}$. For example, the samples of the same category usually form a cluster structure with dense inner connections. As shown in Example 4, a feature is *consistent* with the target concept when it assigns similar values to the samples that are from the same category. Reflecting on the graph $\mathbb{G}$, it assigns similar values to the samples that are near to each other on the graph. Consistent features contain information about the target concept, and therefore help cluster or classify samples correctly.

Given a graph $\mathbb{G}$, we can derive a Laplacian matrix $\mathbf{L}$ (to be discussed in the next section). According to spectral graph theory [33, 58, 17, 124], the structural information of a graph can be obtained by studying its spectrum. For example, it is known that the leading eigenvectors of $\mathbf{L}$ have a tendency to assign similar values to the samples that are near one another on the graph. Below we introduce some basic concepts related to a Laplacian matrix and study its properties. Based on this knowledge, we show how to measure feature relevance using the spectrum of a Laplacian matrix in spectral feature selection. The proposed formulations are applicable for both supervised and unsupervised feature selection.

2.2 The Laplacian Matrix of a Graph

According to sample distribution (or sample class affiliation), a sample similarity matrix $\mathbf{S}$ can be computed to represent the relationships among samples. Given $\mathbf{X}$, we use $\mathbb{G}(V, E)$ to denote an undirected graph constructed from $\mathbf{S}$, where V is the vertex set, and E is the edge set. The i-th vertex v_i of $\mathbb{G}$ corresponds to $\mathbf{x}_i \in \mathbf{X}$, and there is an edge between each vertex pair (v_i, v_j). Given $\mathbb{G}$, its *adjacency matrix*, $\mathbf{A} \in \mathbb{R}^{n \times n}$, is defined as $a_{ij} = s_{ij}$. Let $\mathbf{d} = \{d_1, d_2, ..., d_n\}$, where $d_i = \sum_{k=1}^{n} a_{ik}$, the *degree matrix*, $\mathbf{D} \in \mathbb{R}^{n \times n}$, of $\mathbb{G}$ is defined as

$$\mathbf{D}(i, j) = \begin{cases} d_i, & i = j \\ 0, & otherwise . \end{cases}$$

Obviously $\mathbf{D}$ is a diagonal matrix. Here d_i can be interpreted as an estimation of the density around $\mathbf{x}_i$, since the more data points that are close to $\mathbf{x}_i$, the larger the d_i. Given the adjacency matrix $\mathbf{A}$ and the degree matrix $\mathbf{D}$, the *Laplacian matrix* $\mathbf{L}$ and the *normalized Laplacian matrix* $\mathcal{L}$ are defined as

$$\mathbf{L} = \mathbf{D} - \mathbf{A}; \quad \mathcal{L} = \mathbf{D}^{-\frac{1}{2}} \mathbf{L} \mathbf{D}^{-\frac{1}{2}}. \tag{2.1}$$

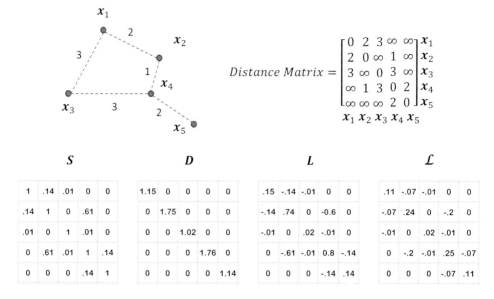

$$
Distance\ Matrix =
\begin{bmatrix}
0 & 2 & 3 & \infty & \infty \\
2 & 0 & \infty & 1 & \infty \\
3 & \infty & 0 & 3 & \infty \\
\infty & 1 & 3 & 0 & 2 \\
\infty & \infty & \infty & 2 & 0
\end{bmatrix}
\begin{matrix}
x_1 \\ x_2 \\ x_3 \\ x_4 \\ x_5
\end{matrix}
$$
$$x_1\ x_2\ x_3\ x_4\ x_5$$

S

1	.14	.01	0	0
.14	1	0	.61	0
.01	0	1	.01	0
0	.61	.01	1	.14
0	0	0	.14	1

D

1.15	0	0	0	0
0	1.75	0	0	0
0	0	1.02	0	0
0	0	0	1.76	0
0	0	0	0	1.14

L

.15	-.14	-.01	0	0
-.14	.74	0	-0.6	0
-.01	0	.02	-.01	0
0	-.61	-.01	0.8	-.14
0	0	0	-.14	.14

$\mathcal{L}$

.11	-.07	-.01	0	0
-.07	.24	0	-.2	0
-.01	0	.02	-.01	0
0	-.2	-.01	.25	-.07
0	0	0	-.07	.11

FIGURE 2.2: A graph and its Laplacian matrices.

Example 5 *A graph and its Laplacian matrices*

Figure 2.2 shows a graph and its Laplacian matrices. In the graph, the number beside each edge is the length of the edge. To compute the similarity between $\mathbf{x}_i$ and $\mathbf{x}_j$, we used the Gaussian radial basis function (RBF) [21], with $\delta = 1$

$$
s_{ij} = exp\left(-\frac{\parallel \mathbf{x}_i - \mathbf{x}_j \parallel^2}{2}\right) = exp\left(-\frac{Distance\text{-}Matrix\,(i,j)^2}{2}\right).
$$

We can see that $\mathbf{D}$ is a diagonal matrix. $\mathbf{S}$, $\mathbf{L}$, and $\mathcal{L}$ are all symmetric matrices. The off-diagonal elements of $\mathbf{L}$ and $\mathcal{L}$ are all negative. We notice that the elements in $\mathcal{L}$ are smaller than those in $\mathbf{L}$. This is due to the fact that $\mathcal{L}_{i,j} = \frac{1}{d_i d_j}\mathbf{L}_{i,j}$. It is also easy for us to verify that $\mathbf{L}\mathbf{1} = \mathbf{0}$, where $\mathbf{1}$ is the vector with all its elements equal to 1.

With the following theorem, we show some properties of $\mathbf{D}$ and $\mathbf{L}$ [33].

Theorem 2.2.1 *Given the Laplacian matrix* $\mathbf{L}$ *of* $\mathbf{G}$, *we have*

1. $\forall\, \mathbf{x} \in \mathbb{R}^n$,

$$\mathbf{x}^\top \mathbf{L} \mathbf{x} = \frac{1}{2} \sum_{i,j=1}^{n} a_{i,j} \, (x_i - x_j)^2. \qquad (2.2)$$

2. $\forall\, \mathbf{x} \in \mathbb{R}^n, \forall\, t \in \mathbb{R}$,

$$(\mathbf{x} - t * \mathbf{1})^\top \mathbf{L}(\mathbf{x} - t * \mathbf{1}) = \mathbf{x}^\top \mathbf{L} \mathbf{x}. \qquad (2.3)$$

3. $\forall\, \mathbf{x} \in \mathbb{R}^n$,

$$\mathbf{x}^\top \mathbf{L} \mathbf{x} \ge 0. \qquad (2.4)$$

4. *Let* $\mathbf{1} = \{1, 1, \ldots, 1\}^\top$ *and* $\mathbf{0} = \{0, 0, \ldots, 0\}^\top$,

$$\mathbf{L} * \mathbf{1} = 0 \times \mathbf{1} = \mathbf{0}. \qquad (2.5)$$

Proof To prove Equation (2.2), we notice that by the definition of d_i, we have

$$
\begin{aligned}
\mathbf{x}^\top \mathbf{L} \mathbf{x} &= \mathbf{x}^\top \mathbf{D} \mathbf{x} - \mathbf{x}^\top \mathbf{S} \mathbf{x} = \sum_{i=1}^{n} d_i x_i^2 - \sum_{i,j=1}^{n} a_{ij} x_i x_j \\
&= \frac{1}{2}\left(\sum_{i=1}^{n} d_i x_i^2 - 2 \sum_{i,j=1}^{n} a_{ij} x_i x_j + \sum_{j=1}^{n} d_j x_j^2 \right) \\
&= \frac{1}{2} \sum_{i,j=1}^{n} a_{i,j} \, (x_i - x_j)^2.
\end{aligned}
$$

Equations (2.3–2.5) can be easily derived from Equation (2.2).

■

Equation (2.4) shows that the Laplacian matrix $\mathbf{L}$ is a positive semi-definite matrix. And Equation (2.4) and Equation (2.5) together suggest that the smallest eigenvalue of $\mathbf{L}$ is 0 and its corresponding eigenvector is $\mathbf{1}$. $(0, \mathbf{1})$ is also called the trivial eigenpair of $\mathbf{L}$.

Theorem 2.2.2 *Given the normalized Laplacian matrix* $\mathcal{L}$ *of* $\mathbf{G}$, *we have*

1. $\forall \mathbf{x} \in \mathbb{R}^n$,

$$\mathbf{x}^\top \mathcal{L} \mathbf{x} = \frac{1}{2} \sum_{i,j=1}^{n} a_{i,j} \left(\frac{x_i}{\sqrt{d_i}} - \frac{x_j}{\sqrt{d_j}} \right)^2. \qquad (2.6)$$

2. $\forall\, \mathbf{x} \in \mathbb{R}^n, \forall\, t \in \mathbb{R}$,

$$(\mathbf{x} - t * \mathbf{d}^{1/2})^\top \mathcal{L}(\mathbf{x} - t * \mathbf{d}^{1/2}) = \mathbf{x}^\top \mathcal{L} \mathbf{x}. \qquad (2.7)$$

3. $\forall\, \mathbf{x} \in \mathbb{R}^n$,

$$\mathbf{x}^\top \mathcal{L} \mathbf{x} \geq 0. \tag{2.8}$$

4. *Given* $\mathbf{d}$,

$$\mathcal{L} * \mathbf{d}^{\frac{1}{2}} = 0 \times \mathbf{d}^{\frac{1}{2}}. \tag{2.9}$$

5. $\forall i, \quad 1 \leq i \leq n$,

$$0 \leq \lambda_i \leq 2. \tag{2.10}$$

Proof The proofs of Equations (2.6)–(2.9) are similar to those in Theorem 2.2.1. Equation (2.10) can be proven by noticing the fact that $\forall i,\ 1 \leq i \leq n$,

$$
\begin{aligned}
\lambda_i \quad &\leq \quad \sup_{\|\mathbf{x}\|=1} \mathbf{x}^\top \mathcal{L} \mathbf{x} \\
&= \quad \sup_{\|\mathbf{x}\|=1} \frac{1}{2} \sum_{i,j=1}^{n} a_{i,j} \left(\frac{x_i}{\sqrt{d_i}} - \frac{x_j}{\sqrt{d_j}} \right)^2 \\
&\leq \quad \sup_{\|\mathbf{x}\|=1} \frac{1}{2} \sum_{i,j=1}^{n} 2a_{i,j} \left(\frac{x_i^2}{d_i} + \frac{x_j^2}{d_j} \right) \\
&= \quad 2\|\mathbf{x}\|_2^2 = 2.
\end{aligned}
$$

In the above derivation, the second inequality holds since $(a + b) \leq 2\left(a^2 + b^2\right)$.

■

Similar to Theorem 2.2.1, Equation (2.8) shows that the normalized Laplacian matrix $\mathcal{L}$ is positive semi-definite. And Equations (2.8) and (2.9) together suggest that the smallest eigenvalue of $\mathcal{L}$ is 0 and $\mathbf{d}^{\frac{1}{2}}$ is the corresponding eigenvector. $(0, \mathbf{d}^{\frac{1}{2}})$ is called the trivial eigenpair of $\mathcal{L}$.

The following examples show us some interesting properties of the eigenvectors of the Laplacian matrix.

Example 6 *The spectrum of a Laplacian matrix*

Figure 2.3 plots the contours of six eigenvectors of a Laplacian matrix $\mathbf{L}$. The Laplacian matrix is constructed from a data set with 90 instances. The instances are drawn from a mixture of three two-dimensional (2D) Gaussian distributions [190, 166], which have a unit variance and a mean at (5,0), (0,5), and (5, 5), respectively. The RBF function defined in Equation (2.25) is used to compute sample similarity with σ being set to 1. Since $\mathbf{L} \in \mathbb{R}^{90 \times 90}$, let ξ be the eigenvectors of $\mathbf{L}$, so we have $\xi \in \mathbb{R}^{90 \times 1}$. Therefore an eigenvector ξ of $\mathbf{L}$ assigns a value to each of the 90 instances sampled from the 2D Gaussian mixture [15].

For any point in the space without a value, we compute its value by averaging the values of the nearby points. Note that only the points that correspond to the 90 instances sampled from the 2D Gaussian mixture are used for computing the values for other points. In the averaging process, the values of their neighbors are weighted by their distance to the points with values.

Let ξ_i denote the eigenvector corresponding to λ_i, which is the i-th smallest eigenvalue of the Laplacian matrix $\mathbf{L}$. Figure 2.3 plots the contours of the eigenvectors ξ_1, ξ_2, ξ_3, ξ_4, ξ_5, and ξ_{20}. The contours show how the eigenvectors assign values to the sample. Basically, the darker the color, the smaller the value. The figure shows that the first eigenvector, ξ_1, assigns the same value to all the instances, which is consistent with Theorem 2.2.1. Since there are three clusters, the second and the third eigenvectors, ξ_2 and ξ_3, capture the cluster structure of the data. The fourth and the fifth eigenvectors, ξ_4 and ξ_5, capture the subcluster structure of the data. And the 20th eigenvector, ξ_{20}, captures the subtle structures of the data, which may be created by noise. We also noticed that λ_1, λ_2, and λ_3 are significantly smaller than the remaining eigenvalues. The example shows that the cluster structure of a data set can be extracted from the leading eigenvectors of its corresponding Laplacian matrix.

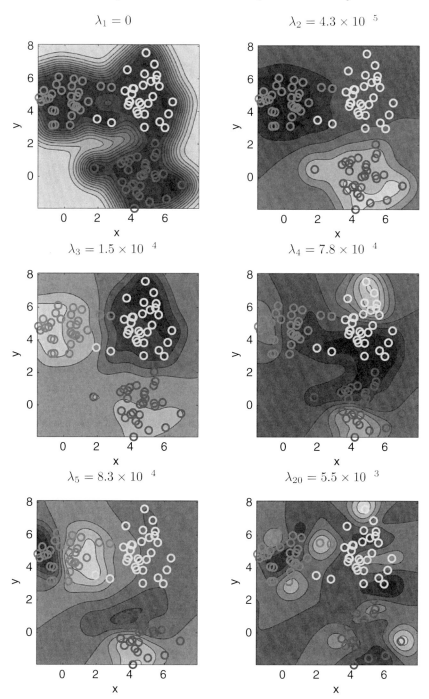

FIGURE 2.3: (**SEE COLOR INSERT**) Contours of the eigenvectors $\xi_1, \xi_2, \xi_3, \xi_4, \xi_5$, and ξ_{20} of **L**.

Example 7 *The spectrum of a normalized Laplacian matrix*

Figure 2.4 plots the contours of six eigenvectors of a normalized Laplacian matrix $\mathcal{L}$: ξ_1, ξ_2, ξ_3, ξ_4, ξ_5, and ξ_{20}. The normal Laplacian matrix is constructed from the same data used in Example 6. The figure shows that the first eigenvector, ξ_1, captures the density information of the data, which is consistent with Theorem 2.2.2. Similar to the last example, the second and the third eigenvectors, ξ_2 and ξ_3, capture the cluster structure of the data. The fourth and the fifth eigenvectors, ξ_4 and ξ_5, capture the subcluster structure of the data. And the 20th eigenvector, ξ_{20}, captures the subtle structures of the data, which might correspond to noise. Again, we observe that λ_1, λ_2, and λ_3 are significantly smaller than the remaining eigenvalues.

According to the spectral graph theory, the eigenvalues of **L** measure the "smoothness" of their corresponding eigenvectors. More specifically, the smaller the eigenvalue, the smoother the corresponding eigenvector. Here the smoothness measures how often an eigenvector assigns similar values to samples that are near each other. This can be explained by Equation (2.2)

$$\lambda_i = \xi_k^\top \mathbf{L} \xi_k = \frac{1}{2} \sum_{i,j=1}^{n} a_{i,j} \left(\xi_{k,i} - \xi_{k,j} \right)^2 .$$

If an eigenvector does not vary much locally (that is, it always assigns similar values to samples that are near to each other on the graph), then its corresponding eigenvalue λ_i will be a very small value. This justifies the usage of the scale of λ_i to measure the smoothness of its corresponding eigenvector ξ_i. Motivated by the above observation, we study below how the graph Laplacian matrix can be used for evaluating feature relevance.

2.3 Evaluating Features on the Graph

Equation (2.2) shows that given **G**, the Laplacian matrix of **G** is a linear operator on vectors

$$< \mathbf{f}, \mathbf{L}\mathbf{f} >= \mathbf{f}^\top \mathbf{L}\mathbf{f} = \frac{1}{2} \sum_{v_i \sim v_j} a_{ij}(f_i - f_j)^2, \quad \mathbf{f} = (f_1, f_2, \ldots, f_n)^\top \in \mathbb{R}^n .$$

$$(2.11)$$

As discussed in the last section, the equation quantifies how much **f** varies locally or how "smooth" it is over **G**. More specifically, the smaller the value of $< \mathbf{f}, \mathbf{L}\mathbf{f} >$, the smoother the vector **f** is on **G**. A smooth vector **f** assigns

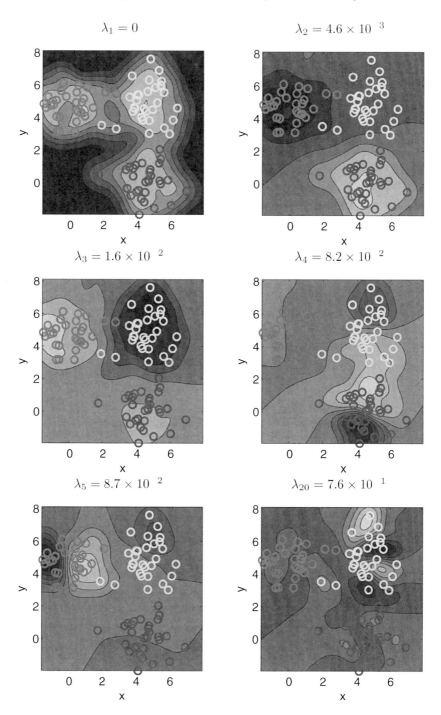

FIGURE 2.4: (**SEE COLOR INSERT**) Contours of the eigenvectors $\xi_1, \xi_2, \xi_3, \xi_4, \xi_5$, and ξ_{20} of $\mathcal{L}$.

similar values to the samples that are close to one another on $\mathbf{G}$, thus it is consistent with the graph structure. $< \mathbf{f}, \mathbf{Lf} >$ can be used to measure the consistency of features on a graph.

However, given a feature vector $\mathbf{f}_i$ and $\mathbf{L}$, two factors affect the value of $< \mathbf{f}_i, \mathbf{Lf}_i >$: the norm of $\mathbf{f}_i$ and the norm of $\mathbf{L}$. The two factors need to be removed, as they do not contain structure information of the data, but can cause the value of $< \mathbf{f}_i, \mathbf{Lf}_i >$ to increase or decrease arbitrarily. The two factors can be removed via normalization. Based on the relationship between $\mathbf{L}$ and $\mathcal{L}$, we have

$$< \mathbf{f}_i, \mathbf{Lf}_i >= \mathbf{f}_i^\top \mathbf{Lf}_i = \mathbf{f}_i^\top \mathbf{D}^{\frac{1}{2}} \mathcal{L} \mathbf{D}^{\frac{1}{2}} \mathbf{f}_i = (\mathbf{D}^{\frac{1}{2}} \mathbf{f}_i)^\top \mathcal{L}(\mathbf{D}^{\frac{1}{2}} \mathbf{f}_i).$$

Let $\widetilde{\mathbf{f}}_i = (\mathbf{D}^{\frac{1}{2}} \mathbf{f}_i)$ denote the weighted feature vector of F_i, and $\hat{\mathbf{f}}_i = \frac{\widetilde{\mathbf{f}}_i}{||\widetilde{\mathbf{f}}_i||}$ the normalized weighted feature vector. The score of F_i can be evaluated by the following function:

$$\varphi_1(F_i) = \hat{\mathbf{f}}_i^\top \mathcal{L} \, \hat{\mathbf{f}}_i. \tag{2.12}$$

With the following theorem, we show the relationship between $\varphi_1(F_i)$ and the normalized cut of a graph. Normalized cut is a concept from spectral graph theory. It measures the capability of a cluster indicator for partitioning the data into well-separated clusters. The following theory suggests that if a feature is relevant, by using the feature as a "soft" cluster indicator, we can obtain a "clear cut," which partitions the data into well-separated clusters.

Theorem 2.3.1 $\varphi_1(F_i)$ *measures the value of the normalized cut [156] by using $\mathbf{f}_i$ as the soft cluster indicator to partition the graph* $\mathbf{G}$.

Proof: The theorem holds as

$$\varphi_1(F_i) = \hat{\mathbf{f}}_i^\top \mathcal{L} \, \hat{\mathbf{f}}_i = \frac{\mathbf{f}_i^\top \mathbf{Lf}_i}{\mathbf{f}_i^\top \mathbf{Df}_i}.$$

■

Given a graph, assume we partition the graph into two clusters C_1 and C_2. The **normalized cut** corresponding to C_1 and C_2 can be calculated by

$$\text{cut}_N(C_1, C_2) = \frac{\text{cut}(C_1, C_2)}{\text{vol}(C_1)} + \frac{\text{cut}(C_2, C_1)}{\text{vol}(C_2)}, \tag{2.13}$$

where $\text{cut}(C_1, C_2)$ measures the total weight of the edges connecting two clusters, and $\text{vol}(C_1)$ measures the total weight of the edges having at least one endpoint in cluster C_1. They are defined as

$$\text{cut}(C_1, C_2) = \sum_{i \subset C_1, j \in C_2} a_{ij}, \quad \text{vol}(C_1) = \sum_{i \in C_1, \forall j} a_{ij}. \tag{2.14}$$

Equation (2.13) shows that the normalized cut prefers a partition with the following two properties. First, the normalized cut prefers a partition, in which the edges between different clusters have low weights, and the edges within each cluster have high weights. Such a partition ensures that the instances in different clusters are different, and the instances within the same cluster are similar. Second, the normalized cut requires the partition to be balanced, since $\text{vol}(C_1 + C_2)$ is a constant, and $1/\text{vol}(C_1) + 1/\text{vol}(C_2)$ is the minimum when $\text{vol}(C_1) = \text{vol}(C_2)$. Let $\mathbf{c} = (c_1, \ldots, c_n)$ be a cluster indicator for C_1, such that if $i \in C_1$, $c_i = 1$, otherwise $c_i = -\frac{\sum_{i \in C_1} d_i}{\sum_{i \in C_2} d_i}$, where d_i is the i-th diagonal element of the degree matrix $\mathbf{D}$. In [157], it is shown that that

$$\frac{\mathbf{c}^\top \mathbf{L} \mathbf{c}}{\mathbf{c}^\top \mathbf{D} \mathbf{c}} = \text{cut}_N(C_1, C_2). \qquad (2.15)$$

Equation (2.15) computes the normalized cut value corresponding to the cluster indicator $\mathbf{c}$. The values of the elements in $\mathbf{c}$ are either 1 or $-\frac{\sum_{i \in C_1} d_i}{\sum_{i \in C_2} d_i}$, therefore it is called a discrete cluster indicator. If we relax this requirement and allow $c_i \in \mathbb{R}$, then the corresponding $\mathbf{c}$ becomes a soft cluster indicator. A good soft cluster indicator leads to a small normalized cut value by assigning similar values to samples that are near one another on the graph. Both theoretical and empirical results show that the normalization step makes the normalized cut more robust to outliers [157, 39, 128].

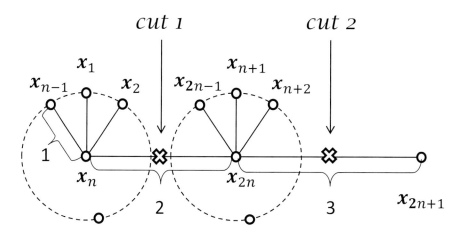

FIGURE 2.5: Two possible cuts of a graph.

Example 8 *The normalized cut of a graph*

In this example, we illustrate the effect of the normalized cut. We compare the normalized cut to the standard cut. Given two clusters C_1 and C_2, in the normalized cut, we define the cluster indicator as

$$c_i = \begin{cases} 1, & i \in C_1 \\ \dfrac{\sum_{i \in C_1} d_i}{\sum_{i \in C_2} d_i}, & i \in C_2 \end{cases}$$

and

$$\mathrm{cut}_N\left(C_1, C_2\right) = \frac{\mathrm{cut}\left(C_1, C_2\right)}{\mathrm{vol}\left(C_1\right)} + \frac{\mathrm{cut}\left(C_2, C_1\right)}{\mathrm{vol}\left(C_2\right)} = \frac{\mathbf{c}^\top \mathbf{L} \mathbf{c}}{\mathbf{c}^\top \mathbf{D} \mathbf{c}}.$$

In the standard cut, the cluster indicator is specified as

$$c_i = \begin{cases} 1, & i \in C_1 \\ -1, & i \in C_2 \end{cases}$$

and

$$\mathrm{cut}\left(C_1, C_2\right) = \frac{1}{4} \mathbf{c}^\top \mathbf{L} \mathbf{c}.$$

Figure 2.5 shows a graph containing three clusters. The first two clusters both have n instances. In each of the two clusters there is a center point, and all other instances in the cluster connect to the center point with a distance of 1. The center points of the two clusters are connected and the distance is 2. The third cluster has only one instance, and the instance is connected to the center point of the second cluster with a distance of 3. The figure shows two possible cuts of the graph. The first one cut the edge connecting the first and the second cluster, and the second one cut the edge connecting the second and the third cluster. Figure 2.6 shows how $\mathrm{cut}\left(C_1, C_2\right)$ and $\mathrm{cut}_N\left(C_1, C_2\right)$ vary with the size of the first and the second clusters.[1] When there is only one instance in the first and the second cluster, both $\mathrm{cut}\left(\cdot\right)$ and $\mathrm{cut}_N\left(\cdot\right)$ assign smaller cut values to cut 2, since cut 2 cuts an edge with a longer distance. In this case both $\mathrm{cut}\left(\cdot\right)$ and $\mathrm{cut}_N\left(\cdot\right)$ prefer cut 2. However, when the number of instances, n, increases, $\mathrm{cut}_N\left(\cdot\right)$ begins to assign a smaller cut value to cut 1, since cut 1 cuts the graph in a more balanced way. Compared with $\mathrm{cut}_N\left(\cdot\right)$, the value of $\mathrm{cut}\left(\cdot\right)$ does not change with n, since it does not consider the size of the clusters.

Given the normalized Laplacian matrix $\mathcal{L}$, we can calculate its eigen-decomposition (λ_i, ξ_i), where λ_i is the eigenvalue and ξ_i is the eigenvector

---

[1] To compute the similarity matrix for the graph, we use a RBF kernel function with $\delta = 2$.

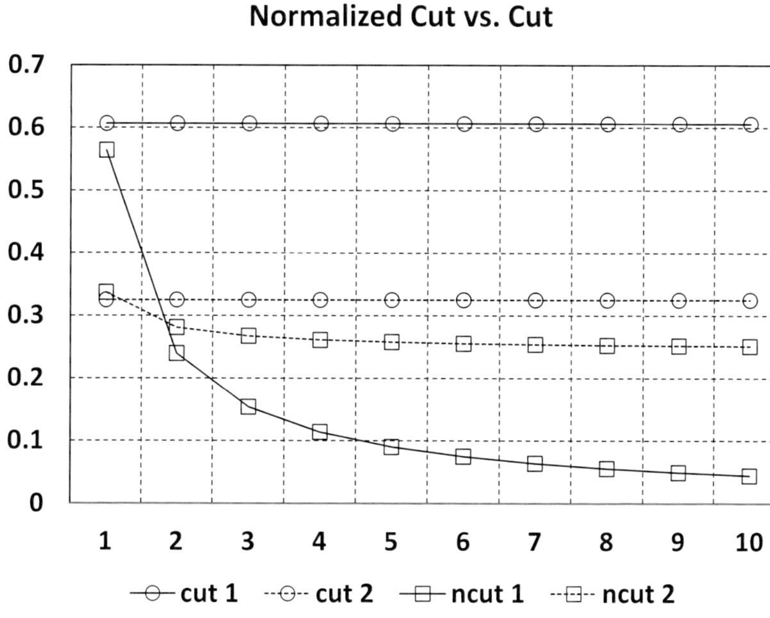

Normalized Cut vs. Cut

FIGURE 2.6: (SEE COLOR INSERT) The cut value (y-axis) of different types of cut under different cluster sizes (x-axis). The x-axis corresponds to the value of n in Figure 2.5.

($1 \leq i \leq n$). Assuming $\lambda_1 \leq \lambda_2 \leq \ldots \leq \lambda_n$, according to Theorem 2.2.1, we have: $\lambda_1 = 0$ and $\xi_1 = \frac{\mathbf{D}^{\frac{1}{2}}\mathbf{1}}{\|\mathbf{D}^{\frac{1}{2}}\mathbf{1}\|}$, which form the trivial eigenpair of the graph. Also we know that all the eigenvalues of $\mathcal{L}$ are in the range of $[0, 2]$. Given a spectral decomposition of $\mathcal{L}$, we can rewrite Equation (2.12) using the eigensystem of $\mathcal{L}$ to achieve a better understanding of the equation.

Theorem 2.3.2 *Let* (λ_j, ξ_j), $1 \leq j \leq n$ *be the eigensystem of* $\mathcal{L}$, *and* $\alpha_j = \cos\theta_j$ *where* θ_j *is the angle between* $\hat{\mathbf{f}}_i$ *and* ξ_j. *Equation (2.12) can be rewritten as*

$$\varphi_1(F_i) = \sum_{j=1}^{n} \alpha_j^2 \lambda_j, \quad where \quad \sum_{j=1}^{n} \alpha_j^2 = 1. \tag{2.16}$$

Proof: Let $\Sigma = \mathrm{DIAG}(\lambda_1, \lambda_2, \ldots, \lambda_n)$ and $U = (\xi_1, \xi_2, \ldots, \xi_n)$. As $\|\hat{\mathbf{f}}_i\| = \|\xi_j\| = 1$, we have $\hat{\mathbf{f}}_i^{\top} \xi_j = \cos\theta_j$. We can rewrite $\hat{\mathbf{f}}_i^{\top} \mathcal{L} \, \hat{\mathbf{f}}_i$ as

$$\hat{\mathbf{f}}_i^{\top} \mathcal{L} \hat{\mathbf{f}}_i = \hat{\mathbf{f}}_i^{\top} U \Sigma U^{\top} \hat{\mathbf{f}}_i = (\alpha_1, \ldots, \alpha_n) \Sigma (\alpha_1, \ldots, \alpha_n)^{\top} = \sum_{i=1}^{n} \alpha_i^2 \lambda_i.$$

Since $\sum_{j=1}^{n} \alpha_j^2 = \hat{\mathbf{f}}_i^{\top} U U^{\top} \hat{\mathbf{f}}_i$, $U U^{\top} = I$ and $\|\hat{\mathbf{f}}_i\| = 1$, we have $\sum_{j=1}^{n} \alpha_j^2 = 1$. ∎

Theorem 2.3.2 suggests that by using Equation (2.12) the score of F_i is calculated by combining the eigenvalues of $\mathcal{L}$, and $\cos\theta_1,\dots,\cos\theta_n$ are the combination coefficients. Note, here $\cos\theta_i$ measures the similarity between the the feature vector and the i-th eigenvector of $\mathcal{L}$. Since $\lambda_1 = 0$, Equation (2.16) can be rewritten as $\hat{\mathbf{f}}_i^\top \mathcal{L} \hat{\mathbf{f}}_i = \sum_{j=2}^n \alpha_j^2 \lambda_j$, meaning that the value obtained from Equation (2.12) evaluates the smoothness of $\hat{\mathbf{f}}_i$ by measuring the similarities between $\hat{\mathbf{f}}_i$ and those nontrivial eigenvectors of $\mathcal{L}$. Assuming that $\mathbf{f}$ aligns closely to the top eigenvectors of $\mathcal{L}$, clearly $\sum_{j=2}^n \alpha_j^2 \lambda_j$ will be small. As shown in Figure 2.4, the top eigenvectors of $\mathcal{L}$ assign similar values to the instances from the same cluster. Therefore if a feature aligns closely with these eigenvectors, it will be smooth on the graph.

Since $\sum_{j=1}^n \alpha_j^2 = 1$ and $\alpha_1 \geq 0$, we have $\sum_{j=2}^n \alpha_j^2 \leq 1$. The bigger the α_1^2, the smaller the $\sum_{j=2}^n \alpha_j^2$ is. The value of $\varphi_1(F_i)$ can be small if $\hat{\mathbf{f}}_i$ is very similar to ξ_1. However, in this case, a small $\varphi_1(F_i)$ value does not indicate better separability, since the trivial eigenvector ξ_1 does not carry any distribution information except the density around samples. To handle this issue, we propose to use $\sum_{j=2}^n \alpha_j^2$ to normalize $\varphi_1(F_i)$, which gives us the following ranking function:

$$\varphi_2(F_i) = \frac{\sum\limits_{j=2}^n \alpha_j^2 \lambda_j}{\sum\limits_{j=2}^n \alpha_j^2} = \frac{\hat{\mathbf{f}}_i^\top \mathcal{L} \hat{\mathbf{f}}_i}{1 - \left(\hat{\mathbf{f}}_i^\top \xi_1\right)^2}. \tag{2.17}$$

A small $\varphi_2(F_i)$ indicates that $\hat{\mathbf{f}}_i$ aligns closely to those nontrivial eigenvectors with small eigenvalues, hence it is smooth on the graph.

According to spectral clustering theory, the leading k eigenvectors of $\mathcal{L}$ form the optimal soft cluster indicators that separate G into k parts. The remaining eigenvectors correspond to the subtle structures formed by noise. Therefore, if k is known, for instance, we know that the data set contains samples from k different categories, which should form k dense clusters. We can also estimate feature relevance by the following function:

$$\varphi_3(F_i) = \sum_{j=2}^k (2 - \lambda_j)\alpha_j^2 . \tag{2.18}$$

By its definition, φ_3 assigns bigger scores to features that are more relevant. This is because if a feature achieves a large score with φ_3, it must align closely to the nontrivial eigenvectors $\xi_2,\dots,\xi_k$, with ξ_2 having the highest priority. By focusing on the leading eigenvectors, φ_3 can effectively reduce noise. Similar mechanisms are also used in principal component analysis (PCA) [15] and spectral dimension reduction [145, 119, 75, 13, 148, 198] for eliminating noise.

Example 9 *Evaluating features with $\varphi_1(\cdot)$, $\varphi_2(\cdot)$, $\varphi_3(\cdot)$*

Figure 2.7 plots the contours of six features: F_1, F_2, F_3, F_4, F_5, and F_6. Among the six features, F_1 and F_2 are relevant features and correspond to the first and second dimensions of the 2D Gaussian mixture generated in Example 6. $F_3, \ldots, F_6$ are randomly generated, with their values following the standard uniform distribution, and thus are irrelevant features. Since $\mathbf{L} \in \mathbb{R}^{90 \times 90}$, $F_i \in \mathbb{R}^{90 \times 1}$, $i = 1, \ldots, 6$, any of the six features will assign a value to each of the 90 instances sampled from the 2D Gaussian mixture. To generate a contour for a feature F_i, for any point in the space without a value, we compute its value by averaging over the values of its nearby points, which are assigned values by F_i. In the averaging process, the values from its neighbors are weighted by their distance to it. The normalized Laplacian matrix $\mathcal{L}$ constructed in Example 7 is used in computing $\varphi_1(\cdot)$, $\varphi_2(\cdot)$, and $\varphi_3(\cdot)$ for feature evaluation.

From Figure 2.7, we can observe that the two relevant features, F_1 and F_2, are smoother than the other four irrelevant features on the graph. They can all be identified as relevant by the three feature ranking functions. The results show that they achieve small values with $\varphi_1(\cdot)$ and $\varphi_2(\cdot)$, and large values with $\varphi_3(\cdot)$.

2.4   An Extension for Feature Ranking Functions

A Laplacian matrix is also used in supervised learning for designing regularization functions to penalize predictors that vary abruptly among adjacent vertices on a graph. In [162], the authors relate the eigenvectors of $\mathcal{L}$ to the Fourier basis [170] and extend the usage of $\mathcal{L}$ to $\gamma(\mathcal{L})$, where $\gamma(\cdot)$ is a spectral matrix function [59] defined as

$$\gamma(\mathcal{L}) = \sum_{j=1}^{n} \gamma(\lambda_j)\xi_j\xi_j^\top. \tag{2.19}$$

In the formulation, $\gamma(\lambda_j)$ is an increasing function that adjusts the eigenvalues of the normalized Laplacian matrix $\mathcal{L}$. It is pointed out in [217] that due to the existence of noise, the difference between the small eigenvalues and the large eigenvalues shrinks. By using a high-order spectral matrix function, we can effectively enlarge this difference.

Given a normalized Laplacian matrix $\mathcal{L}$, its eigenvalues measure the smoothness of the corresponding eigenvectors. The smaller the eigenvalue, the smoother the eigenvector. By applying an increasing function $\gamma(\cdot)$, we

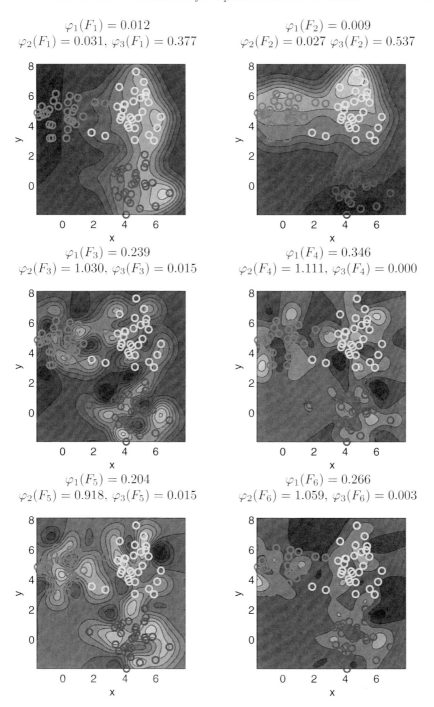

FIGURE 2.7: (**SEE COLOR INSERT**) Contours and the scores of six features. Among these features, F_1 and F_2 are relevant, and $F_3, F_4, F_5,$ and F_6 are irrelevant.

reduce the value of the estimated smoothness of the eigenvectors with large eigenvalues, which usually contain structure information generated by noise. It is shown in [217] that using the $\gamma(\mathcal{L})$ to design the regularization functions can effectively improvement the robustness of an algorithm in a noisy learning environment.

Example 10 *Eigenvalues of a noise-contaminated Laplacian matrix*

Figures 2.8 and 2.9 plot the distributions of the eigenvalues of $\mathcal{L}$, $\tilde{\mathcal{L}}$, and $\tilde{\mathcal{L}}^3$. Here $\mathcal{L}$ is the normalized Laplacian matrix constructed in Example 7. $\tilde{\mathcal{L}}$ is the noise-contaminated Laplacian matrix, with $\frac{\|\tilde{\mathcal{L}}-\mathcal{L}\|}{\|\mathcal{L}\|} = 0.5$. From the figure, we can observe that the noise has two different effects on the distribution of the eigenvalues. First, the slope of the distribution becomes flat. And second, the gaps between the leading eigenvalues become smaller.[2] Comparing $\tilde{\mathcal{L}}^3$ with $\tilde{\mathcal{L}}$, the leading eigenvalues of $\tilde{\mathcal{L}}^3$ are much smaller than those of $\tilde{\mathcal{L}}$, yet on the other hand, the tailing eigenvalues become much bigger. The tail eigenvectors usually contain information generated by noise. In the evaluation process, by using $\tilde{\mathcal{L}}^3$, we penalize the tail eigenvectors by reducing the value of their estimated smoothness.

The above example motivates us to extend our feature ranking functions, $\varphi_1(\cdot)$, $\varphi_2(\cdot)$, and $\varphi_3(\cdot)$ to the following forms for improving their robustness in a noisy learning environment:

$$\hat{\varphi}_1(F_i) = \hat{\mathbf{f}}_i^\top \gamma(\mathcal{L}) \hat{\mathbf{f}}_i = \sum_{j=1}^n \alpha_j^2 \gamma(\lambda_j) \tag{2.20}$$

$$\hat{\varphi}_2(F_i) = \frac{\sum_{j=2}^n \alpha_j^2 \gamma(\lambda_j)}{\sum_{j=2}^n \alpha_j^2} = \frac{\hat{\mathbf{f}}_i^\top \gamma(\mathcal{L}) \hat{\mathbf{f}}_i}{1 - \left(\hat{\mathbf{f}}_i^\top \xi_1\right)^2} \tag{2.21}$$

$$\hat{\varphi}_3(F_i) = \sum_{j=2}^k (\gamma(2) - \gamma(\lambda_j))\alpha_j^2. \tag{2.22}$$

Calculating the spectral decomposition (or eigen decomposition) of $\mathcal{L}$ can be expensive for data with a large number of samples. However, since $\gamma(\cdot)$ is usually a polynomial function $\gamma(\mathcal{L})$ can be calculated efficiently by regarding $\mathcal{L}$ as a variable and applying $\gamma(\cdot)$ on it. For example, assume $\gamma(\lambda) = \lambda^3$, then $\gamma(\mathcal{L}) = \mathcal{L}^3$. For $\hat{\varphi}_3(\cdot)$, the k leading eigenpairs of $\mathcal{L}$ can be obtained efficiently by using fast eigensolvers such as the implicitly restarted Arnoldi method [142].

---

[2]Except the gap between λ_1 and λ_2.

$\lambda\left(\mathcal{L}\right)$

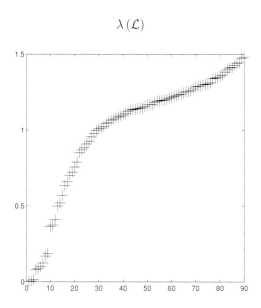

FIGURE 2.8: The distribution of the eigenvalues of $\mathcal{L}$. $\mathcal{L}$ is the Laplacian matrix obtained from the original data.

$\lambda(\tilde{\mathcal{L}})$ $\lambda(\tilde{\mathcal{L}}^3)$

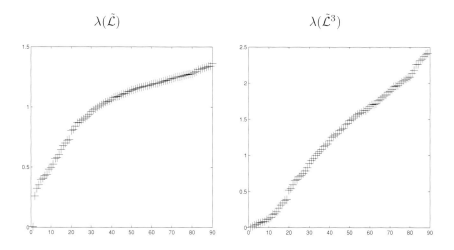

FIGURE 2.9: The distribution of the eigenvalues of $\tilde{\mathcal{L}}$ and $\tilde{\mathcal{L}}^3$. $\tilde{\mathcal{L}}$ is the Laplacian matrix obtained from the noise-contaminated data. $\frac{\|\tilde{\mathcal{L}}-\mathcal{L}\|}{\|\mathcal{L}\|} = 0.5$.

2.5   Spectral Feature Selection via Ranking

The feature evaluation criteria we just presented can be used in a unified framework for spectral feature selection. In this framework, the relevance of a feature is determined by its consistency with the structure of the graph induced from the given, sample similarity. The three feature evaluation functions, $\hat{\varphi}_1(\cdot), \hat{\varphi}_2(\cdot)$, and $\hat{\varphi}_3(\cdot)$, lay the foundation of the framework and enable us to derive families of supervised and unsupervised feature selection in a unified manner. The pseudo-code of the unified framework is shown in Algorithm 1. It selects features in three steps: (1) building the similarity matrix $\mathbf{S}$ and constructing its graphical representation (Lines 1–3); (2) evaluating features using the eigensystem of the graph (Lines 4–6); and (3) ranking features in descending order according to feature relevance, and feature selection is accomplished by choosing the desired number of features from the returned list (Lines 7–8). We name the framework SPEC [222], stemming from the fact that the framework is based on analyzing the spectrums of the normalized Laplacian matrix $\mathcal{L}$. Algorithm 1 shows the framework for evaluating features one by one with a feature evaluation criterion which is independent of any learning algorithm. Therefore, the framework is a filter model for feature selection.

Algorithm 1: SPEC

Input: $\mathbf{X}, \mathbf{y}, \gamma(\cdot), l, \hat{\varphi} \in \{\hat{\varphi}_1, \hat{\varphi}_2, \hat{\varphi}_3\}$
Output: a list of l features
1 construct $\mathbf{S}$, the similarity matrix from $\mathbf{X}$ (or $\mathbf{y}$);
2 construct graph $\mathbb{G}$ from $\mathbf{S}$;
3 build $\mathbf{W}, \mathbf{D}$ and $\mathbf{L}$ from $\mathbb{G}$;
4 **for** *each feature vector* $\mathbf{f}_i$ **do**
5   $\left\lfloor \hat{\mathbf{f}}_i \leftarrow \dfrac{\mathbf{D}^{\frac{1}{2}}\mathbf{f}_i}{||\mathbf{D}^{\frac{1}{2}}\mathbf{f}_i||}; \quad SF_{SPEC}(i) \leftarrow \hat{\varphi}(F_i); \right.$
6 ranking features in descending order according to feature relevance;
7 **return** top l features from the ranked list;

SPEC is a general framework for feature selection. It can be used to systematically derive novel algorithms for different learning contexts. Its three key components are:

1. Sample similarity matrix $\mathbf{S}$

   For example, the matrix constructed using an RBF function introduced in Equation (2.25).

2. Spectral matrix function $\gamma(\cdot)$

   For example, $\gamma(r) = r$, $\gamma(r) = r^3$.

3. Feature rank function $\hat{\varphi}(\cdot)$.

For example, one of the functions in $\{\hat{\varphi}_1(\cdot),\ \hat{\varphi}_2(\cdot),\ \hat{\varphi}_3(\cdot)\}$.

By using different combinations of these components, we can generate families of new algorithms for spectral feature selection. For instance, depending on how label information is used for constructing the similarity matrix $\mathbf{S}$, we can use SPEC to generate algorithms for unsupervised, supervised, or semi-supervised feature selection. Below we show how to apply SPEC in different learning contexts in detail.

2.5.1 SPEC for Unsupervised Learning

When only unlabeled data are provided, the similarity matrix $\mathbf{S}$ can only be constructed in an unsupervised way, and the feature selection algorithms generated by SPEC in this case are unsupervised. Below we list some of the popular functions for computing the similarity among instances in an unsupervised learning context.

1. Linear kernel function:

$$s_{ij} = \mathbf{x}_i^\top \mathbf{x}_j + c. \tag{2.23}$$

The linear kernel function is the simplest kernel function. It is given by the inner product of two instances, plus an optional constant c.

2. Polynomial kernel function:

$$s_{ij} = \left(\alpha \mathbf{x}_i^\top \mathbf{x}_j + c\right)^d. \tag{2.24}$$

The polynomial kernel function is a non-stationary kernel function. In the equation, α is the slope parameter, c is the constant term, and d is the polynomial degree.

3. Radial basis function (RBF):

$$s_{ij} = exp\left(-\frac{\|\mathbf{x}_i - \mathbf{x}_j\|^2}{2\delta^2}\right). \tag{2.25}$$

The adjustable parameter δ plays a very important role in the performance of the function, and should be carefully tuned according to the problem at hand. If overestimated, the exponential will behave almost linearly, and the higher-dimensional projection will start to lose its non-linear power. On the other hand, if underestimated, the function will lack regularization and the decision boundary will be highly sensitive to noise in training data.

4. Cosine similarity function:

$$s_{ij} = \frac{\mathbf{x}_j^\top \mathbf{x}_i}{\|\mathbf{x_i}\| \cdot \|\mathbf{x}_j\|}.$$

Cosine similarity is used to measure the similarity between two vectors by computing the cosine of the angle between them. It is often used for high-dimensional applications such as document clustering and categorization in text mining.

2.5.2 SPEC for Supervised Learning

When class label information is available, the sample similarity matrix can be directly formed from label information. For instance, the following two functions are usually used for constructing a similarity matrix $\mathbf{S}$ in a supervised way:

$$s_{ij} \quad = \quad \left\{ \begin{array}{ll} 1, & y_i = y_j = l \\ 0, & otherwise \end{array} \right. , \tag{2.26}$$

$$s_{ij} \quad = \quad \left\{ \begin{array}{ll} \frac{1}{n_l}, & y_i = y_j = l \\ 0, & otherwise \end{array} \right. . \tag{2.27}$$

In Equation (2.27), n_l is the number of samples in the l class. Comparing with Equation (2.26), Equation (2.27) normalizes the similarity of the samples from the same class by the size of the class. The mechanism is helpful for balancing classes of different sizes. By plugging in a similarity matrix constructed by using the label information, one can obtain a spectral feature selection algorithm for supervised learning.

2.5.3 SPEC for Semi-Supervised Learning

In many real applications, such as text mining and image processing, data are abundant, but labeled data are costly to obtain. It is common to have a high-dimensional data set with a large number of unlabeled samples but only a few labeled samples. The data sets of this kind present a serious challenge to supervised feature selection: the so-called "small labeled-sample problem" [82]. That is, when the labeled sample size is too small to provide sufficient information about the target concept, supervised feature selection algorithms may fail by either unintentionally removing many relevant features or selecting irrelevant features, which seems to be significant only on the small labeled data. Unsupervised feature selection algorithms can be an alternative in this case, as they are able to use the large amount of unlabeled data. However, as these algorithms ignore label information, important hints from labeled data are left out and this will generally downgrade the performance of unsupervised feature selection algorithms. Under the assumption that labeled and unlabeled data are sampled from the same population generated by the target concept, using both labeled and unlabeled data is expected to better estimate feature relevance. Semi-supervised learning is to learn from mixed labeled and unlabeled data [30].

The proposed spectral feature selection framework, SPEC, can be naturally extended to achieve semi-supervised feature selection through a regularization framework, in which a feature's relevance is evaluated by its consistency with both labeled and unlabeled data. The idea can be formulated as

$$\lambda \hat{\varphi}_u (F_i) + (1 - \lambda) \hat{\varphi}_s (F_i). \tag{2.28}$$

The first term and the second terms of Equation (2.28) estimate the consistency of feature F_i with the labeled and the unlabeled data, respectively. To this end, one can construct two similarity matrices, $\mathbf{S}_s$ and $\mathbf{S}_u$, from the labeled and the unlabeled data, respectively. $\hat{\varphi}_s (\cdot)$ and $\hat{\varphi}_u (\cdot)$ can be obtained by applying $\mathbf{S}_s$ and $\mathbf{S}_u$ in SPEC. Note, $\hat{\varphi}_s (\cdot)$ and $\hat{\varphi}_u (\cdot)$ are feature ranking functions, and are chosen from $\{\hat{\varphi}_1 (\cdot), \hat{\varphi}_2 (\cdot), \hat{\varphi}_3 (\cdot)\}$. They are marked with different subscripts, since they are applied to different similarity matrices, $\mathbf{S}_s$ and $\mathbf{S}_u$.

For a feature to be identified as relevant, it must be consistent with the distribution of both the large amount of unlabeled data and the small amount of labeled data. This idea is illustrated in Figure 2.10. The samples with "o" shape are from the negative class, the samples with "+" shape are from positive class, and the remaining ones are unlabeled samples. The ellipses in the figure denote clusters. We have two features, F and F', and they assign the same value to samples that are from the same cluster. Note that the two features are consistent with different cluster structures. As we can see, since the cluster structure of the unlabeled data is ambiguous, feature F and feature F' are equally smooth on the unlabeled data. However, feature F is more consistent with the labeled data, which suggests that F is more relevant.

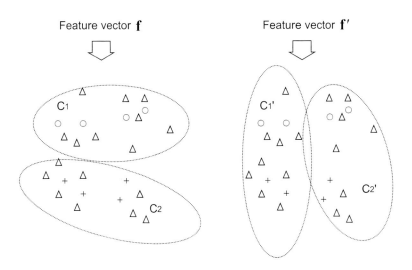

FIGURE 2.10: Use label information in semi-supervised feature selection.

Note, if we replace $\hat{\varphi}_s$ in Equation (2.28) with the normalized mutual information [212] between a feature F_i and the class $\mathbf{y}$, we will obtain the feature evaluation criterion used in *sSelect* [221], which is one of the first semi-supervised feature selection algorithms in the literature.

One issue related to the framework formulated in Equation (2.28) is that the regularization parameter λ is data dependent. That is, for different data, the best value for the regularization parameter may vary quite a bit. Therefore, to find a proper value for the regularization parameter λ is crucial to ensure the performance of the framework. In [219], a parameter tuning mechanism is developed based on studying the cut-value[3] achieved on the data that only contain the selected features. We find the mechanism is often effective, but time-consuming. Therefore developing an efficient and effective technique for determining the value of the regularization parameter remains an open issue.

2.5.4   Time Complexity of SPEC

The time complexity of SPEC largely depends on the cost of (1) building the similarity matrix and the calculation of $\gamma(\cdot)$; (2) feature evaluation with SPEC; and (3) feature ranking.

First, we analyze the time complexity of constructing the similarity matrix and calculating the $\gamma(\cdot)$ in various learning contexts. In the unsupervised case, if we use the RBF function to build the similarity matrix, and $\gamma(\cdot)$ is in the form of $\mathcal{L}^r$, the time complexity of this step is $((rn + m)n^2)$. This is because we need $O(mn^2)$ operations to build $\mathbf{S}$, $\mathbf{D}$, $\mathbf{L}$, and $\mathcal{L}$. We then need $O(rn^3)$ operations to calculate the $\gamma(\mathcal{L})$. In the supervised case, if Equation (2.27) is used to construct the similarity matrix, we need $O(n^2)$ operations to compute $\mathbf{S}$ and $\mathbf{L}$. It can be verified that in this case, $\mathbf{D}$ is an identity matrix, $\mathbf{D} = \mathbf{I}$. $\mathbf{L}$ has c (the number of classes) 0 eigenvalues, and all other eigenvalues are 1. Therefore, we do not need to compute $\mathcal{L}$ and $\gamma(\mathcal{L})$. So in the supervised case, the time complexity for this step is $O(n^2)$. In the semi-supervised case, the similarity matrix is obtained by combining $\mathbf{S}_s$ and $\mathbf{S}_u$, which are the similarity matrices constructed in the supervised and the unsupervised ways, respectively. Therefore, the time complexity of this step is $((rn + m)n^2)$.

Upon obtaining $\gamma(\mathcal{L})$, we need $O(n^2)$ operations to calculate $SF_{SPEC}(i)$ for each feature: transforming $\mathbf{f}_i$ to $\hat{\mathbf{f}}_i$ requires $O(n)$ operations; and calculating $\hat{\varphi}_1$, $\hat{\varphi}_2$, and $\hat{\varphi}_3$ needs $O(n^2)$ operations.[4] Therefore, we need $O(mn^2)$ operations to calculate scores for m features.

Lastly, we need $O(m \log m)$ operations to rank the features.

In summary, the overall time complexity of SPEC is $O\left((rn + m)n^2\right)$ for unsupervised or semi-supervised feature selection, and $O\left(mn^2\right)$ for supervised

---

[3]Given data $\mathbf{X}$, the cut-value can be calculated as follows: first, constructing the adjacent matrix $\mathbf{A}$ from $\mathbf{X}$; then, forming the normalized Laplacian matrix $\mathcal{L}$ using $\mathbf{A}$; last, obtaining the cut-value by calculating the second smallest eigenvalue of $\mathcal{L}$.

[4]For $\hat{\varphi}_3$, using the Arnoldi method to calculate a few eigenpairs of a large sparse matrix needs roughly $O(n^2)$ operations, and calculating $\hat{\varphi}_3$ itself needs $O(k)$ operations.

feature selection. If $\gamma(\cdot)$ is not used for noise reduction, the time complexity of SPEC is $O\left(mn^2\right)$ for all three learning contexts. Note that in the supervised case, the similarity matrix $\mathbf{S}$ is usually of special structure, which can be utilized for improving efficiency. For instance, if Equation (2.27) is used to construct the similarity matrix, the time complexity of SPEC can be improved to $O(cmn)$. In this case, $\mathbf{S}$ has only c nonzero eigenvalues,[5] and $\mathbf{L} = \mathbf{I} - \mathbf{S}$.

Below we analyze the effect of components of SPEC, and provide a guideline for users to choose the proper components according to the reality of different applications.

2.6   Robustness Analysis for SPEC

Being robust is important for feature selection algorithms [146, 211]. A feature selection algorithm is not robust if a small perturbation of the original data can cause a great change in its output. Although the perturbations can be various (e.g., caused by noise), the underlying target concept remains unchanged. Therefore a good feature selection algorithm should be robust to the potential perturbations. Below, we provide a robustness analysis for feature ranking functions $\varphi_1(\cdot)$, $\varphi_2(\cdot)$, and $\varphi_3(\cdot)$. The analysis is based on the perturbation theory developed for symmetric linear systems [38], and can be extended to $\hat{\varphi}_1(\cdot)$, $\hat{\varphi}_2(\cdot)$, and $\hat{\varphi}_3(\cdot)$ easily. We first present two theorems, which serve as the basis for the following analysis.

Theorem 2.6.1 (Weyl) *Let* $\mathbf{A}$ *and* $\mathbf{E}$ *be n-by-n symmetric matrices. Let* $\lambda_1 \leq \ldots \leq \lambda_n$ *be the eigenvalues of* A *and* $\widetilde{\lambda}_1 \leq \ldots \leq \widetilde{\lambda}_n$ *be the eigenvalues of* $\widetilde{\mathbf{A}} = \mathbf{A} + \mathbf{E}$, $\|\lambda_j - \widetilde{\lambda}_j\| \leq \|\mathbf{E}\|_2$.

Assume $\widetilde{\mathbf{A}}$ is the perturbed $\mathbf{A}$, and $\mathbf{E}$ corresponds to noise. Theorem 2.6.1 shows that the eigenvalues of the perturbed matrix $\widetilde{\mathbf{A}}$ are bound by their corresponding eigenvalues of $\mathbf{A}$ and the scale of the perturbation matrix $\mathbf{E}$, which is measured by its norm.

Theorem 2.6.2 *Let* $\mathbf{A}$ *and* $\mathbf{E}$ *be n-by-n symmetric matrices. Let* $\mathbf{A} = \mathbf{Q}\Lambda\mathbf{Q}^\top = \mathbf{Q}diag(\lambda_j)\mathbf{Q}^\top$ *be an eigen decomposition of* $\mathbf{A}$. *Let* $\mathbf{A} + \mathbf{E} = \hat{\mathbf{A}} = \widetilde{\mathbf{Q}}\widetilde{\Lambda}\widetilde{\mathbf{Q}}^\top$ *be the perturbed eigen decomposition. Write* $\mathbf{Q} = [\xi_1, \ldots, \xi_n]$ *and* $\hat{\mathbf{Q}} = [\widetilde{\xi}_1, \ldots, \widetilde{\xi}_n]$, *where* ξ_j *and* $\widetilde{\xi}_j$ *are the unperturbed and perturbed unit eigenvectors, respectively. Let* θ_j *denote the acute angle between* ξ_j *and* $\widetilde{\xi}_j$. *Provided that* $\mathrm{GAP}(j, \mathbf{A} + \mathbf{E}) > 0$, *we have the following inequality*

$$\frac{1}{2}\sin 2\theta_j \leq \frac{\|\mathbf{E}\|_2}{\mathrm{GAP}\left(j, \mathbf{A} + \mathbf{E}\right)}, \tag{2.29}$$

Note that when $\theta_j \ll 1$, *then* $\frac{1}{2}\sin 2\theta_j \approx \sin \theta_j \approx \theta_j$.

---

[5] All these eigenvalues equal 1.

Proofs of the two theorems can be found in Section 5.2 of [38]. In Theorem 2.6.2, $\text{GAP}(j, \mathbf{A} + \mathbf{E})$ denotes the eigengap [129, 128] of λ_j, where λ_j is the j-th eigenvalue of $\mathbf{A} + \mathbf{E}$. Formally we can define $\text{GAP}(j, \mathbf{A} + \mathbf{E})$ as $\text{GAP}(j, \mathbf{A} + \mathbf{E}) = \min_{i \neq j} |\lambda_i - \lambda_j|$. According to Theorems 2.6.1 and 2.6.2, the robustness of the eigenvalues is determined by the scale of the perturbation matrix E, which is measured by its norm. And the robustness of the eigenvectors is determined by the scale of the perturbation matrix E as well as the eigengap of the corresponding eigenvalue.

Example 11 *The effect of noise on the eigensystem*

Figure 2.12 shows how eigenvalues and eigenvectors of $\mathcal{L}$ are affected when different amounts of noise are added to the data. Here $\mathcal{L}$ is the normalized Laplacian matrix constructed in Example 7. Let $\tilde{\mathcal{L}}$ be the noise-contaminated Laplacian matrix, and $\alpha = \frac{\|\tilde{\mathcal{L}} - \mathcal{L}\|}{\|\mathcal{L}\|}$, α reflects how much noise has been added to the data. In the figure, the x-axis corresponds to α. To generate the plots, we gradually increase α from 0 to 0.5. The y-axis of Figure 2.12(a) corresponds to the scale of the eigenvalues. The y-axis of Figure 2.12(b) corresponds to the scale of $\sin(\theta_\epsilon)$, where θ_ϵ is the angle between ξ, the original eigenvector, and $\tilde{\xi}$, the noise-perturbed eigenvector.

Figure 2.11 plots the distribution of the samples when the original data is perturbed using $\alpha = 0.3$. The chart shows that with noise perturbation, the cluster structures of the data become blurred. Figure 2.12(a) plots the values of the λ_2, λ_3, λ_{10}, and λ_{30} under perturbations of different scales. The plot shows that when more noise is added, the leading eigenvalues of $\tilde{\mathcal{L}}$ become bigger and the gap between leading and tail eigenvalues becomes smaller. This corresponds to the fact that when more noise is added, the cluster structures of the perturbed data become blurred. Figure 2.12-(b) plots the values of $\sin(\theta_\epsilon)$ when the scale of the perturbation varies. The plot shows that the leading eigenvectors are more robust to noise, since they have a bigger eigengap, which is consistent with the results presented in Theorem 2.6.2.

Based on the two theorems, we provide an error upper-bound analysis for feature ranking functions $\varphi_1(\cdot)$, $\varphi_2(\cdot)$ and $\varphi_3(\cdot)$, when the original data are perturbed by noise. In general, noise can cause two types of perturbation that will affect the outputs of ranking functions. They are (1) the perturbation of the Laplacian matrix $\mathcal{L}$, which is denoted as $\mathcal{L}_\epsilon$; and (2) the perturbation of the feature vector $\mathbf{f}$, which is denoted as $\mathbf{f}_\epsilon$. Without loss of generality, for the original data and its perturbation, by assuming $\epsilon_\mathcal{L} \geq 0$, we have the following specifications:

$$\tilde{\mathcal{L}} = \mathcal{L} + \mathcal{L}_\epsilon, \|\tilde{\mathcal{L}}\|_2 = \|\mathcal{L}\|_2 = 1, \|\mathcal{L}_\epsilon\|_2 \leq \epsilon_\mathcal{L}. \tag{2.30}$$

$$\alpha = 0.3$$

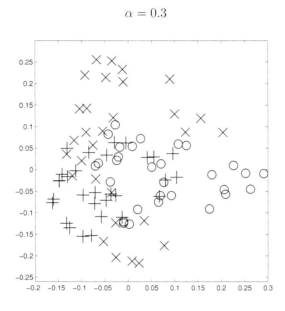

FIGURE 2.11: The effect of noise on sample distribution.

(a) $\lambda_2, \lambda_3, \lambda_{10}, \lambda_{30}$ (b) $\xi_2, \xi_3, \xi_{10}, \xi_{30}$

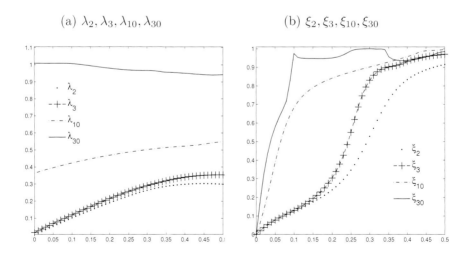

FIGURE 2.12: The effect of noise on eigenvalues and eigenvectors. The x-axis is the α value, which reflects how much noise has been added to the data.

$$\widetilde{\mathbf{f}} = \mathbf{f} + \mathbf{f}_\epsilon, \|\widetilde{\mathbf{f}}\|_2 = \|\mathbf{f}\|_2 = 1, \|\mathbf{f}_\epsilon\|_2 \le \epsilon_\mathbf{f}. \tag{2.31}$$

In the above equations, $\mathcal{L}$ is the original Laplacian matrix; $\widetilde{\mathcal{L}}$ is the perturbed Laplacian matrix; and $\mathcal{L}_\epsilon$ is the corresponding perturbation matrix. A similar relationship holds for $\mathbf{f}$, $\mathbf{f}_\epsilon$, and $\widetilde{\mathbf{f}}$, where $\mathbf{f}$ is a feature vector. With the following theorem, we show that we can bind the perturbation errors of the three feature ranking functions $\varphi_1(\cdot)$, $\varphi_2(\cdot)$, and $\varphi_3(\cdot)$ by $\epsilon_\mathcal{L}$, $\epsilon_\mathbf{f}$, and the eigengap of the eigenvalues of $\widetilde{\mathcal{L}}$.

Theorem 2.6.3 *Assume (λ_j, ξ_j) is the eigensystem of $\mathcal{L}$, and $\alpha_j = \cos\theta_j$, where θ_j is the angle between $\mathbf{f}$ and ξ_j. Also let $(\widetilde{\lambda}_j, \widetilde{\xi}_j)$ be the eigensystem of $\widetilde{\mathcal{L}}$, and $\widetilde{\alpha}_j = \cos\widetilde{\theta}_j$ where $\widetilde{\theta}_j$ is the angle between $\widetilde{\mathbf{f}}$ and $\widetilde{\xi}_j$. We have*

$$\left(\sum_{j=1}^q \widetilde{\alpha}_j^2 \widetilde{\lambda}_j - \sum_{j=1}^q \alpha_j^2 \lambda_j \right) \le \left(q\|\mathcal{L}_\epsilon\|_2 + \sum_{j=1}^q \lambda_j \sin\left(\frac{1}{2}\arcsin 2\epsilon_{j,\,\theta} \right) + \hat{\epsilon}_f \sum_{j=1}^q \lambda_j \right),$$

$$\tag{2.32}$$

where $\epsilon_{j,\,\theta} = \frac{\|\mathcal{L}_\epsilon\|_2}{\mathrm{GAP}(j,\mathcal{L}+\mathcal{L}_\epsilon)}$ and $\hat{\epsilon}_\mathbf{f} = 2\epsilon_\mathbf{f} + \epsilon_\mathbf{f}^2$. Note that when $\arcsin 2\epsilon_{j,\,\theta} \ll 1$,

$$q\|\mathcal{L}_\epsilon\|_2 + \sum_{j=1}^q \lambda_j \sin\left(\frac{1}{2}\arcsin 2\epsilon_{j,\,\theta} \right) + \hat{\epsilon}_f \sum_{j=1}^q \lambda_j$$

$$\approx \left(q\|\mathcal{L}_\epsilon\|_2 + \sum_{j=1}^q \lambda_j \epsilon_{j,\,\theta} + \hat{\epsilon}_f \sum_{j=1}^q \lambda_j \right). \tag{2.33}$$

Proof: We first provide an upper bound for $\widetilde{\alpha}_j^2 \widetilde{\lambda}_j$ using $\epsilon_\mathcal{L}$, $\epsilon_\mathbf{f}$ and the eigengap of $\widetilde{\mathcal{L}}$. For convenience, in the first part of the proof, we drop off the subscript j from $\widetilde{\alpha}_j^2 \widetilde{\lambda}_j$, if it does not cause confusion. Let $\widetilde{\xi} = \xi + \xi_\epsilon, \widetilde{\lambda} = \lambda + \lambda_\epsilon$. We have:

$$
\begin{aligned}
\widetilde{\alpha}^2 \widetilde{\lambda} &= \widetilde{\lambda}\cos^2\left(\widetilde{\theta} \right) = (\lambda + \lambda_\epsilon)\left((\mathbf{f} + \mathbf{f}_\epsilon)^\top (\xi + \xi_\epsilon) \right)^2 \\
&= \lambda\left((\mathbf{f} + \mathbf{f}_\epsilon)^\top (\xi + \xi_\epsilon) \right)^2 + \lambda_\epsilon\left((\mathbf{f} + \mathbf{f}_\epsilon)^\top (\xi + \xi_\epsilon) \right)^2 \\
&\le \lambda\left((\mathbf{f} + \mathbf{f}_\epsilon)^\top (\xi + \xi_\epsilon) \right)^2 + \lambda_\epsilon\left(\|\mathbf{f} + \mathbf{f}_\epsilon\| \|\xi + \xi_\epsilon\| \right)^2 \\
&= \lambda\left((\mathbf{f}^\top (\xi + \xi_\epsilon))^2 + \left(\mathbf{f}_\epsilon^\top (\xi + \xi_\epsilon) \right)^2 + 2\mathbf{f}^\top (\xi + \xi_\epsilon)\,\mathbf{f}_\epsilon^\top (\xi + \xi_\epsilon) \right) + \lambda_\epsilon \\
&\le \lambda\left((\mathbf{f}^\top (\xi + \xi_\epsilon))^2 + (\|\mathbf{f}_\epsilon\|_2 \|\xi + \xi_\epsilon\|_2)^2 + 2\|\mathbf{f}\|_2 \|\xi + \xi_\epsilon\|_2^2 \|\mathbf{f}_\epsilon\|_2 \right) + \lambda_\epsilon.
\end{aligned}
$$

Since $\|\widetilde{\xi}\|_2 = \|\xi\|_2 = 1$ and $\|\widetilde{\mathbf{f}}\|_2 = \|\mathbf{f}\|_2 = 1$, we have

$$\widetilde{\alpha}^2 \widetilde{\lambda} \le \lambda\left((\mathbf{f}^\top (\xi + \xi_\epsilon))^2 + \epsilon_\mathbf{f}^2 + 2\epsilon_\mathbf{f} \right) + \lambda_\epsilon.$$

In the above derivations, we applied the Cauchy-Schwarz inequality: $\mathbf{x}^{\top}\mathbf{y} \leq \|\mathbf{x}\|\|\mathbf{y}\|$. By noticing that $\mathbf{f}^{\top}(\xi + \xi_\epsilon) \leq \cos(\theta - \theta_\epsilon)$, where θ_ϵ is the angle between ξ and $\tilde{\xi}$, we have

$$
\begin{aligned}
\left(\mathbf{f}^{\top}(\xi + \xi_\epsilon)\right)^2 &\leq \cos^2(\theta - \theta_\epsilon) - \cos^2(\theta) + \cos^2(\theta) \\
&= \sin(2\theta - \theta_\epsilon)\sin(\theta_\epsilon) + \cos^2(\theta) \\
&\leq |\sin(\theta_\epsilon)| + \cos^2(\theta).
\end{aligned}
$$

Based on the two sets of results we just obtained, we have the following inequality

$$
\tilde{\alpha}^2\tilde{\lambda} \leq \lambda_\varepsilon + \lambda\left(\epsilon_f^2 + 2\epsilon_f\right) + \lambda|\sin(\theta_\epsilon)| + \lambda\cos^2(\theta),
$$

and

$$
\tilde{\alpha}^2\tilde{\lambda} - \alpha^2\lambda \leq \lambda_\epsilon + \lambda\left(\epsilon_f^2 + 2\epsilon_f\right) + \lambda|\sin(\theta_\epsilon)|.
$$

According to Theorem 2.6.2, we know $\lambda_\epsilon \leq \|\mathcal{L}_\epsilon\|$ and $|\sin(\theta_\epsilon)| \leq \sin\left(\frac{1}{2}\arcsin 2\epsilon_{j,\,\theta}\right)$, where $\epsilon_{j,\,\theta} = \frac{\|\mathcal{L}_\epsilon\|_2}{\mathrm{GAP}(j.\mathcal{L}+\mathcal{L}_\epsilon)}$. We obtain the following result:

$$
\left(\sum_{j=1}^{q}\tilde{\alpha}_j^2\tilde{\lambda}_j - \sum_{j=1}^{q}\alpha_j^2\lambda_j\right) \leq \left(q\|\mathcal{L}_\epsilon\|_2 + \sum_{j=1}^{q}\lambda_j\sin\left(\frac{1}{2}\arcsin 2\epsilon_{j,\,\theta}\right) + \hat{\epsilon}_f\sum_{j=1}^{q}\lambda_j\right).
$$

Also, by noticing that when $\theta \ll 1$, $\frac{1}{2}\sin 2\theta \approx \sin\theta \approx \theta$, we can obtain Equation (2.33).

$\blacksquare$

In $\hat{\varphi}_i(\cdot)$, $i = 1, 2, 3$, and we apply $\gamma(\cdot)$ to rescale the eigenvalues of $\mathcal{L}$ before calculating the feature scores. Based on Theorem 2.6.3, we can also provide a robustness analysis for $\hat{\varphi}_i(\cdot)$. In the analysis we assume $\gamma(\cdot)$ is a rational function and has the form $\gamma(\lambda) = \lambda^r$.

Theorem 2.6.4 *Let (λ_j, ξ_j) be the eigensystem of $\mathcal{L}$, and $\alpha_j = \cos\theta_j$, where θ_j is the angle between $\mathbf{f}$ and ξ_j. Let $(\tilde{\lambda}_j, \tilde{\xi}_j)$ be the eigensystem of $\tilde{\mathcal{L}}$, and $\tilde{\alpha}_j = \cos\tilde{\theta}_j$, where $\tilde{\theta}_j$ is the angle between $\tilde{\mathbf{f}}$ and $\tilde{\xi}_j$. Also let $\tilde{\lambda}_j = \lambda_j + \lambda_{\epsilon,j}$, and assume $\rho\lambda_j \geq \lambda_{\epsilon,j}$, for all $1 \leq i \leq n$. With $\gamma(\lambda) = \lambda^r$, the following inequality holds:*

$$
\left(\sum_{j=1}^{q}\tilde{\alpha}_j^2\tilde{\lambda}_j^r - \sum_{j=1}^{q}\alpha_j^2\lambda_j^r\right)
$$

$$
\leq \sum_{j=1}^{q}\left(\|\mathcal{L}_\epsilon\|_2\frac{(\rho+1)^r - 1}{\rho}\lambda_j^{r-1} + \sin\left(\frac{1}{2}\arcsin 2\epsilon_{j,\,\theta}\right)\lambda_j^r + \hat{\epsilon}_f\lambda_j^r\right), \quad (2.34)
$$

where $\epsilon_{j,\,\theta} = \dfrac{\|\mathcal{L}_\epsilon\|_2}{\mathrm{GAP}(j,\mathcal{L}+\mathcal{L}_\epsilon)}$ and $\hat{\epsilon}_\mathbf{f} - 2\epsilon_\mathbf{f} + \epsilon_\mathbf{f}^2$. Note, when $\arcsin\epsilon_{j,\,\theta} \ll 1$, we have

$$\sum_{j=1}^{q} \left(\|\mathcal{L}_\epsilon\|_2 \frac{(\rho+1)^r - 1}{\rho} \lambda_j^{r-1} + \sin\left(\frac{1}{2}\arcsin 2\epsilon_{j,\,\theta}\right) \lambda_j^r + \hat{\epsilon}_f \lambda_j^r \right)$$

$$\leq \sum_{j=1}^{q} \left(\|\mathcal{L}_\epsilon\|_2 \frac{(\rho+1)^r - 1}{\rho} \lambda_j^{r-1} + \epsilon_{j,\,\theta} \lambda_j^r + \hat{\epsilon}_f \lambda_j^r \right). \tag{2.35}$$

Proof: This is true because of the following inequality

$$
\begin{aligned}
\tilde{\alpha}^2 \tilde{\lambda}^r &= (\lambda + \lambda_\varepsilon)^r \cos^2\left(\tilde{\theta}\right) - \lambda^r \cos^2\left(\tilde{\theta}\right) + \lambda^r \cos^2\left(\tilde{\theta}\right) \\
&= \left((\lambda + \lambda_\varepsilon)^r - \lambda^r\right)\cos^2\left(\tilde{\theta}\right) + \lambda^r \cos^2\left(\tilde{\theta}\right) \\
&= \lambda_\varepsilon \left(\lambda^{r-1} + \lambda_\varepsilon \lambda^{r-2} + \cdots + \lambda_\varepsilon^{r-2}\lambda + \lambda_\varepsilon^{r-1}\right)\cos^2\left(\tilde{\theta}\right) + \lambda^r \cos^2\left(\tilde{\theta}\right) \\
&\leq \lambda_\varepsilon \lambda^{r-1} \left(1 + (1+\rho) + \cdots + (1+\rho)^{r-1}\right)\cos^2\left(\tilde{\theta}\right) + \lambda^r \cos^2\left(\tilde{\theta}\right) \\
&= \lambda_\varepsilon \lambda^{r-1} \frac{(1+\rho)^r - 1}{\rho} \cos^2\left(\tilde{\theta}\right) + \lambda^r \cos^2\left(\tilde{\theta}\right) \\
&\leq \lambda_\varepsilon \lambda^{r-1} \frac{(1+\rho)^r - 1}{\rho} + \lambda^r \cos^2\left(\tilde{\theta}\right).
\end{aligned}
$$

∎

When the original data are perturbed by noise, feature scores will change accordingly. The two theorems show that before and after the perturbation, the difference of the feature scores is bound by $\epsilon_{\mathcal{L}}$, $\epsilon_{\mathbf{f}}$, and the eigengap of $\tilde{\mathcal{L}}$. Among these factors, $\epsilon_{\mathcal{L}}$ corresponds to the matrix perturbation, $\hat{\epsilon}_{\mathbf{f}}$ corresponds to the feature vector perturbation, and the eigengap of $\tilde{\mathcal{L}}$ corresponds to matrix stability [38]. According to spectral clustering theory, if a data set has an easily separable cluster structure, the top eigengaps of its Laplacian matrix should be large. Since the cluster structure of the data is clear, a small amount of noise will not be able to alter the structure easily. Therefore, a Laplacian matrix with larger top eigengaps is considered to be more robust to noise.

Based on the above theorems, we have the following points regarding the robustness of the feature ranking functions $\tilde{\varphi}_1(\cdot)$, $\tilde{\varphi}_2(\cdot)$, and $\tilde{\varphi}_3(\cdot)$

a) Discarding the tail eigenpairs in feature evaluation helps increase robustness. For a graph with well-separable cluster structures, its tail eigenvalues are usually packed in a small range, thus having small eigengaps [128]. Equation (2.34) suggests including eigenpairs with small eigengaps can increase its sensitivity to noise. Also, it is known that for a graph, its tail eigenvectors usually correspond to the subtle structures formed due to noise [188]. Therefore, removing them helps improve robustness.

b) Among the three feature ranking functions, $\varphi_3(\cdot)$ is more robust than $\varphi_1(\cdot)$ and $\varphi_2(\cdot)$, since it discards the least robust tail eigenpairs in evaluation. $\varphi_1(\cdot)$ and $\varphi_2(\cdot)$ are equally robust, since λ_1 and ξ_1 are constants. Although $\varphi_3(\cdot)$ is more robust in theory, to perform well, it needs a proper threshold to determine which tail eigenpairs should be discarded. Discarding either too many or too few eigenpairs may cause loss of information or inclusion of noise. In [128] the authors proposed using a spectrum gap (the eigengap that divides eigenvalues into two well-separable groups) or the known number of clusters to determine the threshold.

c) Theorem 2.6.4 suggests that if only leading eigenpairs are used for computing feature scores, then a high-order rational function can increase robustness, since the leading eigenvalues are usually smaller than one. But, if all eigenpairs are used, the robustness may decrease, as we usually have $\sum \lambda_j^r \geq \sum \lambda_j$. However, in our experiments, we found that even when all eigenpairs are involved, a high-order rational function still helps improve performance. Two points may support our observation. First, $\sum \lambda_j^r$ actually does not increase much compared with $\sum \lambda_j$. For example, in our experiments, we found $\sum \lambda_j^3$ usually increases the value by no more than 25 percent. Second, with a high-order rational function, $\hat{\varphi}_i(\cdot)$ penalizes the large eigenvalues in a harsher way, effectively increasing the gap between the scores of relevant and irrelevant features, which makes the algorithm more robust to perturbations. Therefore, in reality it is reasonable to use high-order rational functions to improve performance.

Example 12 *The effect of noise on the feature ranking functions*

Figure 2.13 shows how feature ranking functions $\hat{\varphi}_1\,(\cdot)$, $\hat{\varphi}_2\,(\cdot)$, and $\hat{\varphi}_3\,(\cdot)$ are affected by noise. In the figure, $\mathcal{L}$ is the normalized Laplacian matrix constructed in Example 7. Let $\tilde{\mathcal{L}}$ be the noise-contaminated Laplacian matrix, and $\alpha = \frac{\|\tilde{\mathcal{L}}-\mathcal{L}\|}{\|\mathcal{L}\|}$, where α reflects how much noise has been added to the data. In the figure, the x-axis corresponds to α. To generate the plots, we gradually increase α from 0 to 1. The y-axis corresponds to the feature scores of each feature. For $\hat{\varphi}_1(\cdot)$ and $\hat{\varphi}_2(\cdot)$, a smaller feature score indicates more relevance. While for $\hat{\varphi}_3(\cdot)$, a bigger feature score indicates more relevance. Six features are tested: F_1, F_2, F_3, F_4, F_5, and F_6. Among the six features, F_1 and F_2 correspond to the first and the second dimension of the 2D Gaussian mixture generated in Example 6, and are relevant features. $F_3, \ldots, F_6$ are randomly generated with their values following the standard uniform distribution. Hence, these features are irrelevant.

We obtain three observations. First, among the three feature ranking functions, $\varphi_3(\cdot)$ is the most robust to perturbations. When $\alpha = 0.8$, both $\varphi_1(\cdot)$ and $\varphi_2(\cdot)$ mix up relevant features with irrelevant ones, while $\varphi_3(\cdot)$ can still separate them.[6] Second, comparing to $\varphi_1(\cdot)$, $\varphi_2(\cdot)$ is more robust due to the fact that the scores returned by $\varphi_2(\cdot)$ offer bigger gaps between the relevant and the irrelevant features. We also notice that the feature scores returned by $\varphi_1(\cdot)$ and $\varphi_2(\cdot)$ actually change in a similar trend as the scale of the perturbation varies. It can be verified that the different behavior of $\varphi_1(\cdot)$ and $\varphi_2(\cdot)$ is caused by the mechanism of removing the trivial eigenpair, $(\lambda_1, \xi_1) = (0, \mathbf{D}^{\frac{1}{2}}\mathbf{1}/\|\mathbf{D}^{\frac{1}{2}}\mathbf{1}\|)$, from consideration. Recall that $\varphi_2(\cdot) = \hat{\mathbf{f}}_i^{\top} \mathcal{L}\, \hat{\mathbf{f}}_i \left(1 - \left(\hat{\mathbf{f}}_i^{\top} \xi_1\right)^2\right)^{-1}$. It turns out that the relevant features are usually far from ξ_1[6], and therefore have denominators near 1. In contrast, the irrelevant ones are often relatively closer to ξ_1 and have smaller denominators. This difference effectively increases the score gaps between the relevant and irrelevant features. Third, a high-order rational function also helps increase the score gap. From the chart, we can observe that although $\varphi_1(\lambda)$ mixes up the relevant with irrelevant features when $\alpha \approx 0.53$, with the help of $\gamma(\cdot) = \lambda^3$, $\hat{\varphi}_1(\lambda)$ does not mix up the relevant with the irrelevant until $\alpha \approx 0.67$. A similar effect can also be observed on the other two feature ranking functions, although these trends are less evident.

---

[6]When $\alpha = 0.8$, the scores generated from $\varphi_3(\cdot)$ for the six features are 0.0206, 0.0501, 0.0096, 0.0154, 0.0023, and 0.0049, respectively.

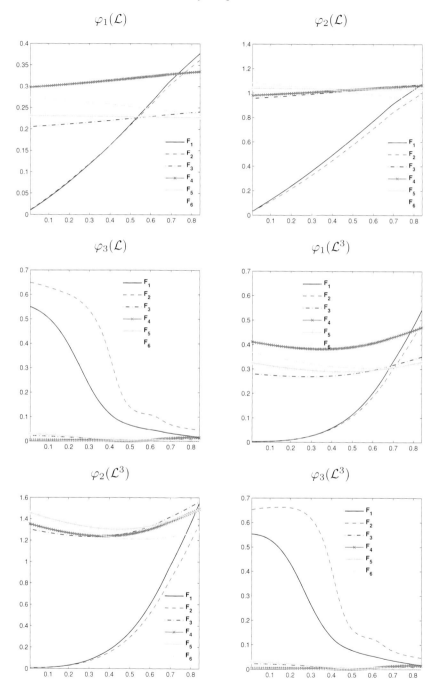

FIGURE 2.13: (**SEE COLOR INSERT**) Effects of noise on the feature ranking functions.

2.7   Discussions

SPEC is a unified spectral feature selection framework for supervised, unsupervised, and semi-supervised feature selection. It is based on three univariate formulations for feature evaluation and is of a filter model. We show that families of effective algorithms can be derived from the framework. We conduct robustness analysis based on perturbation theory. The analysis enables us to obtain better understanding of the behavior of the SPEC in a noisy learning environment.

The proposed framework consists of three components: the similarity matrix $\mathbf{S}$, the ranking function $\hat{\varphi}(\cdot)$, and the spectral function $\gamma(\cdot)$. A proper configuration of the framework ensures good performance. Based on our experimental results and observations, we offer the following guidelines for configuring SPEC: (1) The similarity matrix depicts the relationship among samples. A matrix which reflects the true relationships among samples is important for SPEC to select good features. (2) In noisy learning environments, either $\hat{\varphi}_3(\cdot)$ or a high-order rational function $\gamma(\cdot)$ is helpful for removing noise. (3) For data with a clear spectrum gap, using $\hat{\varphi}_3(\cdot)$ may be very effective. Otherwise $\hat{\varphi}_2(\cdot)$ could be more promising. Compared with $\hat{\varphi}_3(\cdot)$, $\hat{\varphi}_2(\cdot)$ is less aggressive and usually provides robust performance. (4) SPEC generates feature weighting algorithms. However, most feature weighting algorithms do not consider feature redundancy, which may hurt learning performance [212]. To address the problem, we will propose a multivariate formulation for spectral feature selection in Chapter 3.

Chapter 3

Multivariate Formulations for Spectral Feature Selection

Redundant features are those that are relevant to the target concept, but their removal has no negative effect. Usually, a feature becomes redundant when it can be expressed by other features. Redundant features unnecessarily increase data dimensionality [89], which worsens the learning performance. It has been empirically shown that removing redundant features can result in significant performance improvement [69, 40, 56, 210, 6, 43]. In the last section, we introduced the SPEC framework for spectral feature selection. We notice that the feature evaluation criteria in SPEC are univariate: features are evaluated individually, therefore the framework is not capable of handling redundant features.

Example 13 *An example of a redundant feature*

Assume we have three features F_1, F_2, and F_3. Among the three features, F_3 can be expressed as a linear combination of F_1 and F_2:

$$F_3 = aF_1 + bF_2, \quad a, b \in \mathbb{R}.$$

Given any function containing the three features, we can write it as a function that contains only F_1 and F_2:

$$\phi(F_1, F_2, F_3) = \phi(F_1, F_2, aF_1 + bF_2) = \phi'(F_1, F_2).$$

Therefore, in this case, F_3 is redundant due to the existence of F_1 and F_2.

Spectral feature selection can handle redundant features by evaluating the utility of a set of features jointly. In this chapter, we study two multivariate formulations for spectral feature selection, one based on multi-output regression [72] with an $L_{2,1}$-norm regularization, and the other based on matrix comparison. We analyze their capabilities for detecting redundant features, and study their efficiency for problem solving. Before we present the two formulations, we first study an interesting characteristic of the SPEC framework, which we introduced in the last chapter. We show that SPEC selects features by evaluating their capability of preserving the sample similarity specified by the given similarity matrix $\mathbf{S}$. Based on this insight, we present two multivariate formulations for spectral feature selection.

3.1 The Similarity Preserving Nature of SPEC

As shown in Chapter 2, given a similarity matrix $\mathbf{S}$, SPEC selects features aligning well with the top eigenvectors of $\mathcal{L}$. Here $\mathcal{L}$ is the normalized Laplacian matrix derived from $\mathbf{S}$. This fact brings us to the conjecture that if we construct a new sample similarity matrix $\mathbf{K}$, using the features selected by SPEC, $\mathbf{K}$ should be similar to $\mathbf{S}$, in the sense that if the two samples are similar according to $\mathbf{S}$, they should also be similar according to $\mathbf{K}$. To precisely study the similarity preserving nature of SPEC, we reformulate the relevance evaluation criteria used in the SPEC framework in a more general form:

$$\max_{\mathbb{F}_{sub}} \left(\sum_{F \in \mathbb{F}_{sub}} \varphi\left(F\right) \right) = \max_{\mathbb{F}_{sub}} \left(\sum_{F \in \mathbb{F}_{sub}} \hat{\mathbf{f}}^{\top} \, \hat{\mathbf{S}} \, \hat{\mathbf{f}} \right); \quad \hat{\mathbf{f}} \in \mathbb{R}^{n}, \, \hat{\mathbf{S}} \in \mathbb{R}^{n \times n}. \quad (3.1)$$

Basically, we want to find a set of selected features, $\mathbb{F}_{sub}$, such that the objective specified in Equation (3.1) can be maximized. In the above equation, $\hat{\mathbf{f}}$ and $\hat{\mathbf{S}}$ are the normalized feature vector and the normalized sample similarity matrix derived from $\mathbf{f}$ and $\mathbf{S}$, respectively. It is shown in [155] that solving the following problem

$$\max_{\mathbf{K} \succeq 0} \operatorname{Trace}\left(\mathbf{KS}\right) \quad st. \quad \operatorname{Trace}\left(K\right) \leq 1, \quad (3.2)$$

will result in a kernel matrix $\mathbf{K}$, which preserves the sample similarity specified in $\mathbf{S}$. Here, the constraint $\mathbf{K} \succeq 0$ requires the matrix $\mathbf{K}$ to be positive semidefinite. We can write Equation (3.1) in the form of Equation (3.2),

$$\max_{\mathbb{F}_{sub}} \sum_{F \in \mathbb{F}_{sub}} \hat{\mathbf{f}}^{\top} \hat{\mathbf{S}} \, \hat{\mathbf{f}} \;=\; \max_{\mathbb{F}_{sub}} \sum_{F \in \mathbb{F}_{sub}} \operatorname{Trace}\left(\hat{\mathbf{f}} \, \hat{\mathbf{f}}^{\top} \hat{\mathbf{S}}\right)$$

$$=\; \max_{\mathbb{F}_{sub}} \operatorname{Trace}\left(\left(\sum_{F \in \mathbb{F}_{sub}} \hat{\mathbf{f}} \, \hat{\mathbf{f}}^{\top}\right) \hat{\mathbf{S}}\right).$$

We also have $\sum_{F \in \mathbb{F}_{sub}} \hat{\mathbf{f}} \, \hat{\mathbf{f}}^{\top} = \mathbf{X}_{\mathbb{F}_{sub}}^{\top} \mathbf{X}_{\mathbb{F}_{sub}}$. Here $\mathbf{X}_{\mathbb{F}_{sub}}$ is the data containing only the features in $\mathbb{F}_{sub}$. Thus, we have the following equation:

$$\max_{\mathbb{F}_{sub}} \sum_{F \in \mathbb{F}_{sub}} \hat{\mathbf{f}}^{\top} \hat{\mathbf{S}} \, \hat{\mathbf{f}} = \max_{\mathbb{F}_{sub}} \operatorname{Trace}\left(\left(\mathbf{X}_{\mathbb{F}_{sub}}^{\top} \mathbf{X}_{\mathbb{F}_{sub}}\right) \hat{\mathbf{S}}\right). \quad (3.3)$$

This equation shows that $\max_{\mathbb{F}_{sub}} \sum_{F \in \mathbb{F}_{sub}} \hat{\mathbf{f}}^{\top} \hat{\mathbf{S}} \, \hat{\mathbf{f}}$ will select a set of features

$\mathbb{F}_{sub}$, such that the linear kernel constructed from $\mathbf{X}_{\mathbb{F}_{sub}}$ can preserve the pairwise sample similarity specified in $\hat{\mathbf{S}}$. In other words, we can say that the features in $\mathbb{F}_{sub}$ have a strong capability of preserving the pairwise sample similarity specified in $\hat{\mathbf{S}}$. We can also show this in a more intuitive way: since $\hat{\mathbf{f}}^{\top} \hat{\mathbf{S}} \hat{\mathbf{f}} = \sum_i \sum_i \hat{s}_{ij} \hat{f}_i \hat{f}_j$, assuming that features are normalized ($\| \hat{\mathbf{f}} \| = 1$), to obtain a large value from Equation (3.1), a feature must assign similar values to the samples that are similar according to $\hat{\mathbf{S}}$. This ensures that the feature has the strong capability of preserving the sample similarity specified in $\hat{\mathbf{S}}$.

Example 14 *Measuring consistency between matrices*

Trace $(\mathbf{KS})$ can be used to measure the consistency between matrices. To show this, we generated a two-dimensional data set with three classes, whose distribution is shown in Figure 3.1(a). We then generate noise-contaminated data sets by adding different levels of noise to the data set. Figure 3.1(b), (c), and (d) correspond to the data sets containing 30%, 60%, and 90% of noise, respectively. We construct linear kernels on both the original data set and the noise-contaminated data sets, and compute Trace $(\mathbf{KS})$ to measure the consistency between matrices. Here $\mathbf{S}$ is the linear kernel constructed on the original data set, and $\mathbf{K}$ is the linear kernel constructed on either the original data set or a noise-contaminated data set. From the figures the similarity relationships among samples are perturbed proportionally to the level of the noise added to the data. And correspondingly, the value of Trace $(\mathbf{KS})$ decreases. When $\mathbf{K} = \mathbf{S}$, Trace $(\mathbf{KS}) = 1.282$, while when $\mathbf{K}$ is constructed on the data set containing 90% of noise, Trace $(\mathbf{KS})$ decreases to 0.7994.

In the following, we show how SPEC can be reformulated in the form of Equation (3.1). We first study a simple case, in which the spectral matrix function, $\gamma(\cdot)$, is not applied. Using the following theorem, we show that with different definitions of $\hat{\mathbf{f}}$ and $\hat{\mathbf{S}}$, the three feature ranking functions $\varphi_1(\cdot)$, $\varphi_2(\cdot)$, and $\varphi_3(\cdot)$ can be written in a common form: $\max_{\mathbb{F}_{sub}} \sum_{F \in \mathbb{F}_{sub}} \hat{\mathbf{f}}^{\top} \hat{\mathbf{S}} \hat{\mathbf{f}}$. Here, $\hat{\mathbf{f}}$ and $\hat{\mathbf{S}}$ are the normalized versions of $\mathbf{f}$ and $\mathbf{S}$.

Theorem 3.1.1 *Let $\mathbf{S}$ be a similarity matrix, and $\mathbf{D}$ and $\mathcal{L}$ be its degree and normalized Laplacian matrices, respectively. SPEC selects k features, which maximize the following objective function:*

$$\arg\max_{F_{i_1},\ldots,F_{i_k}} \sum_{j=1}^{k} \hat{\mathbf{f}}_{i_j}^{\top} \hat{\mathbf{S}} \hat{\mathbf{f}}_{i_j}. \tag{3.4}$$

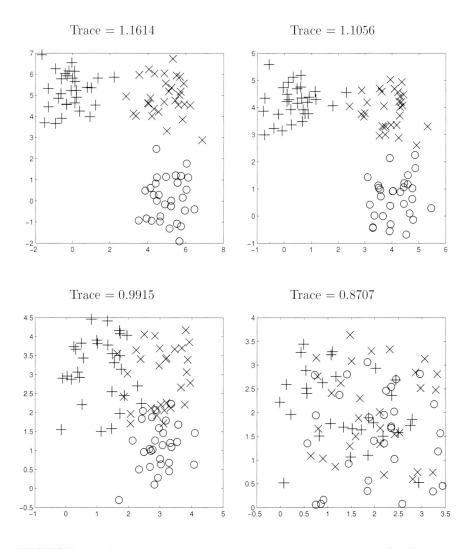

FIGURE 3.1: Measure consistency between matrices via Trace (**KS**).

When $\varphi_1(\cdot)$ is applied, $\hat{\mathbf{f}}$ and $\hat{\mathbf{S}}$ are defined as

$$\hat{\mathbf{f}} = \frac{\mathbf{D}^{\frac{1}{2}}\mathbf{f}}{\|\mathbf{D}^{\frac{1}{2}}\mathbf{f}\|}, \quad \hat{\mathbf{S}} = \mathbf{D}^{-\frac{1}{2}}\,\mathbf{S}\,\mathbf{D}^{-\frac{1}{2}}. \tag{3.5}$$

When $\varphi_2(\cdot)$ is applied, let ξ_1 be the first eigenvector of $\mathcal{L}$, which is equal to $\frac{\mathbf{D}^{-\frac{1}{2}}\mathbf{1}}{\|\mathbf{D}^{-\frac{1}{2}}\mathbf{1}\|_2}$. $\hat{\mathbf{f}}$ and $\hat{\mathbf{S}}$ are defined as

$$\tilde{\mathbf{f}} = \frac{\mathbf{D}^{\frac{1}{2}}\mathbf{f}}{\|\mathbf{D}^{\frac{1}{2}}\mathbf{f}\|}, \quad \hat{\mathbf{f}} = \frac{\tilde{\mathbf{f}} - \tilde{\mathbf{f}}^{\top}\xi_1\xi_1}{\sqrt{1 - \left(\tilde{\mathbf{f}}^{\top}\xi_1\right)^2}}, \quad \hat{\mathbf{S}} = \mathbf{D}^{-\frac{1}{2}}\mathbf{S}\mathbf{D}^{-\frac{1}{2}}. \tag{3.6}$$

When $\varphi_3(\cdot)$ is applied, let $\mathcal{L} = \mathbf{U}\Sigma\mathbf{U}^{\top}$, where $\mathbf{U} = (\xi_1,\ldots,\xi_n)$ and $\Sigma = diag(\lambda_1,\ldots,\lambda_n)$ are the eigen decomposition of $\mathcal{L}$. $\hat{\mathbf{f}}$ and $\hat{\mathbf{S}}$ are defined as:

$$\hat{\mathbf{f}} = \frac{\mathbf{D}^{\frac{1}{2}}\mathbf{f}}{\|\mathbf{D}^{\frac{1}{2}}\mathbf{f}\|}, \quad \hat{\mathbf{S}} = \mathbf{U}_k\left(2\mathbf{I} - \Sigma_k\right)\mathbf{U}_k^{\top}, \tag{3.7}$$

where $\mathbf{U}_k = (\xi_2,\ldots,\xi_k)$, $\Sigma_k = diag(\lambda_2,\ldots,\lambda_k)$.

Proof: We start from $\varphi_1(\cdot)$. It is easy to verify that $\varphi_1(F) = \hat{\mathbf{f}}^{\top}\left(\mathbf{I} - \hat{\mathbf{S}}\right)\hat{\mathbf{f}}$. In SPEC, features are evaluated independently; therefore, using $\varphi_1(\cdot)$ to select k features can be achieved by picking the top k features that have the smallest $\varphi_1(\cdot)$ values. This process can be formulated as the following optimization problem:

$$\arg\min_{F_{i_1},\ldots,F_{i_k}} \sum_{j=1}^{k} \hat{\mathbf{f}}_{i_j}^{\top}\left(\mathbf{I} - \hat{\mathbf{S}}\right)\hat{\mathbf{f}}_{i_j}.$$

Note that in the above equation, features are evaluated independently. Additionally,

$$\arg\min_{F_{i_1},\ldots,F_{i_k}} \sum_{j=1}^{k} \hat{\mathbf{f}}_{i_j}^{\top}\left(\mathbf{I} - \hat{\mathbf{S}}\right)\hat{\mathbf{f}}_{i_j} = \arg\max_{F_{i_1},\ldots,F_{i_k}} \sum_{j=1}^{k} \hat{\mathbf{f}}_{i_j}^{\top}\hat{\mathbf{S}}\,\hat{\mathbf{f}}_{i_j}.$$

Here we assume the features have been normalized, therefore all have unit norm.

In the case of $\varphi_2(\cdot)$, it is easy to verify that $\|\hat{\mathbf{f}}\| = 1$. Since the first eigenvalue of the normalized Laplacian matrix $\mathcal{L}$ is always zero, we have $\xi_1^{\top}\hat{\mathcal{L}}\,\mathbf{x} = 0$ for any $\mathbf{x} \in \mathbb{R}^{n\times1}$. Based on these two facts, we can verify that Equation (3.6) holds.

Similarly, in the case of $\varphi_3(\cdot)$, the following equation holds:

$$\mathbf{f}^{\top}\mathbf{U}_k\left(2\mathbf{I} - \Sigma_k\right)\mathbf{U}_k^{\top}\mathbf{f} = \sum_{j=2}^{k}(2 - \lambda_j)\alpha_j^2 = \varphi_3(F).$$

This proves the equivalence when $\varphi_3(\cdot)$ is used. ∎

Theorem 3.1.1 shows that when $\varphi_1(\cdot)$ or $\varphi_2(\cdot)$ is used, SPEC tries to preserve the sample similarity specified by $\mathbf{D}^{-\frac{1}{2}}\mathbf{S}\mathbf{D}^{-\frac{1}{2}}$, which is the normalized sample similarity matrix. When $\varphi_3(\cdot)$ is used, SPEC tries to preserve the sample similarity specified by $\mathbf{U}_k\left(2\mathbf{I} - \Sigma_k\right)\mathbf{U}_k^\top$, which is derived from $\mathcal{L}$ by adjusting the leading eigenvalues and discarding the tail eigenpairs. In $\varphi_1(\cdot)$ and $\varphi_3(\cdot)$, the features are first reweighted by $\mathbf{D}^{\frac{1}{2}}\mathbf{f}$, which forms the density reweighted features [74]. And they are then normalized to have the unit norm. This step emphasizes the elements in a feature vector, which correspond to the samples from a neighborhood with dense sample distribution. In $\varphi_2(\cdot)$, there is an additional orthogonalization step: features are made to be orthogonal to ξ_1, and then normalized to have unit norm. This step removes ξ_1 from consideration. As we mentioned, by aligning closely with ξ_1, a feature can achieve a large $\varphi_1(\cdot)$ value. However, ξ_1 only captures the density information of the data. The orthogonalization step ensures that we will not assign high relevance scores to features that align closely with ξ_1.

Similarly, when the spectral matrix function $\gamma(\cdot)$ is used in SPEC, using the following theorem, we show that the three feature ranking functions $\hat{\varphi}_1(\cdot)$, $\hat{\varphi}_2(\cdot)$, and $\hat{\varphi}_3(\cdot)$ can also be formulated into the form: $\max_{\mathbb{F}_{sub}} \sum_{F \in \mathbb{F}_{sub}} \hat{\mathbf{f}}^\top \hat{\mathbf{S}} \hat{\mathbf{f}}$.

Theorem 3.1.2 *Let $\mathbf{S}$ be a similarity matrix, and $\mathbf{D}$ and $\mathcal{L}$ be its degree and normalized Laplacian matrices, respectively. Also let $\gamma(\cdot)$ be a spectral matrix function. SPEC selects k features that maximize the objective function:*

$$\arg\max_{F_{i_1}, \ldots, F_{i_k}} \sum_{j=1}^{k} \hat{\mathbf{f}}_{i_j}^\top \hat{\mathbf{S}} \hat{\mathbf{f}}_{i_j}. \tag{3.8}$$

Let $\mathcal{L} = \mathbf{U}\Sigma\mathbf{U}^\top$, where $\mathbf{U} = (\xi_1, \ldots, \xi_n)$ and $\Sigma = diag(\lambda_1, \ldots, \lambda_n)$. When $\hat{\varphi}_1(\cdot)$ is applied, $\hat{\mathbf{f}}$ and $\hat{\mathbf{S}}$ are defined by

$$\hat{\mathbf{f}} = \frac{\mathbf{D}^{\frac{1}{2}}\mathbf{f}}{\|\mathbf{D}^{\frac{1}{2}}\mathbf{f}\|}, \quad \hat{\mathbf{S}} = \mathbf{U}\left(\mathbf{I} - \gamma(\Sigma)\right)\mathbf{U}^\top. \tag{3.9}$$

Let ξ_1 be the first eigenvector of $\mathcal{L}$. When $\hat{\varphi}_2(\cdot)$ is applied, $\hat{\mathbf{f}}$ and $\hat{\mathbf{S}}$ are defined as

$$\tilde{\mathbf{f}} = \frac{\mathbf{D}^{\frac{1}{2}}\mathbf{f}}{\|\mathbf{D}^{\frac{1}{2}}\mathbf{f}\|}, \quad \hat{\mathbf{f}} = \frac{\tilde{\mathbf{f}} - \tilde{\mathbf{f}}^\top \xi_1 \xi_1}{\sqrt{1 - \left(\tilde{\mathbf{f}}^\top \xi_1\right)^2}}, \quad \hat{\mathbf{S}} = \mathbf{U}\left(\mathbf{I} - \gamma(\Sigma)\right)\mathbf{U}^\top. \tag{3.10}$$

When $\hat{\varphi}_3(\cdot)$ is applied, $\hat{\mathbf{f}}$ and $\hat{\mathbf{S}}$ are defined as

$$\hat{\mathbf{f}} = \frac{\mathbf{D}^{\frac{1}{2}}\mathbf{f}}{\|\mathbf{D}^{\frac{1}{2}}\mathbf{f}\|}, \quad \hat{\mathbf{S}} = \mathbf{U}_k\left(\gamma(2\mathbf{I}) - \gamma(\Sigma_k)\right)\mathbf{U}_k^\top, \tag{3.11}$$

$$\mathbf{U}_k = (\xi_2, \ldots, \xi_k), \quad \Sigma_k = diag(\lambda_2, \ldots, \lambda_k).$$

∎

Theorem 3.1.2 can be proved in a way similar to Theorem 3.1.1. Therefore we omit its proof. Theorems 3.1.1 and 3.1.2 together demonstrate the similarity preserving nature of SPEC.

In SPEC, features are evaluated independently. A direct consequence of this is that redundant features cannot be properly handled by the SPEC framework. Redundant features unnecessarily increase dimensionality and can worsen learning performance. They need to be removed in the feature selection process. To achieve this, we propose in the following sections two multivariate formulations for spectral feature selection, which are able to evaluate the utility of a set of features jointly. We show that the multivariate formulations for spectral feature selection can identify redundant features effectively.

3.2 A Sparse Multi-Output Regression Formulation

Let $\mathbf{X} \in \mathbb{R}^{n \times m}$ be a data matrix, where n and m are the numbers of samples and features, respectively. Given a sample similarity matrix $\mathbf{S}$ and a feature F, different feature evaluation criteria in SPEC can be formulated in a common form as

$$\varphi(F, \mathbf{S}) = \hat{\mathbf{f}}^\top \hat{\mathbf{S}} \, \hat{\mathbf{f}} = \sum_{i=1}^{n} \hat{\lambda}_i \left(\hat{\mathbf{f}}^\top \hat{\xi}_i \right)^2 = \sum_{i=1}^{n} \left(\hat{\lambda}_i^{\frac{1}{2}} \hat{\mathbf{f}}^\top \hat{\xi}_i \right)^2, \qquad (3.12)$$

where $\hat{\mathbf{f}}$ is the normalized feature vector, $\hat{\mathbf{S}}$ is the normalized similarity matrix, and $\hat{\lambda}_i$ and $\hat{\xi}_i$ are the i-*th* eigenvalue and eigenvector of $\hat{\mathbf{S}}$, respectively. Equation (3.12) shows that these criteria evaluate features individually, and are therefore unable to identify redundant features.

Let $\mathbf{y}_i = \hat{\lambda}_i^{\frac{1}{2}} \hat{\xi}_i$, Equation (3.12) can be written as

$$\varphi(F, \mathbf{S}) = \sum_{i=1}^{n} \left(\hat{\lambda}_i^{\frac{1}{2}} \hat{\mathbf{f}}^\top \hat{\xi}_i \right)^2 = \sum_{i=1}^{n} \left(\hat{\mathbf{f}}^\top \mathbf{y}_i \right)^2. \qquad (3.13)$$

To identify redundant features, the features must be evaluated jointly. Instead of looking for features that are close to $\mathbf{y}_i$, as formulated in the above equation, we should find a set of l features, such that their linear span [77] is close to $\mathbf{y}_i$. This idea can be formulated as

$$\arg \min_{\mathbb{A}, \mathbf{w}_{i,\mathbb{A}}} \|\mathbf{y}_i - \mathbf{X}_\mathbb{A} \mathbf{w}_{i,\mathbb{A}}\|_2^2,$$

where $\mathbb{A} = \{i_1, \ldots, i_l\} \subseteq \{1, \ldots, m\}$, $\mathbf{X}_\mathbb{A} = (\mathbf{f}_{i_1}, \ldots, \mathbf{f}_{i_l})$, and $\mathbf{w}_i \in \mathbb{R}^{l \times 1}$. Note that in the above equation, we apply the L_2 norm on the difference of two vectors to measure their closeness. When all $\mathbf{y}_i = \hat{\lambda}_i^{\frac{1}{2}} \hat{\xi}_i$ are considered, their joint optimization can be formulated as

$$\arg\min_{\mathbb{A}, \mathbf{w}_{i, \mathbb{A}}} \sum_{i=1}^{n} \|\mathbf{y}_i - \mathbf{X}_{\mathbb{A}} \mathbf{w}_{i, \mathbb{A}}\|_2^2 = \arg\min_{\mathbb{A}, \mathbf{w}_{\mathbb{A}}} \|\mathbf{Y} - \mathbf{X}_{\mathbb{A}} \mathbf{W}_{\mathbb{A}}\|_F^2. \tag{3.14}$$

In the above equation, $\mathbf{Y} = (\mathbf{y}_1, \ldots, \mathbf{y}_n)$, $\mathbf{W}_{\mathbb{A}} = (\mathbf{w}_{1, \mathbb{A}}, \ldots, \mathbf{w}_{n, \mathbb{A}})$. Assuming that $\mathbf{S} = \mathbf{U\Sigma U}^{\top}$ is the SVD of $\hat{\mathbf{S}}$, we have $\mathbf{Y} = \mathbf{U\Sigma}^{1/2}$. And $\|\cdot\|_F$ is the Frobenius norm [59], which is defined as

$$\|\mathbf{R}\|_F = \sqrt{\text{Trace}\left(\mathbf{R}^{\top}\mathbf{R}\right)}. \tag{3.15}$$

We noticed that when $\mathbb{A}$ contains only one feature, the formulation reduces to searching for features that maximize the Equation (3.12).

Given $\mathbf{Y}$ and $\mathbf{X}_{\mathbb{A}}$, the optimal $\mathbf{W}_{\mathbb{A}}$ in Equation (3.14) can be obtained in a closed form. However, feature selection needs to find the optimal $\mathbb{A}$, which is a combinatorial problem being NP-hard. To make the problem solvable, we can approximate the problem as [9, 44, 95, 126, 132, 214, 218, 116, 115]

$$\arg\min_{\mathbf{W}, \lambda} \|\mathbf{Y} - \mathbf{XW}\|_F^2 + \lambda \|\mathbf{W}\|_{2,1}$$

$$s.t. \quad \mathbb{A} = \{i : \|\mathbf{w}^i\|_2 > 0\}, \ Card(\mathbb{A}) = l, \tag{3.16}$$

where $Card(\mathbb{A})$ returns the cardinality of the set $\mathbb{A}$, $\mathbf{w}^i$ denotes the i-*th* row of $\mathbf{W}$, and $\|\mathbf{W}\|_{2,1}$ is the $L_{2,1}$-norm, defined as

$$\|\mathbf{W}\|_{2,1} = \sum_{i=1}^{m} \|\mathbf{w}^i\|_2 \tag{3.17}$$

When applied in regression, the $L_{2,1}$-norm regularization is equivalent to applying a Laplace prior [153] on $\mathbf{w}^i$, which tends to force many rows in $\mathbf{W}$ to become zero row vectors and results in a sparse solution. The effect of the $L_{2,1}$-norm constraint can be demonstrated by the following example.

Example 15 *The effect of the $L_{2,1}$-norm regularization*

In this example, we randomly construct a data set containing 200 samples and 200 features, $\mathbf{X} \in \mathbb{R}^{200 \times 200}$; and $\left(\hat{\lambda}_1^{\frac{1}{2}}, \hat{\xi}_1\right), \ldots, \left(\hat{\lambda}_{100}^{\frac{1}{2}}, \hat{\xi}_{100}\right)$ are used to form $\mathbf{Y}$, $\mathbf{Y} \in \mathbb{R}^{200 \times 100}$. We try different λ values for the regularization and plot the obtained $\mathbf{W}$ in Figure 3.2. In the figure, a light spot corresponds to a nonzero element in $\mathbf{W}$. It shows, when $\lambda = 0$ (no regularization is applied), all features are selected. Since a larger $\|W\|_{2,1}$ applies a more severe penalty on a dense solution, when we increase λ from 0 to 500, more and more rows of $\mathbf{W}$ are set to 0. Because each row of $\mathbf{W}$ corresponds to a feature in $\mathbf{X}$, by setting many rows of $\mathbf{W}$ to zero, we remove many features from consideration, which helps us achieve feature selection.

There are three advantages of the formulation presented in Equation (3.16):

(1) It can find a set of features jointly preserving the sample similarity specified by $\mathbf{S}$.

(2) By jointly evaluating a set of features, it tends to select nonredundant features.

(3) The problem specified in the formulation is tractable.

First, by the following theorem, we show that the formulation can find a set of features jointly preserving the sample similarity specified by $\mathbf{S}$.

Theorem 3.2.1 *Let* $\mathbf{S} = \mathbf{U}\Sigma\mathbf{U}^\top$, $\mathbf{Y} = \mathbf{U}\Sigma^{1/2}$ *and* $\Omega = \mathbf{Y} - \mathbf{X}\mathbf{W}$. *We have*

$$\left\| \mathbf{X}\mathbf{W}\mathbf{W}^\top\mathbf{X}^\top - \mathbf{S} \right\|_F \leq 2(\|\mathbf{Y}\|_F + \|\Omega\|_F)\|\Omega\|_F .$$

Proof: Since $\mathbf{S} = \mathbf{Y}\mathbf{Y}^\top$ and $\|\mathbf{A} + \mathbf{B}\|_F \leq \|\mathbf{A}\|_F + \|\mathbf{B}\|_F$, we have

$$
\begin{aligned}
\|\mathbf{X}\mathbf{W}\mathbf{W}^\top\mathbf{X}^\top - \mathbf{Y}\mathbf{Y}^\top\|_F
&= \|\Omega\mathbf{Y}^\top + \mathbf{Y}\Omega^\top + \Omega\Omega^\top\|_F \\
&\leq \|\Omega\mathbf{Y}^\top\|_F + \|\mathbf{Y}\Omega^\top\|_F + \|\Omega\Omega^\top\|_F \\
&\leq 2\|\mathbf{Y}\|_F\|\Omega\|_F + \|\Omega\|_F^2 \\
&= (2\|\mathbf{Y}\|_F + \|\Omega\|_F)\|\Omega\|_F.
\end{aligned}
$$

In the derivation, we use the inequality $\|\mathbf{A}\mathbf{B}\|_F \leq \|\mathbf{A}\|_F\|\mathbf{B}\|_F$.

∎

In the above theorem, $\mathbf{X}\mathbf{W}$ is a new representation of samples obtained by linearly combining the selected features.[1] And $\mathbf{X}\mathbf{W}\mathbf{W}^\top\mathbf{X}^\top$ computes the pairwise similarity among samples measured by their inner product under this new representation. The theorem shows that by minimizing $\|\Omega\|_F$, we also minimize $\|\mathbf{X}\mathbf{W}\mathbf{W}^\top\mathbf{X}^\top - \mathbf{S}\|_F$, which ensures the selected features can jointly preserve the sample similarity specified by $\mathbf{S}$.

Second, the formulation tends to select nonredundant features. Assume two features $\mathbf{f}_p$ and $\mathbf{f}_q$ satisfy the following conditions: (1) they are equally correlated to $\mathbf{Y}$, i.e., $\mathbf{f}_p^\top\mathbf{Y} = \mathbf{f}_q^\top\mathbf{Y}$; (2) $\mathbf{f}_q$ is highly correlated to $\mathbf{f}_d$, i.e., $\mathbf{f}_q^\top\mathbf{f}_d \rightarrow 1$, and $\mathbf{f}_q$ is less correlated to $\mathbf{f}_d$, i.e., $\mathbf{f}_p^\top\mathbf{f}_d > \mathbf{f}_q^\top\mathbf{f}_d$ (without loss of generality, we assume both $\mathbf{f}_p$ and $\mathbf{f}_q$ are positively correlated to $\mathbf{f}_d$); (3) they are equally correlated to other features, i.e., $\mathbf{f}_p^\top\mathbf{f}_i = \mathbf{f}_q^\top\mathbf{f}_i$, $\forall i \in \{1, \ldots, m\}$, $i \neq d$. Based on these assumptions, we attain the following theorem.

Theorem 3.2.2 *Given the above assumptions, assuming* $\mathbf{f}_d$ *is selected by an optimal solution of Equation (3.16), then* $\mathbf{f}_q$ *has higher priority than* $\mathbf{f}_p$ *to be selected in the optimal solution.*

---

[1] Note that although $\mathbf{W} \in \mathbb{R}^{m \times k}$, many of its rows are $\mathbf{0}^\top$. Therefore, the representation is generated by using only a small subset of selected features.

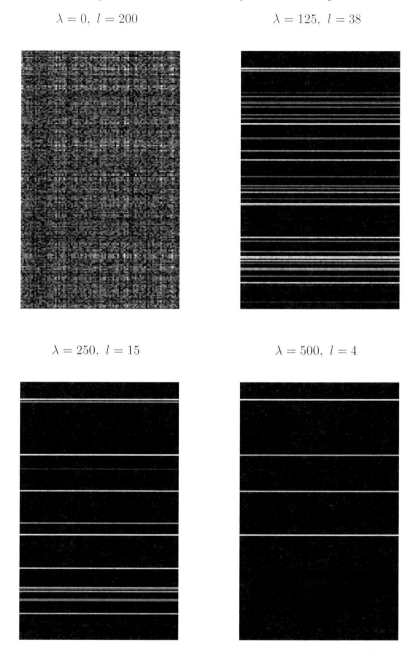

FIGURE 3.2: Different λ values for $L_{2,1}$-norm regularization and their corresponding sparse solutions. l is the number of rows that have nonzero elements. As λ becomes larger, more rows of **S** are set to 0. Note: each row of **W** corresponds to a feature.

Proof: Let $\mathbf{Y} = (\mathbf{y}_1, \cdots, \mathbf{y}_k)$ be the $n \times k$ target matrix, and $\mathbf{W}$ be the $m \times k$ weight matrix. The i-th row and j-th column of $\mathbf{W}$ are denoted by $\mathbf{W}_{i:}$ and $\mathbf{W}_{:j}$, respectively. Recall that $\|\cdot\|_F$ is the Frobenius norm and $\|\mathbf{W}\|_{2,1} = \sum_{i=1}^{m} \|\mathbf{W}_{i:}\|_2$ is the $L_{2,1}$ norm. Let $\overline{\mathbf{W}}$ be the current solution in which two strongly correlated features $\mathbf{f}_d$ and $\mathbf{f}_p$ are selected, i.e., $\|\overline{\mathbf{W}}_{d:}\|_F > 0, \|\overline{\mathbf{W}}_{p:}\|_F > 0$. Using the technique developed in [144], we can show that in the optimal solution of Equation (3.16) $\langle \overline{\mathbf{W}}_{d:}, \overline{\mathbf{W}}_{p:} \rangle > 0$ when $\mathbf{f}_d^\top \mathbf{f}_p \to 1$. Assuming the three conditions specified above hold, we show that as long as $\mathbf{f}_q$ has a sufficiently small correlation with $\mathbf{f}_d$, selecting $\mathbf{f}_q$ rather than $\mathbf{f}_p$ always decreases the objective function. To this end, we define another weight matrix $\tilde{\mathbf{W}}$ as: $\tilde{\mathbf{W}}_{i:} = \overline{\mathbf{W}}_{i:}$ for $\forall\, i \neq p, q$, $\tilde{\mathbf{W}}_{q:} = \overline{\mathbf{W}}_{p:}$, and $\tilde{\mathbf{W}}_{p:} = \mathbf{0}$. Note that (1) $\|\tilde{\mathbf{W}}\|_{2,1} = \|\overline{\mathbf{W}}\|_{2,1}$; and (2) $\tilde{\mathbf{W}}$ and $\overline{\mathbf{W}}$ have no difference except the p-th and q-th rows. Since $\|\mathbf{Y} - \mathbf{X}\mathbf{W}\|_F^2 = \sum_{j=1}^{l} \|\mathbf{y}_i - \mathbf{X}\mathbf{W}_{:j}\|_2^2$, we can show that

$$\|\mathbf{Y} - \mathbf{X}\overline{\mathbf{W}}\|_F^2 - \|\mathbf{Y} - \mathbf{X}\tilde{\mathbf{W}}\|_F^2 = 2\overline{\mathbf{W}}_{p:}\mathbf{Y}^\top (\mathbf{f}_q - \mathbf{f}_p) + 2\langle \overline{\mathbf{W}}_{d:}, \overline{\mathbf{W}}_{p:} \rangle (\rho_{dp} - \rho_{dq}),$$

where, $\rho_{ij} = \mathbf{f}_i^\top \mathbf{f}_j$. In the derivation, we rely on the fact that

$$\sum_{j=1}^{l} \overline{\mathbf{W}}_{pj}\mathbf{y}_j^\top = \overline{\mathbf{W}}_{p:}\mathbf{Y}^\top, \quad \sum_{j=1}^{l} \overline{\mathbf{W}}_{dj}\overline{\mathbf{W}}_{pj} = \langle \overline{\mathbf{W}}_{d:}, \overline{\mathbf{W}}_{p:} \rangle.$$

Based on the equation, we reach the inequality

$$\|\mathbf{Y} - \mathbf{X}\overline{\mathbf{W}}\|_F^2 - \|\mathbf{Y} - \mathbf{X}\tilde{\mathbf{W}}\|_F^2 > 0 \Leftrightarrow$$
$$(\rho_{dp} - \rho_{dq}) > \left(\langle \overline{\mathbf{W}}_{d:}, \overline{\mathbf{W}}_{p:} \rangle \right)^{-1} \overline{\mathbf{W}}_{p:}\mathbf{Y}^\top (\mathbf{f}_p - \mathbf{f}_q).$$

$\|\mathbf{Y}^\top \mathbf{f}_p - \mathbf{Y}^\top \mathbf{f}_q\|_2 = 0$, according to the assumption. As far as $\rho_{dq} < \rho_{dp}$, selecting $\mathbf{f}_q$ rather than $\mathbf{f}_p$ will always decrease the objective function.

∎

The theorem shows that the formulation in Equation (3.16) tends to select features that are the least correlated, ensuring the selection of non-redundant features.

Third, the problem specified in Equation (3.16) is tractable. Given a value for λ, we obtain

$$\arg\min_{\mathbf{W}} \|\mathbf{Y} - \mathbf{X}\mathbf{W}\|_F^2 + \lambda \|\mathbf{W}\|_{2,1}. \tag{3.18}$$

This problem can be solved by applying a general solver [133, 8, 115]. And given l, the number of features to be selected, its corresponding λ value can be found by applying either a grid search or a binary search. Usually, a larger λ value results in selecting fewer features.

Below, we present three efficient solvers for the multivariate spectral feature selection problem defined in Equation (3.16). The first two are based on solving the $L_{2,1}$-regularized regression problem defined in Equation (3.18).

However, for a given l, using the two approaches, we still need to try many different λ values to determine the proper regularization parameter, which results in the selection of exact l features. This requires us to run a solver many times, which is computationally inefficient. The third solver is a path-following approach [205, 73, 48] based on solving the multivariate spectral feature selection problem defined in Equation (3.16) directly. Therefore, the solver is more efficient comparing to the first two. Note, in Equation (3.18), we assume λ is given, while in Equation (3.16) we do not assume this. Finding the proper regularization parameter λ is part of the objective defined in Equation (3.16).

3.3   Solving the $L_{2,1}$-Regularized Regression Problem

Assuming the regularization parameter λ in Equation (3.18) is known, the two most efficient solvers for the $L_{2,1}$-regularized regression problem specified in Equation (3.18) are the *coordinate gradient descent method* [185, 29, 186] and the *accelerated gradient descent method* [127, 12, 115, 116], and they are both iterative methods. The difference between the two methods is that in each iteration, the coordinate gradient descent method picks one row of the weight matrix $\mathbf{W}$ to optimize, while the accelerated gradient method optimizes the whole weight matrix. Although the two methods use different strategies for optimization, they are based on solving the same model function, which is defined as

$$
\begin{aligned}
\mathcal{M}_{\mathbf{W}_j,\lambda}(\mathbf{W}) \;=\; & \frac{1}{2}\|\mathbf{X}\mathbf{W}_j - \mathbf{Y}\|_F^2 + \lambda\|\mathbf{W}\|_{2,1} \\
+ \;& \mathrm{Trace}\left((\mathbf{X}\mathbf{W}_j - \mathbf{Y})^\top \mathbf{X}\,(\mathbf{W}_j - \mathbf{W})\right) \\
+ \;& \frac{L_j}{2}\mathrm{Trace}\left((\mathbf{W}_j - \mathbf{W})^\top (\mathbf{W}_j - \mathbf{W})\right).
\end{aligned}
$$

In the above function, $\mathbf{W}_j$ and λ are given, and $\mathbf{W}$ is unknown. $\mathcal{M}_{\mathbf{W}_j,\lambda}(\mathbf{W})$ forms a quadratic approximation of the original objective function defined in Equation (3.18).

Let

$$
\mathrm{loss}\,(\mathbf{W}) = \frac{1}{2}\,\|\mathbf{Y} - \mathbf{X}\mathbf{W}\|_F^2 + \lambda\,\|\mathbf{W}\|_{2,1}\,.
$$

We can verify that

$$
\frac{\partial\|\mathbf{X}\mathbf{W} - \mathbf{Y}\|_F^2}{\partial\mathbf{W}} = 2\mathbf{X}^\top (\mathbf{X}\mathbf{W} - \mathbf{Y})\,.
$$

Therefore, $\mathcal{M}_{\mathbf{W}_j,\lambda}(\mathbf{W})$ can be rewritten as

$$
\begin{aligned}
\mathcal{M}_{\mathbf{W}_j,\lambda}(\mathbf{W}) &= \operatorname{loss}(\mathbf{W}_j) + \operatorname{Trace}\left(\operatorname{loss}'(\mathbf{W}_j)^\top (\mathbf{W} - \mathbf{W}_j)\right) + \lambda \|\mathbf{W}\|_{2,1} \\
&+ \frac{L_j}{2} \operatorname{Trace}\left((\mathbf{W}_j - \mathbf{W})^\top (\mathbf{W}_j - \mathbf{W})\right).
\end{aligned}
\tag{3.19}
$$

The above equation shows that the first two terms of the model function $\mathcal{M}_{\mathbf{W}_j,\lambda}(\mathbf{W})$ form the first-order Taylor expansion of $\|\mathbf{Y} - \mathbf{XW}\|_F^2$ at the point $\mathbf{W}_j$. $\|\mathbf{Y} - \mathbf{XW}\|_F^2$ is differentiable anywhere in the domain of $\mathbf{W}$, and $\|\mathbf{W}\|_{2,1}$ is not differentiable at the points $\mathbf{w}^i = \mathbf{0}$, $i = 1, \ldots, m$. Therefore, in $\operatorname{loss}(\mathbf{W})$, $\|\mathbf{Y} - \mathbf{XW}\|_F^2$ forms the smooth part, and $\lambda \|\mathbf{W}\|_{2,1}$ forms the non-smooth part. We put the nonsmooth part of the loss function directly into the model function. The regularization term $\operatorname{Trace}\left((\mathbf{W}_j - \mathbf{W})^\top (\mathbf{W}_j - \mathbf{W})\right)$ puts a constraint on the distance between $\mathbf{W}_j$ and $\mathbf{W}$, and prevents $\mathbf{W}$ from being too far from $\mathbf{W}_j$. This term ensures that the model function can be a good approximation to the original loss function in the neighborhood of $\mathbf{W}_j$.

Let $\mathbf{w}^i$ be the i-th row of $\mathbf{W}$. We can also write Equation (3.19) as

$$
\begin{aligned}
\mathcal{M}_{\mathbf{W}_j,\lambda}(\mathbf{W}) &= \frac{1}{2} \|\mathbf{XW}_j - \mathbf{Y}\|_F^2 + \sum_{i=1}^m <\mathbf{f}_i^\top (\mathbf{Y} - \mathbf{XW}_j), \mathbf{w}_j^i - \mathbf{w}^i> \\
&+ \lambda \|\mathbf{W}\|_{2,1} + \frac{L_j}{2} \sum_{i=1}^m <\mathbf{w}_j^i - \mathbf{w}^i, \mathbf{w}_j^i - \mathbf{w}^i>,
\end{aligned}
\tag{3.20}
$$

where $< \cdot >$ is the inner product operator on vectors, $<\mathbf{x}, \mathbf{y}> = \mathbf{x}^\top \mathbf{y}$. It is easy to see that when $\mathbf{W}^\star$ is the optimal solution of Eq. (3.18), we have

$$
\mathbf{W}^\star = \arg \min_{\mathbf{W}} \mathcal{M}_{\mathbf{W}^\star,\lambda}(\mathbf{W}).
\tag{3.21}
$$

.

Both the coordinate gradient descent method and the accelerated gradient method try to generate a sequence of $\mathbf{W}_j$ to approach the optimal solution of Equation (3.18). Assuming $\mathbf{W}_j$ is the current solution, the next solution in the sequence is obtained by solving the following problems,

$$
\arg \min_{\mathbf{W}} \mathcal{M}_{\mathbf{W}_j,\lambda}(\mathbf{W}), \quad \text{Accelerated gradient descent method}; \tag{3.22}
$$

$$
\arg \min_{\mathbf{w}^i} \mathcal{M}_{\mathbf{W}_j,\lambda}(\mathbf{W}), \quad \text{Coordinate gradient method}. \tag{3.23}
$$

We will study how the sequence is generated in detail later.

It turns out that Equation (3.22) and Equation (3.23) have closed form solutions. Let's assume

$$
\mathbf{V} = \mathbf{W}_j - \frac{1}{L_j} \mathbf{X}^\top (\mathbf{XW}_j - \mathbf{Y}), \ \rho = \frac{\lambda}{L_j}.
\tag{3.24}
$$

Then we can reformulate $\arg\min_{\mathbf{W}} \mathcal{M}_{\mathbf{W}_j,\lambda}(\mathbf{W})$ in the following form:

$$\arg\min_{\mathbf{W}} \mathcal{M}_{\mathbf{W}_j,\lambda}(\mathbf{W}) = \arg\min_{\mathbf{W}} \frac{1}{2}\|\mathbf{W} - \mathbf{V}\|_F^2 + \rho\|\mathbf{W}\|_{2,1}. \tag{3.25}$$

This equation can be simply verified by plugging $\mathbf{V}$ and ρ on the right side of the equation. Since $\|\mathbf{A}\|_F^2 = \text{Trace}\left(A^\top A\right) = \sum_i \mathbf{a}^i$, where $\mathbf{a}^i$ is the i-th row of $\mathbf{A}$, we have

$$\arg\min_{\mathbf{W}} \mathcal{M}_{\mathbf{W}_j,\lambda}(\mathbf{W}) = \arg\min_{\mathbf{W}} \left(\sum_{i=1}^{m} \frac{1}{2}\|\mathbf{w}^i - \mathbf{v}^i\|_2^2 + \rho\|\mathbf{w}^i\|_2 \right).$$

Therefore, the minimization of $\mathbf{w}^i$ is independent of the other rows of $\mathbf{W}$, and the original problem can be decomposed into m independent sub-problems:

$$\arg\min_{\mathbf{w}^i} \frac{1}{2}\|\mathbf{w}^i - \mathbf{v}^i\|_2^2 + \rho\|\mathbf{w}^i\|_2, \quad i = 1, \ldots, m. \tag{3.26}$$

To obtain the minimizer of the model function $\mathcal{M}_{\mathbf{W}_j,\lambda}(\mathbf{W})$, we notice that $\left\|\mathbf{w}^i - \mathbf{v}^i\right\|_2^2$ is differentiable in the domain of $\mathbf{w}^i$, and its gradient is given by

$$\frac{\partial \left\|\mathbf{w}^i - \mathbf{v}^i\right\|_2^2}{\partial \mathbf{w}^i} = 2\left(\mathbf{w}^i - \mathbf{v}^i\right). \tag{3.27}$$

Since $\left\|\mathbf{w}^i\right\|_{2,1}$ is not differentiable at $\mathbf{0}$, it has only subgradient [18, 131], which is given by

$$\frac{\partial\left\|\mathbf{w}^i\right\|_{2,1}}{\partial \mathbf{w}^i} = \begin{cases} \dfrac{\mathbf{w}^i}{\|\mathbf{w}^i\|}, & \text{when } \mathbf{w}^i \neq 0 \\ \mathbf{u} \in \mathbb{R}^{1\times k}, \|\mathbf{u}\| \leq 1, & \text{when } \mathbf{w}^i = 0 \end{cases}. \tag{3.28}$$

Since $\mathcal{M}_{\mathbf{W}_j,\lambda}(\mathbf{W})$ is convex, according to convex optimization theory [18], we know it has a unique minimal, and its optimal solution can be obtained by solving the problem

$$\frac{\partial \mathcal{M}_{\mathbf{W}_j,\lambda}(\mathbf{W})}{\partial \mathbf{w}^i} = 0. \tag{3.29}$$

By plugging the following equation back into Equation (3.29), we can verify that it is the optimal solution of Equation (3.29). Therefore, it is also the optimal solution of Equation (3.26).

$$\mathbf{w}^i = \begin{cases} \mathbf{v}^i\left(1 - \dfrac{\rho}{\|\mathbf{v}^i\|}\right), & \text{when } \|\mathbf{v}^i\|_2 > \rho \\ \mathbf{0}, & \text{when } \|\mathbf{v}^i\|_2 \leq \rho \end{cases}. \tag{3.30}$$

Below we present the coordinate gradient descent method and the accelerated gradient method for solving the $L_{2,1}$-regularized regression problem defined in Equation (3.18).

3.3.1 The Coordinate Gradient Descent Method (CGD)

In the coordinate gradient descent (CGD) method, we generate the solution sequence by iteratively updating the rows of $\mathbf{W}$. This boils down to solving the sub-problems of Equation (3.25), which is defined as:

$$\arg\min_{\mathbf{w}^i} \frac{1}{2}\|\mathbf{w}^i - \mathbf{v}^i\|_2^2 + \rho\|\mathbf{w}^i\|_2, \quad i = 1, \ldots, m.$$

The pseudo-code of the coordinate gradient descent method is shown in Algorithm 2. The method contains two major steps: (1) Line 2–Line 15, update each row of the weight matrix $\mathbf{W}$, $\mathbf{w}^i$; and (2) Line 16–Line 21, test whether the solution converges.[2]

Algorithm 2: The coordinate gradient descent method

Input: $\mathbf{X}$, $\mathbf{Y}$, λ, $\mathbf{W}_0$, $L_0 > 0$
Output: $\mathbf{W}$

1 $\mathbf{W} = \mathbf{W}_0$, $j = 1$;
2 **for** $i = 1 \ldots m$ **do**
3   **for** $L = L_{j-1}$, $2L_{j-1}$, $4L_{j-1}$, $\ldots$ **do**
4          $\mathbf{v}^i = \mathbf{w}^i - \frac{1}{L}\mathbf{f}_i^\top (\mathbf{XW} - \mathbf{Y})$, $\rho = \lambda/L$;
5          $\mathbf{w} = \arg\min_{\mathbf{w}} \frac{1}{2}\|\mathbf{w} - \mathbf{v}^i\|_2^2 + \rho\|\mathbf{w}\|_2$;
6   **if** $\|\mathbf{Y} - \mathbf{XW}_{\mathbf{w}^i=\mathbf{w}}\|_F^2 + \lambda\|\mathbf{W}_{\mathbf{w}^i=\mathbf{w}}\|_{2,1} \leq \mathcal{M}_{\mathbf{W},\,\lambda}\left(\mathbf{W}_{\mathbf{w}^i=\mathbf{w}}\right)$ **then**
7   **break**;
8      $\mathbf{d} = \mathbf{w}^i - \mathbf{w}$;
9   **if** $\mathbf{d} \neq \mathbf{0}$ **then**
10         $\alpha \leftarrow$ line search;
11         $\mathbf{w}^i = \mathbf{w}^i + \alpha\mathbf{d}$;
12 $j = j + 1$, $L_j = L$;
13 **if** *converge* **then**
14   **return** $\mathbf{W}$;
15 **else**
16   **goto** line 2

The first step of the algorithm can be further divided into two sub-steps: (a) In Line 2–Line 9, we compute the $\mathbf{w}$ for updating $\mathbf{w}^i$ based on the current solution. To ensure the validity of the $\mathbf{w}$ obtained in Line 5, L in Equation (3.19) should be large enough so that $\mathcal{M}_{\mathbf{W},\,\lambda}\left(\mathbf{W}_{\mathbf{w}^i=\mathbf{w}}\right)$ can bound $\|\mathbf{Y} - \mathbf{XW}_{\mathbf{w}^i=\mathbf{w}}\|_F^2 + \lambda\|\mathbf{W}_{\mathbf{w}^i=\mathbf{w}}\|_{2,1}$ from above. (b) In Line 10–Line 14, instead of replacing $\mathbf{w}^i$ with $\mathbf{w}$, we adopt a more sophisticated way for updating $\mathbf{w}^i$: we first compute the update direction $\mathbf{d} = \mathbf{w}^i - \mathbf{w}$ (Line 12), then use line

---

[2]The convergence of the solution can be measured by the norm of difference between $\mathbf{W}_i$ and $\mathbf{W}_{i+1}$, e.g., $\|\mathbf{W}_{i+1} - \mathbf{W}_i\|_2 < \varepsilon$.

search to determine how far we should go with this direction, and update $\mathbf{w}^i$ using $\mathbf{w}^i = \mathbf{w}^i + \alpha \mathbf{d}$ (Line 13). The reason for doing this is that using $\mathbf{w}$ to replace $\mathbf{w}^i$ can be too aggressive, which may interfere with the convergence. The pseudo-code of the line search procedure is shown in Algorithm 3.

Algorithm 3: Line search

    Input: $\mathbf{X}$, $\mathbf{Y}$, λ, $\mathbf{W}$, i, $\mathbf{d} \in \mathbb{R}^{1 \times k}$, $\alpha_0 > 0$, $\delta > 0$, $\sigma > 0$
    Output: α

1   $\Delta = \mathbf{d}^\top \left(\mathbf{Y} - \mathbf{X}\mathbf{W}^\top \right) \mathbf{f}_i + \lambda \|\mathbf{w}^i + \mathbf{d}\|_2 + \frac{L_j}{2}\|\mathbf{d}\|_2^2 - \lambda\|\mathbf{w}^i\|_2$;

2   **for** $\alpha = \alpha_0,\ \delta\alpha_0,\ \delta^2\alpha_0,\ \ldots$ **do**

3   **if** $f\left(\mathbf{W}_{\mathbf{w}^i=\mathbf{w}^i+\alpha\mathbf{d}}\right) - f\left(\mathbf{W}\right) \leq \alpha\sigma\Delta$ **then**

4   **break**;

5 **return** α;

Algorithm 3 presents an inexact line search procedure using the Armijo rule [131]. In the procedure, $\alpha_0 > 0$, $\delta > 0$, $\sigma > 0$ are input parameters, and Δ is the improvement of model function by using $\mathbf{w} = \mathbf{w}^i + \mathbf{d}$ as the new solution.

It is shown in [186] that Algorithm 2 has a local linear convergence rate under certain conditions. Although the algorithm is reported to be very efficient [213] in real-world applications, its global rate of convergence is still unknown.

3.3.2   The Accelerated Gradient Descent Method (AGD)

In the accelerated gradient descent (AGD) method, we generate a sequence of solutions by iteratively updating the $\mathbf{W}$. The pseudo-code of the accelerate gradient descent method is shown in Algorithm 4. The method is based on generating two sequences: $\{\mathbf{W}_j\}_{j=1,2,\ldots}$ (Lines 4–9) and $\{\mathbf{S}_j\}_{j=1,2,\ldots}$ (Line 3). $\{\mathbf{W}_j\}_{j=1,2,\ldots}$ is the sequence of approximate solutions, which asymptotically approaches the optimal solution of Equation (3.18). And $\{\mathbf{S}_j\}_{j=1,2,\ldots}$ is the sequence of the search points. A search point $\mathbf{S}_i$ is the affine combination of $\mathbf{W}_j$ and $\mathbf{W}_{j-1}$ And $\mathbf{W}_j$ is computed by minimizing the model function $\mathcal{M}_{\mathbf{S}_{j-1},\lambda}\left(\mathbf{W}\right)$. In Line 6, we check whether the L in Equation (3.19) is large enough, so that $\mathcal{M}_{\mathbf{S}_j,\ \lambda}\left(\mathbf{W}_{j+1}\right)$ can bound $\|\mathbf{Y} - \mathbf{X}\mathbf{W}_{j+1}\|_F^2 + \lambda\|\mathbf{W}_{j+1}\|_{2,1}$ from above.

As shown in [116] the accelerated gradient method has a global convergence rate of O($\frac{1}{M^2}$), where M is the number of iterations. Let m be the number of features, n the number of samples, and C the number of columns of $\mathbf{Y}$. The time complexity of the accelerated gradient method is given by

$$O\left(mnCMl_L\right), \tag{3.31}$$

where M is the maximal number of iterations specified in Algorithm 4, and

---

Algorithm 4: Accelerated gradient descent method

Input: $\mathbf{X}$, $\mathbf{Y}$, λ, $\mathbf{W}_0$, $L_0 > 0$, M

Output: $\mathbf{W}_{M+1}$

1 $\mathbf{W}_1 = \mathbf{W}_0$, $\alpha_{-1} = 0$, $\alpha_0 = 1$, $L = L_0$;

2 **for** $j = 1 \ldots M$ **do**

3 $\quad$ $\beta_j = \frac{\alpha_{j-2}-1}{\alpha_{j-1}}$, $\mathbf{S}_j = \mathbf{W}_j + \beta_j (\mathbf{W}_j - \mathbf{W}_{j-1})$;

4 $\quad$ **for** $L = L_{j-1}$, $2L_{j-1}$, $4L_{j-1}$, $\ldots$ **do**

5 $\quad\quad$ $\mathbf{W}_{j+1} = \arg\min_{\mathbf{W}} \mathcal{M}_{\mathbf{S}_j,\lambda}(\mathbf{W})$;

6 $\quad\quad$ **if** $\frac{1}{2}\|\mathbf{Y} - \mathbf{X}\mathbf{W}_{j+1}\|_F^2 + \lambda \|\mathbf{W}_{j+1}\|_{2,1} \leq \mathcal{M}_{\mathbf{S}_j,\lambda}(\mathbf{W}_{j+1})$ **then**

7 $\quad\quad\quad$ **break**;

8 $\quad$ $L_j = L$, $\alpha_{j+1} = \frac{1+\sqrt{1+4\alpha_i^2}}{2}$;

9 **return** $\mathbf{W}_{M+1}$;

---

l_L is the averaged number of ties for searching the proper L in the validation process. The above equation shows that the time complexity of the accelerated gradient method is linear in terms of the number of samples and the number of features. Therefore, it is very efficient.

3.4 Efficient Multivariate Spectral Feature Selection

The two methods presented in the last section solve the $L_{2,1}$-regularized regression problem specified in Equation (3.18), which has the form

$$\arg\min_{\mathbf{W}} \|\mathbf{Y} - \mathbf{X}\mathbf{W}\|_F^2 + \lambda \|\mathbf{W}\|_{2,1}.$$

It may be inefficient for us to use them to solve the multivariate spectral feature selection problem specified in Equation (3.16), which has the form

$$\arg\min_{\mathbf{W},\lambda} \|\mathbf{Y} - \mathbf{X}\mathbf{W}\|_F^2 + \lambda \|\mathbf{W}\|_{2,1}$$

$$s.t. \ \ \mathbb{A} = \{i : \|\mathbf{w}^i\|_2 > 0\}, \ Card(\mathbb{A}) = l.$$

In the above formulation, λ is not given. Instead, we are given l, the number of features to be selected. One can solve this problem indirectly by solving Equation (3.18). However, this will not be efficient, since it requires us to solve Equation (3.18) multiple times for searching a proper λ value, which leads to the selection of exact l features. Here we present an efficient path-following solver for the problem specified in Equation (3.16). It can automatically detect the points when a new feature enters its active set,[3] and update its parameters accordingly. It can efficiently generate a solution path for selecting the specified number of features.

We start by deriving the necessary and sufficient conditions for a feature to have nonzero weight (i.e., being selected) in an optimal solution of Equation (3.18).

Let

$$Loss\left(\mathbf{W}, \lambda\right) = \|\mathbf{Y} - \mathbf{XW}\|_F^2 - \lambda \|\mathbf{W}\|_{2,1}.$$

We notice that $Loss\left(\mathbf{W}, \lambda\right)$ is convex, but it is nonsmooth when $\mathbf{w}^i = \mathbf{0}$. According to the convex optimization theorem [18], $\mathbf{W}_*$ minimizes $Loss\left(\mathbf{W}, \lambda\right)$ if and only if:

$$\mathbf{0} \in \partial_{\mathbf{w}^i} Loss\left(\mathbf{W}, \lambda\right)|_{\mathbf{W}=\mathbf{W}_*}, \ i = 1, \ldots, m.$$

Here, $\partial_{\mathbf{w}^i}\left(\mathbf{W}, \lambda\right)$ is the subdifferential of $Loss\left(\mathbf{W}, \lambda\right)$ on $\mathbf{w}^i$, and has the following form:

$$\partial_{\mathbf{w}^i} Loss\left(\mathbf{W}, \lambda\right) = \mathbf{f}_i^\top \left(\mathbf{Y} - \mathbf{XW}\right) + \lambda \mathbf{v}_i$$

$$\mathbf{v}_i = \frac{\mathbf{w}^i}{\|\mathbf{w}^i\|}, \ \text{if} \ \mathbf{w}^i \neq 0$$

$$\mathbf{v}_i \in \left\{\mathbf{u} | \mathbf{u} \in \mathbb{R}^{1 \times k}, \|\mathbf{u}\|_2 \leq 1\right\}, \ \text{if} \ \mathbf{w}^i = 0. \tag{3.32}$$

Therefore, $\mathbf{W}_*$ is an optimal solution if and only if:

$$-\lambda \mathbf{v}_i = \mathbf{f}_i^\top \left(\mathbf{Y} - \mathbf{XW}\right)|_{\mathbf{W}=\mathbf{W}_*}, \ \forall i \in \{1, \ldots, m\}. \tag{3.33}$$

Based on this observation, we give necessary conditions (weak), and both necessary and sufficient conditions (strong) for $\mathbf{W}$ to be optimal. We show that a suboptimal solution, which satisfies the *necessary* conditions, can be easily obtained. And the obtained suboptimal solution can be efficiently adjusted to generate an optimal solution, which satisfies the *necessary and sufficient* conditions.

Theorem 3.4.1 *Assuming* $\mathbf{w}^i$ *is the i-th row of* $\mathbf{W}$, *the necessary conditions for* $\mathbf{W}$ *to be optimal are:* $\forall i \in \{1, \ldots, m\}$,

$$\mathbf{w}^i \neq 0 \ \Rightarrow \ \|\mathbf{f}^\top \left(\mathbf{Y} - \mathbf{XW}\right)\|_2 = \lambda$$
$$\mathbf{w}^i = 0 \ \Rightarrow \ \|\mathbf{f}^\top \left(\mathbf{Y} - \mathbf{XW}\right)\|_2 \leq \lambda. \tag{3.34}$$

The theorem suggests that for a feature to be selected, its correlation to the residual, $\mathbf{R} = \mathbf{Y} - \mathbf{XW}$, must be equal to λ. Here, the correlation between a feature and the residual is measured by $\|\mathbf{f}^\top \mathbf{R}\|_2$. A feature is selected if it has a nonzero weight vector in the optimal solution. The above property is also called the *equal correlation condition* for these features, since they are equally

---

[3]An active set contains the indices of the features that have nonzero weights in $\mathbf{W}$.

correlated to the residual. A solution satisfying this condition can be easily obtained via applying a forward stepwise search strategy, which is similar to that introduced in the least angle regression (LARS) [48].

Theorem 3.4.2 *Assuming* $\mathbf{w}^i$ *is the i-th row of* $\mathbf{W}$, *the necessary and sufficient conditions for* $\mathbf{W}$ *to be optimal are:* $\forall i \in \{1, \dots, m\}$,

$$\mathbf{w}^i \neq 0 \quad \Rightarrow \quad \mathbf{f}^\top (\mathbf{Y} - \mathbf{X}\mathbf{W}) = -\lambda \frac{\mathbf{w}^i}{\|\mathbf{w}^i\|_2}$$

$$\mathbf{w}^i = 0 \quad \Rightarrow \quad \|\mathbf{f}^\top (\mathbf{Y} - \mathbf{X}\mathbf{W})\|_2 \leq \lambda. \tag{3.35}$$

Algorithm 5: MRSF: Minimal redundancy spectral feature selection

---

Input: $\mathbf{X}$, $\mathbf{Y}$, l
Output: $\mathbf{W}$

1   $\mathbf{W}^{[1]} = 0$, $\lambda_1 = +\infty$, $i = 1$ and $\mathbf{R}^{[1]} = \mathbf{Y}$;

2   Compute the initial active set: $\mathbb{A}_1 = \arg\max_j \|\mathbf{f}_j^\top \mathbf{R}^{[1]}\|_2^2$;

3   **while** $i \leq l$ **do**

4   Compute the walking direction $\gamma_{\mathbb{A}_i}$: $\gamma_{\mathbb{A}_i} = \left(\mathbf{X}_{\mathbb{A}_i}^\top \mathbf{X}_{\mathbb{A}_i}\right)^{-1} \mathbf{X}_{\mathbb{A}_i}^\top \mathbf{R}^{[i]}$;

5   **for** *each* $j \notin \mathbb{A}_i$ *and an arbitrary* $t \in \mathbb{A}_i$ **do**

6   Compute the step size α_j in direction $\gamma_{\mathbb{A}_i}$ for $\mathbf{f}_j$ to enter $\mathbb{A}_i$.
     $\|\mathbf{f}_j^\top \left(\mathbf{R}^{[i]} - \alpha_j \mathbf{X}_{\mathbb{A}_i} \gamma_{\mathbb{A}_i}\right)\|_2 = (1 - \alpha_j)\|\mathbf{f}_t^\top \mathbf{R}^{[i]}\|_2$;

7     $j^* = \arg\min_{j \notin \mathbb{A}_i} \alpha_j$;

8     $\hat{\mathbf{W}} = \left(\left(\mathbf{W}^{[i]} + \alpha_{j^*} \gamma_{\mathbb{A}_i}\right)^\top, \mathbf{0}\right)^\top$;

9     $\hat{\mathbb{A}} = \mathbb{A}_i \bigcup \{j^*\}$, $\lambda_i = (1 - \alpha_{j^*})\|\mathbf{f}_t^\top \mathbf{R}^{[i]}\|_2$;

10   Solve the smaller optimization problem,
    $\min_{\tilde{\mathbf{W}}} \|\mathbf{Y} - \mathbf{X}_{\hat{\mathbb{A}}}\tilde{\mathbf{W}}\|_F^2 + \lambda_i\|\tilde{\mathbf{W}}\|_{2,1}$, using a general solver with $\hat{\mathbf{W}}$ as the starting point;

11    $\tilde{\mathbf{R}} = \mathbf{Y} - \mathbf{X}_{\hat{\mathbb{A}}}\tilde{\mathbf{W}}$;

12   **if** $\forall i \notin \hat{\mathbb{A}}$, $\|\mathbf{f}_i^\top \tilde{\mathbf{R}}\|_2 \leq \lambda_i$ **then**

13     $\mathbb{A}_{i+1} = \hat{\mathbb{A}}$, $\mathbf{W}^{[i+1]} = \tilde{\mathbf{W}}$, $\mathbf{R}^{[i+1]} = \tilde{\mathbf{R}}$, $i = i + 1$;

14   **else**

15     $\hat{\mathbb{A}} = \left\{i : \|\tilde{\mathbf{w}}^i\| \neq 0\right\} \bigcup \left\{j : \|\mathbf{f}_j^\top \tilde{\mathbf{R}}\|_2 > \lambda_i\right\}$;

16   Remove $\tilde{\mathbf{w}}^i$ from $\tilde{\mathbf{W}}$, if $\|\tilde{\mathbf{w}}^i\| = 0$,
    $\hat{\mathbf{W}} = \left(\tilde{\mathbf{W}}^\top, \mathbf{0}, \dots, \mathbf{0}\right)^\top$, **Goto** line 11;

17 Extend $\mathbf{W}^{[l]}$ to $\mathbf{W}$ by adding empty rows to $\mathbf{W}^{[l]}$;

18 **return** $\mathbf{W}^{[l]}$;

Based on the above two theorems, we propose an efficient solver for multivariate spectral feature selection based on $L_{2,1}$-regularized regression. Its pseudo-code can be found in Algorithm 5. In the algorithm, $\mathbb{A}_i$ is the "active set" of the i-*th* run, and contains the features selected in that run. Algorithm 5 contains two major steps.

1. In Lines 4–8, the algorithm determines $\gamma_{\mathbb{A}_i}$, the direction for updating $\mathbf{W}^{[i]}$ (Line 4), and α_{j^*}, the step size for updating $\mathbf{W}^{[i]}$ (Lines 5–8). It then updates the active set and computes the λ_i (Line 10). We can verify that when the regularization parameter is set to λ_i, the $\hat{\mathbf{W}}$ generated in this step is a suboptimal solution satisfying the equal correlation condition specified in Theorem 3.4.1.

2. In Lines 11–18, the algorithm finds an optimal solution corresponding to the λ_i obtained in step 1. Given λ_i, it first solves an $L_{2,1}$-norm regularized regression problem using a general solver (e.g., either the coordinate gradient descent method or the accelerated gradient method) (Line 11). Note that this problem is of much smaller scale, since it is based only on the features in the current active set, but not the whole set. For example, in the i-th iteration, there are only i features in the active set, and $i \ll m$. Also $\check{\mathbf{W}}$ is used as a starting point to accelerate the convergence of the solver. It then checks whether the obtained solution is also optimal on the whole data (Line 13) by using the conditions specified in Theorem 3.4.2. If it is true, the algorithm records the current optimal solution and proceeds to Line 4 for the next run (Line 14). Otherwise, it adjusts the active set, updates the $\hat{\mathbf{W}}$ to remove the unselected features, and makes space to accommodate the newly selected features. It then returns to Line 11 (Line 17). In this step, we adjust the suboptimal solution obtained in the first step and compute the optimal solution corresponding to λ_i.

Theorem 3.4.3 *(1) Let $\mathbf{W}^{[i]}$ be the optimal solution obtained in the i-th iteration. The $\hat{\mathbf{W}}$ generated in step 1 (Line 9) satisfies the equal correlation condition specified in Theorem 3.4.1. (2) The $\mathbf{W}^{[i+1]}$ computed in step 2 (Line 14) is an optimal solution corresponding to λ_i.*

Proof: To prove the first part of the theorem, let $\mathbf{W}^{[i]}$ be the optimal solution obtained in the i-th step. Its corresponding residual and regularization parameters are $\mathbf{R}^{[i]} = \mathbf{Y} - \mathbf{X}_{\mathbb{A}_i}\mathbf{W}^{[i]}$ and λ_i, respectively. When $\hat{\mathbf{W}} = \left(\left(\mathbf{W}^{[i]} + \alpha_{j^*}\gamma_{\mathbb{A}_i} \right)^{\top}, \mathbf{0} \right)^{\top}$ and $\hat{\mathbb{A}} = \mathbb{A}_i \bigcup \{j^*\}$, the corresponding residue can be written as

$$
\begin{aligned}
\hat{\mathbf{R}} &= \mathbf{Y} - (\mathbf{X}_{\mathbb{A}_i}, \mathbf{f}_{j^*}) \left(\left(\mathbf{W}^{[i]} + \alpha_{j^*}\gamma_{\mathbb{A}_i} \right)^{\top}, \mathbf{0} \right)^{\top} \\
&= \mathbf{Y} - \mathbf{X}_{\mathbb{A}_i} \left(\mathbf{W}^{[i]} + \alpha_{j^*}\gamma_{\mathbb{A}_i} \right) \\
&= \mathbf{R}^{[i]} - \alpha_{j^*}\mathbf{X}_{\mathbb{A}_i}\gamma_{\mathbb{A}_i}.
\end{aligned}
$$

Therefore, we have

$$
\mathbf{f}_t^{\top}\hat{\mathbf{R}} = \mathbf{f}_t^{\top}\mathbf{R}^{[i]} - \alpha_{j^*}\mathbf{f}_t^{\top}\mathbf{X}_{\mathbb{A}_i}\gamma_{\mathbb{A}_i}, \ \forall t \in \mathbb{A}_i \cup \{j^*\}.
$$

When $t \in \mathbb{A}_i$, we have

$$\mathbf{f}_t^\top \mathbf{R}^{[i]} - \alpha_{j^*} \mathbf{f}_t^\top \mathbf{X}_{\mathbb{A}_i} \gamma_{\mathbb{A}_i} = (1 - \alpha_{j^*}) \mathbf{f}_t^\top \mathbf{R}^{[i]}.$$

To obtain this equation, we need to show

$$\mathbf{f}_t^\top \mathbf{X}_{\mathbb{A}_i} \gamma_{\mathbb{A}_i} = \mathbf{f}_t^\top \mathbf{X}_{\mathbb{A}_i} (\mathbf{X}_{\mathbb{A}_i}^\top \mathbf{X}_{\mathbb{A}_i})^{-1} \mathbf{X}_{\mathbb{A}_i}^\top \mathbf{R}^{[i]} = \mathbf{f}_t^\top \mathbf{R}^{[i]}, \ \forall t \in \mathbb{A}_i.$$

Let $\mathbf{X}_{\mathbb{A}_i} = \mathbf{U}\mathbf{\Sigma}\mathbf{V}^\top$ be the SVD of $\mathbf{X}_{\mathbb{A}_i}$. Since $\mathbf{f}_t$ is a column of $\mathbf{X}_{\mathbb{A}_i}$, we have

$$\mathbf{f}_t = \mathbf{U}\mathbf{a}, \ \mathbf{a} = \mathbf{\Sigma}\mathbf{v}^{q\top},$$

where $\mathbf{v}^q$ is the q-th row of $\mathbf{V}$, and $\mathbf{f}_t$ is the q-th column of $\mathbf{X}_{\mathbb{A}_i}$. Based on this equation, we can obtain the following equation,

$$
\begin{aligned}
\mathbf{f}_t^\top \left(\mathbf{X}_{\mathbb{A}_i} (\mathbf{X}_{\mathbb{A}_i}^\top \mathbf{X}_{\mathbb{A}_i})^{-1} \mathbf{X}_{\mathbb{A}_i}^\top \right) &= \mathbf{f}_t^\top \mathbf{U}\mathbf{\Sigma}\mathbf{V}^\top (\mathbf{V}\mathbf{\Sigma}^2\mathbf{V}^\top)^{-1} \mathbf{V}\mathbf{\Sigma}\mathbf{U}^\top \\
&= \mathbf{f}_t^\top \mathbf{U}\mathbf{\Sigma}\mathbf{V}^\top \mathbf{V}\mathbf{\Sigma}^{-2}\mathbf{V}^\top \mathbf{V}\mathbf{\Sigma}\mathbf{U}^\top \\
&= \mathbf{f}_t^\top \mathbf{U}\mathbf{U}^\top = (\mathbf{U}\mathbf{a})^\top \mathbf{U}\mathbf{U}^\top \\
&= \mathbf{a}^\top \mathbf{U}^\top \mathbf{U}\mathbf{U}^\top = \mathbf{a}^\top \mathbf{U}^\top \\
&= \mathbf{f}_t^\top.
\end{aligned}
$$

$\mathbf{M} = \mathbf{X}_{\mathbb{A}_i} (\mathbf{X}_{\mathbb{A}_i}^\top \mathbf{X}_{\mathbb{A}_i})^{-1} \mathbf{X}_{\mathbb{A}_i}^\top \in \mathbb{R}^{n \times n}$ defines a projection matrix, which projects any n-dimensional vector to the space spanned by the columns of $\mathbf{X}$. Since $\mathbf{f}_t$ is a column of $\mathbf{X}_{\mathbb{A}_i}$, it is already in the space spanned by the columns of $\mathbf{X}$. The above equation shows that in this case, the projection matrix $\mathbf{M}$ will project $\mathbf{f}_t$ into itself. Based on this observation, for $\forall t \in \mathbb{A}_i$ we can obtain the equation

$$
\begin{aligned}
\|\mathbf{f}_t^\top \hat{\mathbf{R}}\|_2 &= \|\mathbf{f}_t^\top \left(\mathbf{Y} - \mathbf{X}_{\mathbb{A}_i} \left(\mathbf{W}^{[i]} + \alpha_{j^*} \gamma_{\mathbb{A}_i} \right) \right)\|_2 \\
&= (1 - \alpha_{j^*}) \|\mathbf{f}_t^\top \mathbf{R}^{[i]}\|_2.
\end{aligned}
$$

Since $\|\mathbf{f}_p^\top \mathbf{R}\|_2 = \|\mathbf{f}_q^\top \mathbf{R}\|_2$ for $\forall p, q \in \mathbb{A}_i$ (due to the optimality of $\mathbf{W}^{[i]}$), we have

$$\|\mathbf{f}_p^\top \hat{\mathbf{R}}^{[i]}\|_2 = \|\mathbf{f}_q^\top \hat{\mathbf{R}}^{[i]}\|_2, \ \ \forall p, q \in \mathbb{A}_i. \tag{3.36}$$

When $t = j^*$, $\mathbf{f}_j^*$ will be the feature that is about to enter the active set. According to Line 6 of the algorithm, $\forall t \in \mathbb{A}_i$, we have

$$
\begin{aligned}
\|\mathbf{f}_{j^*}^\top \hat{\mathbf{R}}\|_2 &= \|\mathbf{f}_{j^*}^\top \left(\mathbf{R}^{[i]} - \alpha_{j^*} \mathbf{X}_{\mathbb{A}_i} \gamma_{\mathbb{A}_i} \right)\|_2 \\
&= (1 - \alpha_{j^*}) \|\mathbf{f}_t^\top \mathbf{R}^{[i]}\|_2 \\
&= \|\mathbf{f}_t^\top \hat{\mathbf{R}}^{[i]}\|_2. \tag{3.37}
\end{aligned}
$$

By combining Equation (3.36) and Equation (3.37), we proved the first part of the theorem.

The second part of the theorem can be simply verified by applying the necessary and sufficient conditions for an optimal solution specified in Theorem 3.4.2.

■

To select l features, Algorithm 5 runs at most $l-1$ iterations to shrink the regularization parameter λ from $+\infty$ to a proper value, so that exact l features can be selected. In each iteration, the algorithm decreases λ by a certain amount to allow a new feature to enter the active set. Let $\mathbf{W}^{[i]}$ and λ_i be the optimal solution and the corresponding regularization parameter obtained in the i-th iteration. According to Theorem 3.4.1, we know that all the active features in $\mathbf{W}^{[i]}$ are equally correlated to the residual: $\|\mathbf{f}^\top \left(\mathbf{Y} - \mathbf{X}\mathbf{W}^{[i]}\right)\|_2 = \lambda_i$. And all the inactive features are less correlated. In the $(i+1)$-th iteration, to activate a new feature, the algorithm first determines a direction $\gamma_{\mathbb{A}_{i+1}}$. In the proof of Theorem 3.4.3, we show that by updating $\mathbf{W}^{[i+1]}$ using $\alpha\gamma_{\mathbb{A}_{i+1}}$, the equal correlation condition always holds for $\mathbf{W}^{[i+1]} + \alpha\gamma_{\mathbb{A}_{i+1}}$, $\forall \alpha \leq 0$. However, we cannot set the α value arbitrarily. Let $\mathbf{f}_t$ be an arbitrary feature in the active set. We find the α value by solving the problem

$$\alpha^* = \arg \min_{j \notin \mathbb{A}_{i+1}} \left(\|\mathbf{f}_j^\top \left(\mathbf{R}^{[i+1]} - \alpha\mathbf{X}_{\mathbb{A}_{i+1}}\gamma_{\mathbb{A}_{i+1}}\right)\|_2 = (1-\alpha)\|\mathbf{f}_t^\top \mathbf{R}^{[i+1]}\|_2\right).$$

(3.38)

The obtained α^* is the minimal step size for activating a new feature. It is easy to verify that when $\alpha < \alpha^*$, all the inactive features are still less correlated to the residual

$$\|\mathbf{f}_j^\top \left(\mathbf{R}^{[i+1]} - \alpha\mathbf{X}_{\mathbb{A}_{i+1}}\gamma_{\mathbb{A}_{i+1}}\right)\|_2 < (1-\alpha)\|\mathbf{f}_t^\top \mathbf{R}^{[i+1]}\|_2.$$

And when $\alpha = \alpha^*$, the inactive feature corresponding to α^* starts satisfying the equal correlation condition, which provides us a hint that this feature may become active[4] when we update $\mathbf{W}^{[i+1]}$ by $\alpha^*\gamma_{\mathbb{A}_{i+1}}$. Given the equivalence between the feature-residual correlation and the λ, shown in the Theorem 3.4.1, we set the value of λ_{i+1} using the equation

$$\lambda_{i+1} = (1-\alpha^*)\|\mathbf{f}_t^\top \mathbf{R}^{[i+1]}\|_2.$$

We also update the weight matrix and the active set to include the newly activated feature in the tentative solution. Note that the updated weight matrix only stratifies the necessary condition for an optimal solution. So it may not be the optimal one. Therefore, in the second step of the algorithm, we adjust this weight matrix to an optimal one. Note that it is possible that the optimal active set may be different from the one determined in the first step.

The second step of the algorithm can be done efficiently. First, in Line 11, we solve an $L_{2,1}$-norm regularized regression problem based only on the features in the active set, which is of a much smaller scale compared with that of the whole feature set; second, we compute the optimal solution based on the tentative solution obtained in the first step. It turns out that the

---

[4]If several features correspond to α^*, they all satisfy the equal correlation condition, when $\alpha = \alpha^*$. In this case, at least one of them may become active.

tentative solution is usually close to the optimal one. Therefore, the solver often converges in just a few iterations for solving the problem specified in Line 11.

Let m be the number of features, n the number of samples, C the number of columns of $\mathbf{Y}$, and l the number of selected features. The time complexity of MRSF is

$$O\left(\left(lmnC + l^2 nCMl_L \right) l_V + \left(l^3 + lmC \right) n \right), \tag{3.39}$$

where M is the maximal number of iterations specified in Algorithm 4, l_L is the averaged number of ties for searching the proper L in the validation process, and l_V is the number of the backtraces for adjusting $\mathbb{A}$ in Lines 16 and 17 of Algorithm 5. If assuming $l < CMl_L l_V$, Equation (3.39) can be simplified to

$$O\left(lnC \left(m + lMl_L \right) l_V \right). \tag{3.40}$$

Example 16 *An empirical study of the efficiency of MRSF*

We construct an artificial data set by randomly generating a data matrix $\mathbf{X} \in \mathbb{R}^{1000 \times 10000}$ (1000 samples and 10000 features) and a target matrix $\mathbf{Y} \in \mathbb{R}^{1000 \times 10}$.

For comparison, we first apply the accelerated gradient descent method (AGD) on the artificial data with different λ values for regularization. The performance of AGD is reported in Table 3.1. From the table we can observe that as λ decreases, more and more features are selected, which leads to smaller residual values. On the artificial data, on average, it takes 0.22 seconds for AGD to run one iteration.[5] And on average, AGD converges in about 500 iterations. When $\lambda = 0.5$, AGD selects 54 features, which takes about 122 seconds.

We then apply MRSF to select 50 features on the artificial data. MRSF runs 40 iterations,[6] which takes about 32 seconds, almost 4 times faster than the case for AGD on the whole data set. The residual of the solution is 9.79.

Figure 3.3 shows the run time of each AGD solver call in MRSF, which takes 0.42 ± 0.14 seconds on average. Figure 3.4 presents the number of iterations for each AGD call to converge. On average, it takes about 30 iterations. This suggests that the run time of each AGD iteration is about 0.02 seconds, which is 10 times faster than the time used by the AGD solver on the whole data. The reason is that in this case, the AGD solver runs on a much smaller problem containing only the features activated in the tentative solution (see Line 11 of Algorithm 5). We notice that the number of iterations for the AGD solver to converge is also much smaller in this case. It suggests that the tentative solution is close to the optimal solution.

Figure 3.5 shows the number of features selected by MRSF in each iteration. It verifies that MRSF may select more than one feature in each iteration, if more than one feature violates the global optimal condition (Lines 16 and 17 of Algorithm 5) in the validation step. Figure 3.6 presents the number of AGD calls in each iteration. It shows that on the artificial data used in this experiment, on average l_V, the number of the backtraces in the validation step of MRSF, is about 1.25, which is quite small.

This example demonstrates that MRSF is an efficient solver for selecting a specific number of features by generating a solution path.

---

[5] The experiment is run on a computer with an Intel Core 2 Duo CPU and 4GB memory. The operating system is Mirosoft Windows 7 64bit. MRSF is implemented using Matlab. The AGD solver is downloaded from http://www.public.asu.edu/ jye02/Software/SLEP/, which also runs in MATLAB.

[6] MRSF may select more than one feature in each iteration, if more than one feature violates the global optimal condition (Lines 16-17 of Algorithm 5) in the validation step.

TABLE 3.1: The performance of AGD on the artificial data.

λ	1.0	0.9	0.7	0.5	0.3	0.1	0.0
selected features	0	5	17	54	97	196	10000
iterations	2	362	555	561	828	1017	441
time (sec)	0.94	79.30	122.79	122.21	175.59	223.44	96.21
time per iteration	0.47	0.22	0.22	0.22	0.21	0.22	0.22
residual	50.80	15.06	10.95	9.78	9.60	9.05	0.00

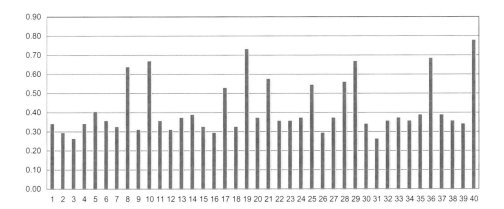

FIGURE 3.3: MRSF, run time of each AGD solver call.

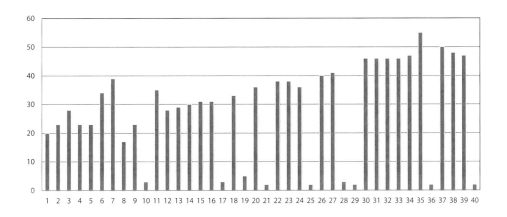

FIGURE 3.4: MRSF, number of iterations for each AGD call to converge.

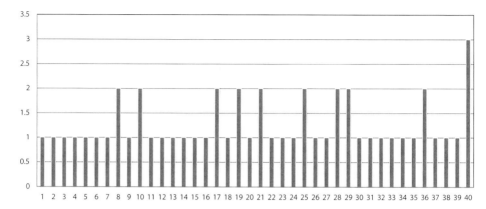

FIGURE 3.5: MRSF, number of features selected in each iteration.

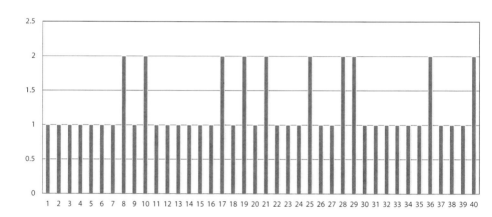

FIGURE 3.6: MRSF, number of AGD calls in each iteration.

3.5   A Formulation Based on Matrix Comparison

In spectral feature selection, we try to select features that can preserve the sample similarity specified in a given similarity matrix **S**. In Equation (3.16), this is achieved by solving a sparse multi-output regression problem, in which the weighted eigenvectors of **S** are used as the target. As shown in Theorem 3.2.1, using this formulation, we can find a set of features, such that the linear kernel based on the linear combination of the selected features is very close to **S**. When the Frobenius norm is used to measure the closeness of two matrices, this problem can be formulated as:

$$arg \min_{\mathbf{W}} \left\| \mathbf{XWW}^\top \mathbf{X}^\top - \mathbf{S} \right\|_F$$

$$s.t. \quad \mathbb{A} = \{i : \left\| \mathbf{w}^i \right\|_2 > 0\}, \; Card\,(\mathbb{A}) = l.$$

We can simplify the problem as selecting a set of features such that the linear kernel obtained based on the selected features is close to $\mathbf{S}$:

$$\min_{\mathcal{A}} \left\| \mathbf{S} - \mathbf{X}_{\mathcal{A}} \mathbf{X}_{\mathcal{A}}^\top \right\|, \tag{3.41}$$

$$\text{where} \quad \mathbf{X}_{\mathcal{A}} = (\mathbf{f}_{i_1}, \ldots, \mathbf{f}_{i_l}), \; i_j \in \mathcal{A}, \; j = 1, \ldots, k.$$

Treating $\left\| \mathbf{S} - \mathbf{X}_{\mathcal{A}} \mathbf{X}_{\mathcal{A}}^\top \right\|$ as a feature selection criterion, we can use it with the traditional forward search strategy for feature selection. The algorithm is named MCSF, which stands for *M*atrix *C*omparison for *S*pectral *F*eature selection. The pseudo-code of the algorithm can be found in Algorithm 6. Note that the card $(\cdot)$ in Line 2 returns the size of a set, and Lines 3 and 7 make use of the fact

$$\mathbf{S} - \mathbf{X}_{\mathcal{A}} \mathbf{X}_{\mathcal{A}}^\top = \mathbf{S} - \sum_{i \in \mathcal{A}} \mathbf{f}_i \mathbf{f}_i^\top,$$

$$\text{where} \quad \mathbf{X}_{\mathcal{A}} = (\mathbf{f}_{i_1}, \ldots, \mathbf{f}_{i_k}), \; i_j \in \mathcal{A}, \; j = 1, \ldots, k.$$

The above equation shows that once a feature $\mathbf{f}_i$ is selected, we can remove $\mathbf{f}_i \mathbf{f}_i^\top$ from $\mathbf{S}$, and use the obtained residual $\mathbf{R}$ in the later steps. This strategy eliminates the redundant computations and makes the algorithm efficient. To select l features, the algorithm needs to run l iterations. In each iteration, it greedily picks one feature that is most consistent with the current residue $\mathbf{R}$, adds the feature to $\mathbb{A}$, and updates the residue by $\mathbf{R} = \mathbf{R} - \mathbf{f}_i \mathbf{f}_i^\top$.

In each iteration, features are compared to $\mathbf{R}$. Note that $\mathbf{R}$ is obtained by substracting the sum of the outer products of the selected features from $\mathbf{S}$. So, features are not evaluated independently. And the formulation promotes the selection of uncorrelated features.

The condition specified in Line 4 of Algorithm 6 guarantees that $\|\mathbf{R}\|_F^2$ monotonically decreases after each step. It can be shown that the time complexity of the algorithm is $O\left(lmn^2\right)$, where l is the number of selected features. Assuming features have been normalized to have unit norm, $\|\mathbf{f}_i\| = 1$, we have the following equation:

$$\arg\min_{i \notin \mathcal{A}} \left\| \mathbf{R} - \mathbf{f}_i \mathbf{f}_i^\top \right\|_F^2 = \arg\max_{i \notin \mathcal{A}} \mathbf{f}_i^\top \mathbf{R} \mathbf{f}_i.$$

Therefore the problem specified in Line 3 can be solved in $O(mn^2)$ operations. When l features are selected, the total time complexity of the algorithm is $O(lmn^2)$.

Algorithm 6: MCSF: Matrix comparison for spectral feature selection

---

Input: $\mathbf{f}_1, \ldots, \mathbf{f}_m$, $\mathbf{S}$, l
Output: $\mathcal{A}$ - the selected features

1 $\mathbb{A} = \phi, \mathbf{R} = \mathbf{S}$;
2 **while** $card(\mathcal{A}) < l$ **do**
3 $\quad$ $i^* = \arg\min_{i \notin \mathcal{A}} \|\mathbf{R} - \mathbf{f}_i \mathbf{f}_i^\top\|_F^2$;
4 $\quad$ **if** $\|\mathbf{R} - \mathbf{f}_i \mathbf{f}_i^\top\|_F^2 > \|\mathbf{R}\|_F^2$ **then**
5 $\quad\quad$ | **return** $\mathbb{A}$;
6 $\quad$ **else**
7 $\quad\quad$ | $\mathbb{A} = \mathbb{A} \cup \{i^*\}$; $\mathbf{R} = \mathbf{R} - \mathbf{f}_i \mathbf{f}_i^\top$;

8 **return** $\mathcal{A}$;

3.6 Feature Selection with Proposed Formulations

The proposed multivariate formulations can be used for both supervised and unsupervised feature selection. The key is how to construct the similarity matrix $\mathbf{S}$ in different learning settings. To address this, the methods introduced in Section 2.5.1 can be used.

In a supervised learning setting, if Equation (3.16) is used for feature evaluation, it is more efficiently for us to construct the target matrix $\mathbf{Y}$ directly from the label information. For example, we can define $\mathbf{Y}$ as

$$
\mathbf{Y}_{i,j} = \begin{cases} \sqrt{\frac{n}{n_j}} - \sqrt{\frac{n_j}{n}} & y_i = j \\ -\sqrt{\frac{n_j}{n}} & \text{otherwise} \end{cases}, \tag{3.42}
$$

or

$$
\mathbf{Y}_{i,j} = \begin{cases} 1 & y_i = j \\ -1 & \text{otherwise} \end{cases}. \tag{3.43}
$$

Interestingly, in Section 4.2, we will show that when these $\mathbf{Y}$ are used in Equation (3.16), we can actually obtain sparse solutions for the Least Square Linear Discriminant Analysis (LSLDA) [204] and the Least Square Support Vector Machine (LSSVM) [178], respectively.

In the next chapter, we will study the connections among spectral feature selection and some representative dimension reduction algorithms. We will show that spectral feature selection not only unifies many supervised and unsupervised feature selection algorithms, but also connects feature selection with feature extraction via its multivariate formulations.

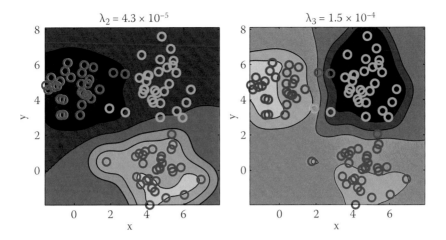

COLOR FIGURE 1.9: The contour of the second and third eigenvectors of a Laplacian matrix derived from a similarity matrix **S**. The numbers on the top are the corresponding eigenvalues.

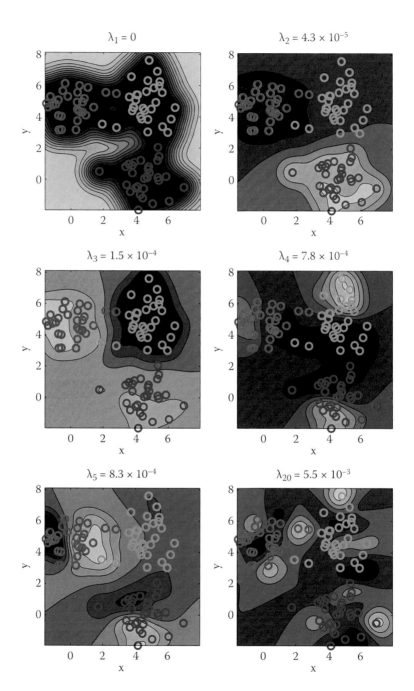

COLOR FIGURE 2.3: Contours of the eigenvectors $\xi_1, \xi_2, \xi_3, \xi_4, \xi_5$, and ξ_{20} of **L**.

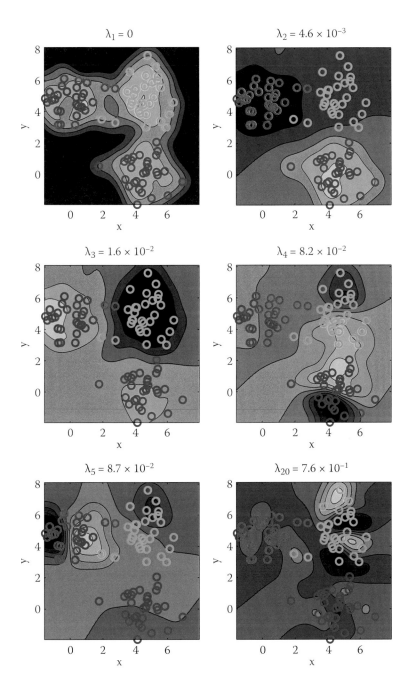

COLOR FIGURE 2.4: Contours of the eigenvectors $\xi_1, \xi_2, \xi_3, \xi_4, \xi_5$, and ξ_{20} of $\mathcal{L}$.

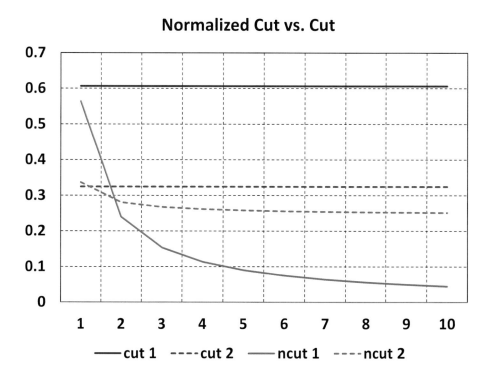

COLOR FIGURE 2.6: The cut value (y-axis) of different types of cut under different cluster sizes (x-axis). The x-axis corresponds to the value of n in Figure 2.5.

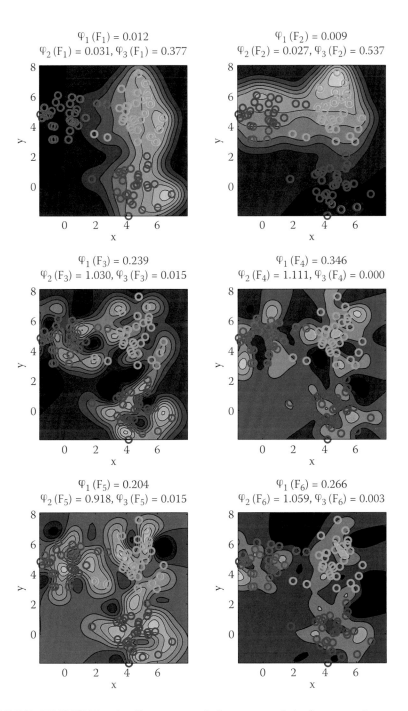

COLOR FIGURE 2.7: Contours and the scores of six features. Among these features, F_1 and F_2 are relevant, and $F_3, F_4, F_5,$ and F_6 are irrelevant.

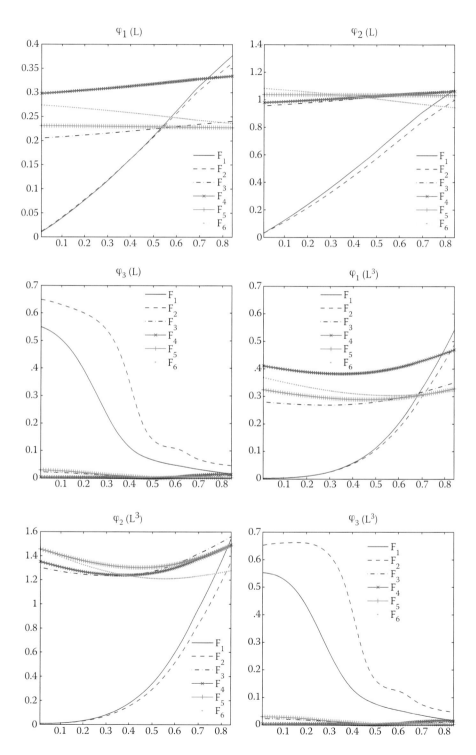

COLOR FIGURE 2.13: Effects of noise on the feature ranking functions.

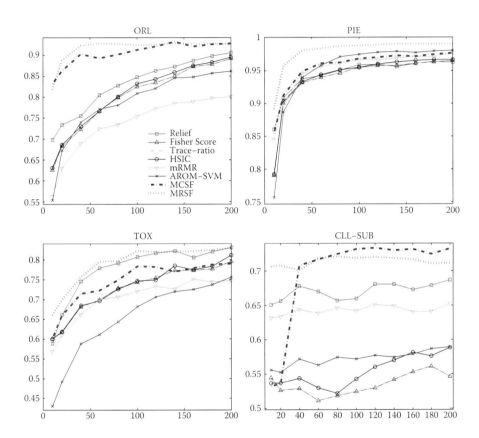

COLOR FIGURE 4.4: Study of supervised cases: Plots for accuracy (*y*-axis) vs. different numbers of selected features (*x*-axis) on the six data sets. The higher the accuracy, the better.

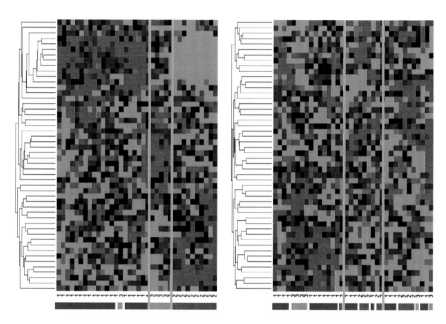

COLOR FIGURE 6.7: Cluster analysis on the genes selected by KOFS$_{\text{Prob}}$ (left) and GO-REL-PROP (right), respectively. The color lines on the bottom of the figure correspond to the samples from patients of B-cell ALL (blue), T-cell ALL (red), and B-cell ALL with the MLL/AF4 chromosomal rearrangement (green), respectively.

Chapter 4

Connections to Existing Algorithms

Spectral feature selection is a general framework. In this section we show that a number of existing feature selection algorithms are essentially special cases of spectral feature selection. These algorithms include Relief and ReliefF [158], Laplacian Score [74], Fisher Score [45], HSIC [165], and Trace Ratio [130]. These algorithms are designed to achieve different goals. For instance, Fisher Score and ReliefF are designed to optimize sample separability, Laplacian Score is designed to retain sample locality, and HSIC is designed to maximize feature class dependency. We can show that these algorithms actually select feature by evaluating features' capability to preserve sample similarity in similar ways.

In this chapter, we also study the connections between multivariate spectral feature selection and a number of well-known learning models, including principal component analysis (PCA) [85], linear discriminant analysis (LDA) [199], and least square support vector machine (LS-SVM) [178]. The study provides us an interesting insight into these existing models, and allows us to utilize the efficient solvers developed in Chapter 3 to generate sparse solutions for the models. We notice that spectral feature selection is for selecting original features, while PCA and LDA are for extracting new features from the original ones. So the multivariate formulations for spectral feature selection form a bridge connecting the two different types of dimensionality reduction techniques.

4.1 Connections to Existing Feature Selection Algorithms

We first show how a number of existing feature selection algorithms can be unified with our univariate formulations for spectral feature selection. To achieve this, we prove that all these algorithms can be reformulated in a common form:

$$\max_{\mathbb{F}_{sub}} \sum_{F \in \mathbb{F}_{sub}} \varphi(F) = \max_{\mathbb{F}_{sub}} \sum_{F \in \mathbb{F}_{sub}} \hat{\mathbf{f}}^\top \hat{\mathbf{S}} \, \hat{\mathbf{f}}, \tag{4.1}$$

$$\hat{\mathbf{f}} \in \mathbb{R}^n, \quad \hat{\mathbf{S}} \in \mathbb{R}^{n \times n}.$$

Here $\mathbb{F}_{sub}$ is the set of selected features, and $\hat{\mathbf{f}}$ and $\hat{\mathbf{S}}$ are the normalized feature vector and the normalized sample similarity matrix, respectively. The only difference among these feature selection algorithms is that they use different ways to compute $\hat{\mathbf{f}}$ and $\hat{\mathbf{S}}$. As we have analyzed in Section 3.1, if a feature selection criterion is in the form of Equation (4.1), it will select features by evaluating features' capability of preserving the sample similarity specified by $\hat{\mathbf{S}}$, and can be treated as a special case of spectral feature selection.

4.1.1   Laplacian Score

Laplacian Score [74] is an unsupervised feature weighting algorithm that uses a filter model. Given an adjacency matrix $\mathbf{S}$, let $\mathbf{D}$ and $\mathbf{L}$ be its corresponding degree and Laplacian matrices, respectively. The Laplacian Score of $\mathbf{f}$ can be calculated via the equation

$$\varphi_L(\mathbf{f}) = \frac{\tilde{\mathbf{f}}^\top \mathbf{L} \tilde{\mathbf{f}}}{\tilde{\mathbf{f}}^\top \mathbf{D} \tilde{\mathbf{f}}}, \quad \text{where} \quad \tilde{\mathbf{f}} = \mathbf{f} - \frac{\mathbf{f}^\top \mathbf{D} \mathbf{1}}{\mathbf{1}^\top \mathbf{D} \mathbf{1}} \mathbf{1}. \tag{4.2}$$

We show that $\varphi_2(\mathbf{f}) = \varphi_L(\mathbf{f})$ in the theorem below. Here $\varphi_2(\cdot)$ is the feature ranking function defined in Equation (2.17) in Chapter 2.

Theorem 4.1.1 *The Laplacian Score [74], an unsupervised feature selection algorithm, is a special case of SPEC, when $\hat{\varphi}(\cdot) = \varphi_2(\cdot)$.*

Proof: The feature evaluation criterion of the Laplacian Score is

$$\varphi_L(F) = \frac{\tilde{\mathbf{f}}^\top \mathbf{L} \tilde{\mathbf{f}}}{\tilde{\mathbf{f}}^\top \mathbf{D} \tilde{\mathbf{f}}}, \quad \text{where} \quad \tilde{\mathbf{f}} = \mathbf{f} - \frac{\mathbf{f}^T \mathbf{D} \mathbf{1}}{\mathbf{1}^T \mathbf{D} \mathbf{1}} \mathbf{1}.$$

Plugging $\tilde{\mathbf{f}}$ in $\varphi_L(F)$, we have

$$\varphi_L(F) = \frac{\mathbf{f}^\top \mathbf{L} \mathbf{f}}{\mathbf{f}^\top \mathbf{D} \mathbf{f} - \frac{(\mathbf{f}^\top \mathbf{D} \mathbf{1})^2}{\mathbf{1}^\top \mathbf{D} \mathbf{1}}} = \frac{(\mathbf{D}^{\frac{1}{2}} \mathbf{f})^\top \mathcal{L} (\mathbf{D}^{\frac{1}{2}} \mathbf{f})}{(\mathbf{D}^{\frac{1}{2}} \mathbf{f})^\top (\mathbf{D}^{\frac{1}{2}} \mathbf{f}) - \frac{\left((\mathbf{D}^{\frac{1}{2}} \mathbf{f})^\top (\mathbf{D}^{\frac{1}{2}} \mathbf{1})\right)^2}{(\mathbf{D}^{\frac{1}{2}} \mathbf{1})^\top (\mathbf{D}^{\frac{1}{2}} \mathbf{1})}}.$$

If we let ξ_1 be the first eigenvector of the normalized Laplacian matrix $\mathcal{L}$, we have $\xi_1 = \frac{\mathbf{D}^{\frac{1}{2}} \mathbf{1}}{||\mathbf{D}^{\frac{1}{2}} \mathbf{1}||}$. Also in $\varphi_2(\cdot)$, $\hat{\mathbf{f}} = \frac{\mathbf{D}^{\frac{1}{2}} \mathbf{f}}{||\mathbf{D}^{\frac{1}{2}} \mathbf{f}||}$. Therefore, the following equation holds:

$$\varphi_L(F) = \frac{\hat{\mathbf{f}}^\top \mathcal{L} \, \hat{\mathbf{f}}}{1 - \left(\hat{\mathbf{f}}^\top \xi_1\right)^2} = \varphi_2(\cdot)$$

■

Theorem 4.1.1 shows that the Laplacian Score is a special case of SPEC, and based on this theorem, we have the following theorem.

Theorem 4.1.2 *Let $\hat{\mathbf{S}}$ be the similarity matrix, selecting l features using the Laplacian Score can be achieved by maximizing the objective function*

$$\arg\max_{F_{i_1},\ldots,F_{i_l}} \sum_{j=1}^{l} \hat{\mathbf{f}}_{i_j}^{\top} \, \hat{\mathbf{S}} \, \hat{\mathbf{f}}_{i_j},$$

where $\hat{\mathbf{f}}$ and $\hat{\mathbf{S}}$ are defined as

$$\tilde{\mathbf{f}} = \frac{\mathbf{D}^{\frac{1}{2}}\mathbf{f}}{\|\mathbf{D}^{\frac{1}{2}}\mathbf{f}\|}, \quad \hat{\mathbf{f}} = \frac{\tilde{\mathbf{f}} - \tilde{\mathbf{f}}^{\top}\xi_1\xi_1}{\sqrt{1 - \left(\tilde{\mathbf{f}}^{\top}\xi_1\right)^2}}, \quad \hat{\mathbf{S}} = \mathbf{D}^{-\frac{1}{2}}\mathbf{S}\mathbf{D}^{-\frac{1}{2}}.$$

∎

4.1.2 Fisher Score

Fisher Score [45] is a supervised feature weighting algorithm with a filter model. Given the class label $\mathbf{y} = \{y_1, \ldots, y_n\}$, Fisher Score prefers features that assign similar values to the samples from the same class and different values to the samples from different classes. The evaluation criterion used in the Fisher Score can be formulated as

$$\varphi_F(F_i) = \frac{\sum_{j=1}^{c} n_j \left(\mu_j - \mu\right)^2}{\sum_{j=1}^{c} n_j \sigma_j^2}, \tag{4.3}$$

where μ is the mean of the feature $\mathbf{f}_i$, n_j is the number of samples in the jth class, and μ_j and σ_j are the mean and the variance of $\mathbf{f}_i$ on the class j, respectively.

As shown in [74], when the similarity matrix $\mathbf{S}$ is derived from the class label using the equation

$$\mathbf{S}_{ij}^{FIS} = \begin{cases} \frac{1}{n_l}, & y_i = y_j = l \\ 0, & otherwise \end{cases}. \tag{4.4}$$

Laplacian Score and Fisher Score are equivalent in the sense that

$$\varphi_L(F_i) = \frac{1}{1 + \varphi_F(F_i)}. \tag{4.5}$$

Therefore, we have the following theorem.

Theorem 4.1.3 *Let $\hat{\mathbf{S}}$ be the similarity matrix defined in Equation (4.4). To select l features using Fisher Score can be achieved by maximizing the following objective function:*

$$\arg\max_{F_{i_1},\ldots,F_{i_l}} \sum_{j=1}^{l} \hat{\mathbf{f}}_{i_j}^{\top} \, \hat{\mathbf{S}} \, \hat{\mathbf{f}}_{i_j}.$$

Here $\hat{\mathbf{f}}$ *and* $\hat{\mathbf{S}}$ *are defined as:*

$$\tilde{\mathbf{f}} = \frac{\mathbf{D}^{\frac{1}{2}}\mathbf{f}}{\|\mathbf{D}^{\frac{1}{2}}\mathbf{f}\|}, \quad \hat{\mathbf{f}} = \frac{\tilde{\mathbf{f}} - \tilde{\mathbf{f}}^{\top}\xi_1\xi_1}{\sqrt{1 - \left(\tilde{\mathbf{f}}^{\top}\xi_1\right)^2}}, \quad \hat{\mathbf{S}} = \mathbf{D}^{-\frac{1}{2}}\mathbf{S}\mathbf{D}^{-\frac{1}{2}}.$$

∎

4.1.3   Relief and ReliefF

Relief [90] and its multiclass extension, ReliefF [94], are supervised feature weighting algorithms using the filter model. Assuming M instances are randomly sampled from the data, the feature evaluation criterion of Relief is defined as

$$\varphi_R\left(F_i\right) = \frac{1}{2}\sum_{t=1}^{M}\left(\|x_{t,i} - NM(\mathbf{x}_t)_i\| - \|x_{t,i} - NH(\mathbf{x}_t)_i\|\right).$$

In the equation, $x_{t,i}$ denotes the value of instance $\mathbf{x}_t$ on feature $\mathbf{f}_i$. $NH(\mathbf{x})$ and $NM(\mathbf{x})$ denote the nearest points to $\mathbf{x}$ in the data with the same and different labels, respectively, and $\|\cdot\|$ is a distance measurement. To handle multiclass problems, the above evaluation metric is extended in ReliefF to the equation

$$\varphi_R\left(F_i\right) = \frac{1}{M}\cdot\sum_{t=1}^{M}\left\{-\frac{1}{M_{t,CL(\mathbf{x}_t)}}\sum_{\mathbf{x}_j\in NH(\mathbf{x}_t)}\|x_{t,i} - x_{j,i}\|\right.$$

$$\left. + \sum_{C\neq CL(\mathbf{x}_t)}\left(\frac{P(C)}{1 - P\left(CL(\mathbf{x}_t)\right)}\times\frac{1}{M_{t,C}}\times\sum_{\mathbf{x}_j\in NM(\mathbf{x}_t,C)}\|x_{t,i} - x_{j,i}\|\right)\right\}.$$
$$(4.6)$$

Here, $CL(\mathbf{x}_t)$ returns the class label of the instance $\mathbf{x}_t$, and $P(C)$ is the probability of instances belonging to the class C. $x_{t,i}$ is the value of the feature $\mathbf{f}_i$ on the instance $\mathbf{x}_t$. $NH(\mathbf{x})$ denotes the set of samples that are nearest to $\mathbf{x}$ and with the same class of $\mathbf{x}$. A sample in $NH(\mathbf{x})$ is called a "nearest hit" of $\mathbf{x}$. $NM(\mathbf{x}, C)$ denotes the set of samples that are nearest to $\mathbf{x}$ and with the class label C ($C \neq CL(\mathbf{x}_t)$). And a sample in $NM(\mathbf{x})$ is called a "nearest miss" of $\mathbf{x}$. $M_{t,CL(\mathbf{x}_t)}$ is the size of $NH(\mathbf{x})$, and $M_{t,C}$ is the size of $NM(\mathbf{x}, C)$. Usually, the sizes of both $NH(\mathbf{x})$ and $NM(\mathbf{x}, C)$ are set to a prespecified constant.

The relevance evaluation criteria of Relief and ReliefF show that the two algorithms seek features that contribute to the separation of samples from different classes.

Assume that the training data have c classes with p instances in each class; there are h instances in both $NH(\mathbf{x})$ and $NM(\mathbf{x}, C)$; and all features have been normalized to have the unit norm. As shown in [222], under the specified assumptions, the feature relevance evaluation criterion of ReliefF can be formulated as

$$\sum_{i=1}^{n} \left(\sum_{j \in NH(\mathbf{x}_i)} \frac{1}{h}(f_i - f_j)^2 - \sum_{C \neq y_i} \frac{\sum_{j \in NM(C, \mathbf{x}_i)} (f_i - f_j)^2}{(c-1)h} \right). \qquad (4.7)$$

In the above equation, f_i is the value of the feature $\mathbf{f}$ on the i-th instance, $\mathbf{x}_i$. Here we use the Euclidean distance to calculate the difference between two values, and use all training data to train ReliefF. To study the connection between ReliefF and spectral feature selection, we define a similarity matrix $\mathbf{S}$ as

$$\mathbf{S}_{i,j}^{REL} = \begin{cases} 1 & i = j \\ -\frac{1}{k} & x_j \in NH(\mathbf{x}_i) \\ \frac{1}{(c-1)k} & x_j \in NM(\mathbf{x}_i, CL(\mathbf{x}_i)) \end{cases}. \qquad (4.8)$$

To ensure that $\mathbf{S}^{REL}$ is symmetric, we assume that if $x_j \in NH(\mathbf{x}_i)$, we also have $x_i \in NH(\mathbf{x}_j)$; and if $x_j \in NM(\mathbf{x}_i, CL(\mathbf{x}_i))$, we also have $x_i \in NM(\mathbf{x}_j, CL(\mathbf{x}_j))$. By applying Theorem 2.2.1, it is easy to verify that $\mathbf{D} = \mathbf{I}$, and $\varphi_R(F_i) = -1 + \mathbf{f}^\top \mathbf{S}^{REL} \mathbf{f}$ is equivalent to the evaluation criterion defined in Equation (4.7). Since $\varphi_1(F_i) = -1 + \mathbf{f}^\top \mathbf{S}^{REL} \mathbf{f}$, where $\varphi_1(\cdot)$ is the feature evaluation criterion defined in Equation (2.12), we can see that under these assumptions, ReliefF also forms a special case of SPEC. Based on the above observation, we have the following theorem.

Theorem 4.1.4 *Let $\hat{\mathbf{S}}$ be the similarity matrix defined in Equation (4.8). Selecting l features using ReliefF can be achieved by maximizing the objective function*

$$\arg\max\nolimits_{F_{i_1}, \dots, F_{i_l}} \sum_{j=1}^{l} \hat{\mathbf{f}}_{i_j}^\top \, \hat{\mathbf{S}} \, \hat{\mathbf{f}}_{i_j}.$$

Here, $\hat{\mathbf{f}}$ and $\hat{\mathbf{S}}$ are defined as

$$\hat{\mathbf{f}} = \frac{\mathbf{D}^{\frac{1}{2}} \mathbf{f}}{\|\mathbf{D}^{\frac{1}{2}} \mathbf{f}\|}, \quad \hat{\mathbf{S}} = \mathbf{D}^{-\frac{1}{2}} \, \mathbf{S} \, \mathbf{D}^{-\frac{1}{2}}. \qquad (4.9)$$

∎

4.1.4 Trace Ratio Criterion

The Trace Ratio Criterion for feature selection is proposed in [130]. It defines two adjacency matrices, $\mathbf{S}_w$ and $\mathbf{S}_b$. $\mathbf{S}_w$ represents the within-class or local adjacency relationship of instances, whereas $\mathbf{S}_b$ represents the between-class or the global counterpart. Two graphs, $\mathbb{G}_w$ and $\mathbb{G}_b$, can be constructed, and their corresponding graph Laplacian matrices are $\mathbf{L}_w$ and $\mathbf{L}_b$, respectively. Assuming we want to select k features, $\mathbf{W} = [\mathbf{w}_{i_1}, \mathbf{w}_{i_2}, \cdots, \mathbf{w}_{i_k}] \in \mathbb{R}^{n \times k}$ is the selection matrix, where the column vector $\mathbf{w}_{i_j}$ has one and only one "1" at its i_j-th element, and $\{i_1, i_2, \cdots, i_k\} \in \{1, 2, \cdots, n\}$. The Trace Ratio Criterion tries to find the best selection matrix $\mathbf{W}$ by maximizing the following objective function

$$\mathbf{W}^{\star} = \arg\max_{\mathbf{W}} = \frac{trace(\mathbf{W}^{\top}\mathbf{X}^{\top}\mathbf{L}_b\mathbf{X}\mathbf{W})}{trace(\mathbf{W}^{\top}\mathbf{X}^{\top}\mathbf{L}_w\mathbf{X}\mathbf{W})}. \tag{4.10}$$

As shown in [130], the optimal solution of the problem can be obtained by iteratively solving the following two subproblems. First, when λ_i is mixed, we solve problem (P1):

$$(\text{P1}): \quad \mathbf{W}_{i+1} = \arg\max_{\mathbf{W}} trace\left(\mathbf{W}^{\top}\mathbf{X}^{\top}(\mathbf{L}_b - \lambda_i\mathbf{L}_w)\mathbf{X}\mathbf{W}\right). \tag{4.11}$$

Second, when $\mathbf{W}_i$ is fixed, we solve problem (P2):

$$(\text{P2}): \quad \lambda_{i+1} = \frac{trace(\mathbf{W}_{i+1}^{\top}\mathbf{X}^{\top}\mathbf{L}_b\mathbf{X}\mathbf{W}_{i+1})}{trace(\mathbf{W}_{i+1}^{\top}\mathbf{X}^{\top}\mathbf{L}_w\mathbf{X}\mathbf{W}_{i+1})}. \tag{4.12}$$

Since

$$trace\left(\mathbf{W}^{\top}\mathbf{X}^{\top}(\mathbf{L}_b - \lambda\mathbf{L}_w)\mathbf{X}\mathbf{W}\right) = \sum_{i \in \{i_1, i_2, \cdots, i_k\}} \mathbf{f}_i^{\top}(\mathbf{L}_b - \lambda\mathbf{L}_w)\,\mathbf{f}_i,$$

it is easy to verify that when λ is fixed, the subproblem (P1) can be solved by picking the top k features with large $\mathbf{f}_i^{\top}(\mathbf{L}_b - \lambda\mathbf{L}_w)\,\mathbf{f}_i$ values. Therefore, although the Trace Ratio Criterion is proposed for subset feature selection, features are actually evaluated independently in the feature selection process. We have the following theorem to build a connection between the Trace Ratio Criterion and the SPEC framework.

Theorem 4.1.5 *Assume λ^* is optimal for Equation (4.10). Selecting l features using the Trace Ratio Criterion can be achieved by maximizing the following objective function:*

$$\arg\max_{F_{i_1}, \ldots, F_{i_l}} \sum_{j=1}^{l} \hat{\mathbf{f}}_{i_j}^{\top}\,\hat{\mathbf{S}}\,\hat{\mathbf{f}}_{i_j}.$$

Here, $\hat{\mathbf{f}}$ and $\hat{\mathbf{S}}$ are defined as

$$\hat{\mathbf{f}} = \mathbf{f}, \quad \hat{\mathbf{S}} = (\mathbf{L_b} - \lambda^*\mathbf{L_w}). \tag{4.13}$$

∎

The theorem suggests that to maximize $\mathbf{f}^{\top}(\mathbf{L}_b - \lambda\mathbf{L}_w)\,\mathbf{f}$, a feature needs to simultaneously maximize $\mathbf{f}^{\top}\mathbf{L}_b\,\mathbf{f}$, which requires assigning different values to samples that are from different classes; and minimize $\mathbf{f}^{\top}\mathbf{L}_w\,\mathbf{f}$, which requires assigning similar values to samples that are from the same class.[1] The Trace Ratio Criterion selects features in a similar way as the Fisher score. Actually, it is shown in [130] that with specific definitions for $\mathbf{L}_w$ and $\mathbf{L}_b$, The Trace Ratio Criterion is equivalent to the Fisher Score method.

---

[1]λ is used to balance the two components in the criterion.

4.1.5 Hilbert-Schmidt Independence Criterion (HSIC)

The Hilbert-Schmidt Independence Criterion (HSIC) was first proposed in [62] for measuring the dependence between two kernels. In [165], HSIC is applied for feature selection, and the basic idea is to select a subset of features, such that the kernel constructed using the feature subset maximizes HSIC when compared to a given kernel $\mathbf{K}$. In [165], an unbiased estimator of HSIC is given as:

$$\varphi_H\left(\mathbf{F}\right) = \frac{1}{n(n-3)}\left[\text{Trace}\left(\mathbf{K_F}\mathbf{K}\right) + \frac{\mathbf{1}^\top\mathbf{K_F}\mathbf{11}^\top\mathbf{K1}}{(n-1)(n-2)}\frac{2}{n-2}\mathbf{1}^\top\mathbf{K_F}\mathbf{K1}\right].(4.14)$$

In the equation, $\mathbf{F}$ is a subset of the original features and $\mathbf{K_F}$ is the kernel obtained from $\mathbf{F}$. To achieve an unbiased estimation, HSIC requires the diagonal elements of $\mathbf{K}$ and $\mathbf{K_F}$ to be set to 0. Based on HSIC, features can be selected via either backward elimination or forward selection. Using a general kernel in HSIC can be very time-consuming, due to the complexity of the kernel construction step in each iteration. Therefore, a linear kernel is usually used. It is shown in [164] that when a linear kernel is used for constructing $\mathbf{K_F}$, selecting k features using HSIC can be achieved as solving the problem

$$\arg\max_{F_{i_1},\dots,F_{i_l}}\sum_{j=1}^{l}\mathbf{f}_{i_j}^\top\,\mathbf{S}_{HSIC}\,\mathbf{f}_{i_j},$$

where

$$\mathbf{S}_{HSIC} = \frac{1}{n(n-3)}\left[\mathbf{K} + \left(\mathbf{11}^T - \mathbf{I}\right)\frac{\mathbf{1}^T\mathbf{K1}}{(n-1)(n-2)}\frac{2}{n-2}\left(\mathbf{K11}^T - \text{diag}\left(\mathbf{K1}\right)\right)\right].$$
$$(4.15)$$

It is clear that in this case, HSIC forms a special case of SPEC, which is formally stated in the following theorem.

Theorem 4.1.6 *When a linear kernel is applied, selecting l features using HSIC can be achieved by maximizing the following objective function:*

$$\arg\max_{F_{i_1},\dots,F_{i_l}}\sum_{j=1}^{l}\hat{\mathbf{f}}_{i_j}^\top\,\hat{\mathbf{S}}\,\hat{\mathbf{f}}_{i_j},\quad\hat{\mathbf{f}}=\mathbf{f},\quad\hat{\mathbf{S}}=\mathbf{S}_{HSIC}.$$

∎

4.1.6 A Summary of the Equivalence Relationships

We show that five existing representative feature selection algorithms, including Laplacian Score, Fisher Score, ReliefF, Trace Ratio, and HSIC, all fit into the framework formulated in Equation (3.1). In Table 4.1, we summarize the sample similarity matrix and the corresponding normalization criteria used

TABLE 4.1: The similarity matrices and feature vectors used in different algorithms.

Algorithm	Sample Similarity Matrix	Feature Normalization
SPEC - $\hat{\varphi}_1(\cdot)$	$\hat{\mathbf{S}} = \mathbf{U}(\mathbf{I} - \gamma(\Sigma))\mathbf{U}^\top$	$\hat{\mathbf{f}} = \dfrac{\mathbf{D}^{\frac{1}{2}}\mathbf{f}}{\|\mathbf{D}^{\frac{1}{2}}\mathbf{f}\|}$
SPEC - $\hat{\varphi}_2(\cdot)$	$\hat{\mathbf{S}} = \mathbf{U}(\mathbf{I} - \gamma(\Sigma))\mathbf{U}^\top$	$\tilde{\mathbf{f}} = \dfrac{\mathbf{D}^{\frac{1}{2}}\mathbf{f}}{\|\mathbf{D}^{\frac{1}{2}}\mathbf{f}\|}, \ \hat{\mathbf{f}} = \dfrac{\tilde{\mathbf{f}} - \tilde{\mathbf{f}}^\top\xi_1\xi_1}{\sqrt{1-\left(\tilde{\mathbf{f}}^\top\xi_1\right)^2}}$
SPEC - $\hat{\varphi}_3(\cdot)$	$\mathbf{S} = \mathbf{U}_k\left(\gamma(2\mathbf{I}) - \gamma(\Sigma_k)\right)\mathbf{U}_k^\top$	$\hat{\mathbf{f}} = \dfrac{\mathbf{D}^{\frac{1}{2}}\mathbf{f}}{\|\mathbf{D}^{\frac{1}{2}}\mathbf{f}\|}$
Laplacian Score	$\mathbf{D}^{-\frac{1}{2}}\mathbf{S}\mathbf{D}^{-\frac{1}{2}}$	$\tilde{\mathbf{f}} = \dfrac{\mathbf{D}^{\frac{1}{2}}\mathbf{f}}{\|\mathbf{D}^{\frac{1}{2}}\mathbf{f}\|}, \ \hat{\mathbf{f}} = \dfrac{\tilde{\mathbf{f}} - \tilde{\mathbf{f}}^\top\xi_1\xi_1}{\sqrt{1-\left(\tilde{\mathbf{f}}^\top\xi_1\right)^2}}$
Fisher Score	$\mathbf{S}^{FIS}$	$\tilde{\mathbf{f}} = \dfrac{\mathbf{D}^{\frac{1}{2}}\mathbf{f}}{\|\mathbf{D}^{\frac{1}{2}}\mathbf{f}\|}, \ \hat{\mathbf{f}} = \dfrac{\tilde{\mathbf{f}} - \tilde{\mathbf{f}}^\top\xi_1\xi_1}{\sqrt{1-\left(\tilde{\mathbf{f}}^\top\xi_1\right)^2}}$
ReliefF	$\mathbf{S}^{REL}$	$\hat{\mathbf{f}} = \dfrac{\mathbf{D}^{\frac{1}{2}}\mathbf{f}}{\|\mathbf{D}^{\frac{1}{2}}\mathbf{f}\|}$
Trace Ratio Criterion	$\mathbf{L}_b - \lambda^*\mathbf{L}_w$	$\hat{\mathbf{f}} = \mathbf{f}$
HSIC	$\mathbf{S}_{HSIC}$	$\hat{\mathbf{f}} = \mathbf{f}$

in these algorithms. It turns out that although these algorithms were originally designed to achieve different goals, they actually select features via estimating their capability toward preserving sample similarity. One limitation seen in all these algorithms is that they evaluate features independently, causing them to be unable to handle redundant features. This is a common drawback of these algorithms. To address this drawback, the multivariate formulations presented in Chapter 3 for spectral feature selection can be utilized.

4.2   Connections to Other Learning Models

In the last section, we showed that many existing feature selection algorithms can be reformulated as special cases of the univariate formulations for spectral feature selection. In this section, we show that the multivariate formulation for spectral feature selection,

$$\arg \min_{\mathbf{W},\, \lambda} \|\mathbf{Y} - \mathbf{XW}\|_F^2 + \lambda \|\mathbf{W}\|_{2,1}$$
$$s.t. \quad \mathbb{A} = \{i : \|\mathbf{w}^i\|_2 > 0\}, \; Card\,(\mathbb{A}) = l, \tag{4.16}$$

can also be connected to some well-known learning models, including the principal component analysis (PCA) [85], the linear discriminant analysis (LDA) [51], and the support vector machine (SVM) [187], through their least square formulations [178, 176]. These connections provide us interesting insights, and allow us to compute sparse (or sparser) solutions for these models using the techniques developed in Chapter 3. Note that spectral feature selection is for selecting original features, while PCA and LDA are for extracting new features from the original ones. Therefore, the multivariate formulations for spectral feature selection form a bridge that effectively connects two different types of dimensionality reduction techniques and allows for their joint study.

4.2.1   Linear Discriminant Analysis

Linear Discriminant Analysis (LDA) [51, 200, 204, 207, 202, 203, 201, 196] is a supervised feature extraction approach. Assuming samples are from k different classes. LDA tries to generate a $k - 1$ dimensional space to represent the data, such that in this space the samples from different classes are well separable. LDA extracts new features by linearly combining the original features.

Example 17 *Linear Discriminant Analysis (LDA)*

Figure 4.1 shows how linear discriminant analysis works. In this example, the data $\mathbf{X} \in \mathbb{R}^{n \times 2}$ distribute in a two-dimensional space (x-y axes), and the samples are from two different classes. LDA determines a weight vector $\mathbf{w} \in \mathbb{R}^{2 \times 1}$, and uses $\mathbf{w}$ to project the samples to generate one-dimensional data

$$\hat{\mathbf{X}} = \mathbf{X}\mathbf{w}, \quad \hat{\mathbf{X}} \in \mathbb{R}^{n \times 1}.$$

Let $SEP\left(\hat{\mathbf{W}}\right)$ be a measurement that evaluates the separability of the one-dimensional data $\hat{\mathbf{X}}$, e.g., the measurement defined in Equation (4.20). LDA tries to find the $\mathbf{w}$ that maximizes $SEP\left(\hat{\mathbf{W}}\right)$. Note that, in this example, $\hat{\mathbf{X}}$ contains only one feature, and it is a linear combination of the original features in $\mathbf{X}$.

Below, we present the sample separability measurement used in LDA. To this end, we first define the total covariance matrix and the between-class covariance matrix. We then define the sample separability measurement based on the two covariance matrices.

Let n be the number of samples, n_j the number of samples in the j-th class, $\mathbf{x}_i$ the i-th sample, $\mathbf{c}$ the mean of the data, and $\mathbf{c}_j$ the mean of the data in the j-th class.[2] The total covariance matrix $\mathbf{S}_t$ and the between-class covariance matrix $\mathbf{S}_b$ are defined as

$$\mathbf{S}_t = \frac{1}{n} \sum_{i=1}^{n} (\mathbf{x}_i - \mathbf{c})(\mathbf{x}_i - \mathbf{c})^T,$$

$$\mathbf{S}_b = \frac{1}{n} \sum_{j=1}^{k} n_j \left(\mathbf{c}^{(j)} - \mathbf{c}\right)\left(\mathbf{c}^{(j)} - \mathbf{c}\right)^T,$$

$$\text{where } \mathbf{c} = \frac{1}{n} \sum_{i=1}^{n} \mathbf{x}_i, \quad \mathbf{c}^{(j)} = \frac{1}{n_i} \sum_{i \in \text{class}j} \mathbf{x}_i.$$

Let $\hat{\mathbf{X}} = \mathbf{X}\mathbf{W}$ be the data obtained by projecting the original data $\mathbf{X}$ into the lower-dimensional space generated by LDA, where $\mathbf{W} \in \mathbb{R}^{m \times (c-1)}$ is the projection matrix.[3] Let $\hat{\mathbf{S}}_t$ and $\hat{\mathbf{S}}_b$ be the total and the between-class covariance matrices of the data in the lower dimensional space, respectively.

---

[2]$\mathbf{x}_i, \mathbf{c}, \mathbf{c}_j \in \mathbb{R}^{m \times 1}$ are column vectors.

[3]m is the number of features, c is the number of classes. Note that $\mathbf{W}$ has $c - 1$ columns, since $rank\left(\mathbf{S}_b\right) = c - 1$.

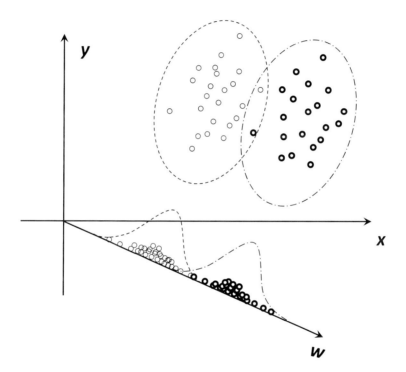

FIGURE 4.1: Linear discriminant analysis.

We have

$$\hat{\mathbf{S}}_t = \mathbf{W}^\top \mathbf{S}_t \mathbf{W}, \tag{4.17}$$

$$\hat{\mathbf{S}}_b = \mathbf{W}^\top \mathbf{S}_b \mathbf{W}. \tag{4.18}$$

Based on the the total and the between-class covariance matrices, a popular criterion for measuring sample separability in LDA [199] is defined as

$$Trace\left(\mathbf{S}_t^{-1}\mathbf{S}_b\right). \tag{4.19}$$

It can be verified that for a data set, when samples from the same class are near one another, and samples from different classes are far apart, the above equation will return a large value [201]. Based on this observation, the projection matrix $\mathbf{W}$ in LDA is obtained by solving the problem

$$\mathbf{W}^* = arg\max_{\mathbf{W}}\left(Trace\left(\hat{\mathbf{S}}_t^{-1}\hat{\mathbf{S}}_b\right)\right). \tag{4.20}$$

It can be shown that the $c-1$ columns of $\mathbf{W}^*$ are given by the $c-1$ eigenvectors of $\mathbf{S}_t^{-1}\mathbf{S}_b$, corresponding to the $c-1$ largest eigenvalues [199].

In Least Square LDA (LSLDA) [204], instead of solving an eigenvalue problem, we compute $\mathbf{W}$ by solving a least square problem. Let y_i be the label of the i-th sample. We can define a target matrix, $\mathbf{Y}$ as

$$\mathbf{Y}_{i,j}^{LDA} = \begin{cases} \sqrt{\frac{n}{n_j}} - \sqrt{\frac{n_j}{n}} & y_i = j \\ -\sqrt{\frac{n_j}{n}} & \text{otherwise.} \end{cases} \tag{4.21}$$

Assuming that $\mathbf{X}$ is centralized, we can verify that the following equation holds:

$$\mathbf{S}_b = \frac{1}{n}\mathbf{X}\mathbf{Y}^{LDA}\mathbf{Y}^{LDA^\top}\mathbf{X}^\top, \quad \mathbf{S}_t = \mathbf{X}\mathbf{X}^\top. \tag{4.22}$$

And the objective of LSLDA is defined as

$$\min_{\mathbf{W}} \|\mathbf{X}\mathbf{W} - \mathbf{Y}^{LDA}\|_F^2, \quad \mathbf{W} \in \mathbb{R}^{m \times k}. \tag{4.23}$$

In [204], it is shown that when $rank(\mathbf{S}_t) = rank(\mathbf{S}_w) + rank(\mathbf{S}_b)$, LSLDA is strictly equivalent to LDA. It turns out that this condition is quite mild, and it usually holds when the dimensionality of the data is high.

Comparing Equation (4.16) with Equation (4.23), we can see that the multivariate formulation for spectral feature selection and LSLDA share similar objective functions. Their sole difference is that the former one applies a sparse regularization to ensure that only l features are used to construct the optimal solution. Therefore, when $\mathbf{Y}^{LDA}$ is used as the target matrix in Equation (4.16), we can obtain a sparse solution for LSLDA, and the linear combination of the selected feature will form a lower dimensional space, in which samples from different classes can be separated well. This analysis shows that the sparse LSLDA (SLSLDA) forms a special case of the multi-variate spectral feature selection by using $\mathbf{Y}^{LDA}$ as the target matrix. Also we can show that when $\mathbf{S}$ is the matrix defined in Equation (4.4), $\mathbf{K}_{LSLDA}$ can be formulated as

$$\mathbf{K}_{LSLDA} = (\mathbf{Y}^{LDA})(\mathbf{Y}^{LDA})^{\top} = n\mathbf{S}^{FIS} - \mathbf{1}\mathbf{1}^{\top}. \tag{4.24}$$

Since the matrix $\mathbf{1}\mathbf{1}^{\top}$ and n are constant, it turns out that the Fisher Score and the LSLDA essentially specify the same simple similarity. Unlike the Fisher Score, the LSLDA is a supervised feature extraction algorithm, which generates new features by combining original features.

4.2.2 Least Square Support Vector Machine

Support Vector Machine (SVM) [34, 36, 167, 150, 73, 229, 27, 22, 34] is a supervised learning model that has been widely applied in various data mining applications [216, 83, 68, 103, 184, 55, 20, 84].

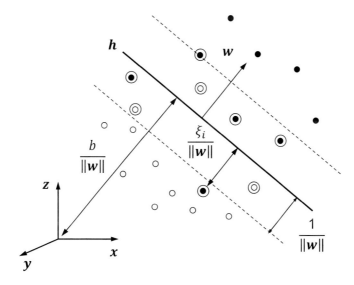

● Support vectors of the positive class

◎ Support vectors of the negative class

FIGURE 4.2: A linear separating hyperplane of support vector machine.

As shown in Figure 4.2, given a binary classification problem, SVM tries to find a hyperplane, which can separate the samples from different classes with a large margin. This idea can be formulated using the following equation.

$$\min \|\mathbf{w}\|$$
$$s.t. \quad y_i \left(\mathbf{x}_i^\top \mathbf{w} + b\right) \geq 1 - \xi_i, \ \forall i$$
$$\xi_i \geq 0, \ \sum_{i=1}^{n} \xi_i \leq C. \tag{4.25}$$

In the above equation, $\mathbf{x}_i$ is the i-th sample, and $y_i \in \{-1, 1\}$ is its label. $\mathbf{w}$ and b are the weight vector and the interception defining the hyperplane $\mathbf{h} = \{\mathbf{x}|\mathbf{x}^\top \mathbf{w} + b = 0\}$. Given a sample $\mathbf{x}$, $\mathbf{x}^\top \mathbf{w} + b$ computes the distance from $\mathbf{x}$ to the hyperplane $\mathbf{h}$. It is easy to verify that if $\mathbf{x}$ is below the hyperplane, $\mathbf{x}^\top \mathbf{w} + b \leq 0$, otherwise $\mathbf{x}^\top \mathbf{w} + b \geq 0$.

Let the region below $\mathbf{h}$ correspond to the negative class, and the other side corresponds to the positive class. The condition, $y_i \left(\mathbf{x}_i^\top \mathbf{w} + b\right) \geq 1$, forces all the samples to stay in the region that their classes belong to. And additionally, they must be at least $\frac{1}{\|\mathbf{w}\|}$ away from the hyperplane $\mathbf{h}$ [72]. Therefore, $\frac{1}{\|\mathbf{w}\|}$ measures the size of the margin corresponding to classifying the samples using the hyperplane $\mathbf{h}$.

Since the samples are not always linearly separable, slack variables ξ_i, $i = 1, \ldots, n$ are introduced to allow some samples to stay on the wrong side:

$$y_i \left(\mathbf{x}_i^\top \mathbf{w} + b\right) \geq 1 - \xi_i, \quad \forall i.$$

Obviously, if $y_i \left(\mathbf{x}_i^\top \mathbf{w} + b\right) < 0$, $\mathbf{x}_i$ will be on the wrong side, and correspondingly, $\xi_i > 0$. Similarly, if $y_i \left(\mathbf{x}_i^\top \mathbf{w} + b\right) > 1$, $\mathbf{x}_i$ will be on the correct side, and correspondingly, $\xi_i = 0$. This observation suggests that $\sum \xi_i$ can be used to bound the total number of training misclassifications. In SVM, all the samples that satisfy $y_i \left(\mathbf{x}_i^\top \mathbf{w} + b\right) \leq 1$ are called *support vectors*, and they are either in the margin area, or on the wrong side of the hyperplane $\mathbf{h}$.

The training of SVM involves solving a convex *quadratic optimization* problem (QP). Solving QP is computationally expensive, due to the need to compute a dense Hessian matrix. Solving the QP with a general-purpose QP solver would have a time complexity of $O(n^3)$ [18], which is not scalable. To address this problem, powerful optimization techniques such as the interior point method [194] and the coordinate descent method [29] have been applied for solving the problem in very efficient ways.

Instead of solving a QP problem, in the least square SVM (LSSVM) [178], the SVM formulation is approximated and reformulated as a least square problem:

$$\min_{\mathbf{W}} \ \|\mathbf{X}\mathbf{W} - \mathbf{Y}^{SVM}\|_F^2, \quad \mathbf{W} \in \mathbb{R}^{m \times k},$$
$$\mathbf{Y}_{i,j}^{SVM} = \begin{cases} 1 & y_i = j \\ -1 & \text{otherwise.} \end{cases} \tag{4.26}$$

In [208], it is shown that for high-dimensional data, LSSVM and SVM behave similarly.

Comparing Equation (4.16) with Equation (4.26), we can see that when $\mathbf{Y}_{i,j}^{SVM}$ is used in both equations, the only difference between the multi-variate formulation for spectral feature selection and the LSSVM is that the former applies a sparse regularization to ensure that only l features are used to construct the solution. Therefore, when $\mathbf{Y}^{SVM}$ is used as the target matrix in Equation (4.16), we can obtain a sparse solution for LSSVM. This analysis shows that sparse LSSVM (SLSSVM) forms a special case of multivariate spectral feature selection by using $\mathbf{Y}^{SVM}$ as the target matrix.

4.2.3 Principal Component Analysis

Principal component analysis (PCA) [85] is an unsupervised feature extraction approach. Given a data set $\mathbf{X}$, the PCA generates a set of principal components (the new features), which maximizes the variance of the data projected on them. Given the covariance matrix $\mathbf{C} = \frac{1}{n} \sum_{i=1}^{n} (\mathbf{x}_i - \mathbf{c})(\mathbf{x}_i - \mathbf{c})^T$, the principal components of $\mathbf{X}$ can be obtained by computing the top eigenvectors of $\mathbf{C}$ corresponding to the largest eigenvalues.

Example 18 *Principal components of two-dimensional data*

Figure 4.3 shows the distribution of a two-dimensional data set $\mathbf{X}$. Since $\mathbf{X} \in \mathbb{R}^{n \times 2}$, its covariance matrix $\mathbf{C}$ is of rank 2, $\mathbf{C} \in \mathbb{R}^{2 \times 2}$. Therefore, using PCA we can obtain two principal components for $\mathbf{X}$: $\mathbf{w}_1$ and $\mathbf{w}_2$. $\mathbf{w}_1$ is the largest principal component. It is the direction that maximizes the variances of the projected data, $\mathbf{X}\mathbf{w}_1$. $\mathbf{w}_2$ is the smallest principal component. $\mathbf{w}_1$ and $\mathbf{w}_2$ are orthogonal.

If we let $\mathbf{P} = \mathbf{I} - \frac{1}{n}\mathbf{1}\mathbf{1}^\top$, we have $\mathbf{C} = (\mathbf{PX})^\top (\mathbf{PX})$. Based on this observation, we can compute the variance of $\mathbf{X}\mathbf{w}_1$ using the equation

$$Var(\mathbf{X}\mathbf{w}_1) = (\mathbf{PX}\mathbf{w}_1)^\top (\mathbf{PX}\mathbf{w}_1) = \mathbf{w}_1^\top \mathbf{C}\mathbf{w}_1.$$

To maximize the above equation, we have $\mathbf{w}_1 = \xi_1$, where ξ_1 is the eigenvector of $\mathbf{C}$ corresponding to the largest eigenvalue. Similarly, let $\mathbf{X}$ be an m-dimensional data, $\mathbf{X} \in \mathbb{R}^{n \times m}$. Its first l principal components can be obtained by computing the top l eigenvectors of $\mathbf{C}$, which corresponds to the l largest eigenvalues.

Below we show the connection between the multivariate formulation for spectral feature selection and the least square formulation for PCA.

Assume that $m \geq n$, and $\mathbf{X} = \mathbf{U}\Sigma\mathbf{V}^\top$ is the SVD of $\mathbf{X}$. Let $\mathbf{U} = \{\mathbf{u}_1, \ldots, \mathbf{u}_n\}$, $\mathbf{V} = \{\mathbf{v}_1, \ldots, \mathbf{v}_n\}$, and $\Sigma = \text{diag}\{\lambda_1, \ldots, \lambda_n\}$. It is shown in [230]

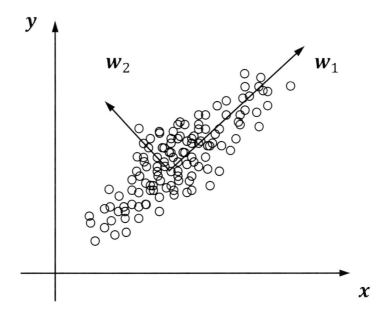

FIGURE 4.3: The principal components determined by PCA.

that the principal components generated by PCA can be equally obtained by solving the following problem:

$$\mathbf{w}_i = \arg\max_{\mathbf{w}_i} \|\mathbf{y}_i - \mathbf{X}\mathbf{w}_i\|_2,$$
$$\mathbf{y}_i = \lambda_i \mathbf{v}_i, \quad i = 1, \ldots, k. \tag{4.27}$$

Based on this observation, the authors in [230] proposed to obtain the sparse solutions for PCA by solving an L_1-norm regularization problem:

$$\mathbf{w}_i = \arg\max_{\mathbf{w}_i} \|\mathbf{y}_i - \mathbf{X}\mathbf{w}_i\|_2,$$
$$\|\mathbf{w}_i\|_1 \leq t,$$
$$\mathbf{y}_i = \lambda_i \mathbf{v}_i \quad i = 1, \ldots, k. \tag{4.28}$$

By considering the k principal components together, Equation (4.28) can be written as:

$$\mathbf{W} = \arg\max_{\mathbf{W}} \|\mathbf{Y} - \mathbf{X}\mathbf{W}\|_F,$$
$$\mathbf{W} = \{\mathbf{w}_1, \ldots, \mathbf{w}_k\}, \ \|\mathbf{w}_i\|_1 \leq t,$$
$$\mathbf{Y} = \mathbf{V}_k \Sigma_k, \tag{4.29}$$

where $\mathbf{V}_k = \{\mathbf{v}_1, \ldots, \mathbf{v}_k\}$, and $\Sigma_k = \text{diag}\{\lambda_1, \ldots, \lambda_k\}$.

Comparing Equation (4.27) and Equation (4.29) with Equation (4.16), it is clear that PCA eccentrically projects samples to a lower-dimensional space, where the similarity between samples measured by their inner product (in the original space) is best preserved. Therefore, the sparse PCA formulation, specified in Equation (4.28), can be regarded as a special case of the multivariate spectral feature selection, when a linear kernel is used to define the similarity among samples. As compared to sparse PCA, the usage of the $L_{2,1}$ norm in Equation (4.16) makes the formulation more suitable for feature selection. The L_1-norm used in Equation (4.28) ensures that each $\mathbf{w}_i$ is sparse. However, in different $\mathbf{w}_i$, different features are used. When considering all $\mathbf{w}_i$ together, many features may still be used in the obtained $\mathbf{W}$. In contrast, the $L_{2,1}$ norm ensures that only a small set of the features are used in constructing the whole $\mathbf{W}$.

4.2.4 Simultaneous Feature Selection and Extraction

Feature selection achieves dimensionality reduction by selecting a small set of the original features. Feature extraction reduces dimensionality by generating a small set of new features via combining the original features. Currently, feature selection and feature extraction are largely studied independently. The above analysis shows that feature selection and feature extraction can actually be done simultaneously with the multivariate formulation for spectral feature selection.

By applying feature selection, the redundant and irrelevant features can be removed. This helps us effectively reduce the noise in the data. By applying feature extraction, we can combine the selected features and generate a smaller set of new features. Compared to the original features, the newly generated features may possess stronger discriminative power, and usually result in better learning performance. The multivariate formulations for spectral feature selection form a bridge connecting feature selection with feature extraction, and allow us to take full advantage of both techniques.

4.3 An Experimental Study of the Algorithms

In this section we empirically evaluate the performance of various spectral feature selection algorithms in both supervised and unsupervised learning contexts. In the experiments, we compare nine feature selection algorithms. For supervised learning, eight feature selection algorithms are chosen for comparison: ReliefF, Fisher Score, Trace Ratio Criterion, HSIC, MRSF, MCSF, mRMR [40], and AROM-SVM [192]. The first six are spectral feature selection algorithms. The last two are existing state-of-the-art feature selection algorithms. Both of the algorithms are able to handle redundant features, and are used in the experiment as the baseline algorithms for comparison. For un-

TABLE 4.2: Summary of the benchmark data sets

Data Set	# Features	# Instances	# Classes
PIE10P	2400	210	10
ORL10P	10000	100	10
TOX	5748	171	4
CLL-SUB	11340	111	3

supervised learning, six algorithms are used for comparison: Laplacian Score, SPEC, Trace Ratio Criterion, HSIC, MRSE, and MCSF. They are all spectral feature selection algorithms. For MRSF and MCSF, in supervised learning context, $\mathbf{S}$ is calculated by Equation (4.4); and in unsupervised learning, $\mathbf{S}$ is calculated by the Gaussian RBF kernel function. Four high-dimensional data sets are used in the experiment. They are two image data sets: PIE10P[4] and ORL10P[5]; and two microarray data sets: TOX and CLL-SUB.[6] Detailed information of the benchmark data sets is listed in Table 4.2.

Let $\mathbf{F}$ be a set of the selected features, and $\mathbf{X_F}$ is the data set only containing the features in $\mathbf{F}$. In the supervised learning setting, algorithms are compared on (1) **classification accuracy** and (2) **redundancy rate**. The redundancy rate is measured by

$$\mathrm{RED}\,(\mathbf{F}) = \frac{1}{m(m-1)} \sum_{f_i, f_j \in \mathbf{F}, i > j} \rho_{i,j},$$

where $\rho_{i,j}$ measures the correlation between the i-th and j-th features. A large value of $\mathrm{RED}\,(\mathbf{F})$ indicates that many selected features are strongly correlated and thus redundancy is expected to exist in $\mathbf{F}$.

In the unsupervised learning setting, three measurements are used to compare the performance of the feature selection algorithms: (1) **redundancy rate** defined in Equation (4.3); (2) **scale of the residue**; and (3) **Jaccard score** [81]. The scale of the residue is computed by the equation

$$\|\mathbf{X_F X_F}^\top - \mathbf{K}\|_F^2.$$

The Jaccard score is computed by the equation

$$\mathrm{JAC}\,(\mathbf{K_F}, \mathbf{K}, k) = \frac{1}{n} \sum_{i=1}^{n} \frac{NB\,(i, k, \mathbf{K_F}) \cap NB\,(i, k, \mathbf{K})}{NB\,(i, k, \mathbf{K_F}) \cup NB\,(i, k, \mathbf{K})},$$

where $\mathbf{K_F} = \mathbf{X_F X_F^\top}$ and $\mathbf{K}$ are the linear kernel constructed using the selected

---

[4]http://peipa.essex.ac.uk/ipa/pix/faces/manchester/. Images are subsampled down to the size of 60×40.

[5]http://www.uk.research.att.com/facedatabase.html. Images are subsampled down to size of 100×100.

[6]Both data are retrieved from the Gene Expression Omnibus gene expression repository (http://www.ncbi.nlm.nih.gov/geo/) with retrieval IDs: GDS1454 and GDS968.

features and the input similarity matrix, respectively. Here $NB(i, k, \mathbf{K})$ returns the k nearest neighbors of the i-th instance according to the pairwised similarity specified by $\mathbf{K}$. The Jaccard score measures the averaged overlapping of the neighborhoods specified by $\mathbf{K_F}$ and $\mathbf{K}$. A high Jaccard score indicates that the pairwised similarities specified by the two similarity matrices are consistent. The scale of the residue and the Jaccard score are used to assess an algorithm's capability of preserving the sample similarity in the continuous and the discrete ways, respectively.

In the supervised learning context, for each data set, we randomly sample 50% data for training, and the remaining for testing. The process is repeated 20 times. Different algorithms are evaluated. The results are averaged to obtain the final results. Linear SVM is used for classification. The parameters for feature selection algorithms and the SVM are tuned with cross-validation, if necessary. The Student's t-test is used to evaluate the statistical significance with p-value < 0.05. For the unsupervised learning setting, all the samples are used for feature selection. The selected features are evaluated using the three measurements mentioned above.

4.3.1 A Study of the Supervised Case

4.3.1.1 Accuracy

The classification accuracy results are shown in Figure 4.4 and Table 6.5. Figure 4.4 contains the plots of the accuracy of the SVM classifier using the top 10, 20, ..., 200 features selected by each algorithm. Table 6.5 shows the *aggregated accuracy* of different algorithms on each data set. The aggregated accuracy is obtained by averaging the averaged accuracy achieved by SVM using the top 10, 20, ..., 200 features selected by each algorithm. The value in the parentheses is the p-Value. In Figure 4.4 and Table 6.5, we can observe that MRSF produces superior classification performance compared to the other algorithms. The performance of MCSF is also good, which is the second best in the test.

4.3.1.2 Redundancy Rate

Table 4.4 presents the averaged redundancy rates of the top n features selected by different algorithms, where n is the number of samples. We choose n, as when the number of selected features is larger than n, any feature can be expressed by a linear combination of the remaining ones, which introduces unnecessary redundancy in evaluation. In the table, the boldfaced values are the lowest redundancy rates or the ones without significant difference to the lowest. The results from the redundancy rates show that MRCF and MRSF all attain low redundancy rates, which suggests that the redundancy removal mechanisms in both algorithms are effective. We also observe that the two baseline algorithms mRMR and AROM-SVM also produce low redundancy

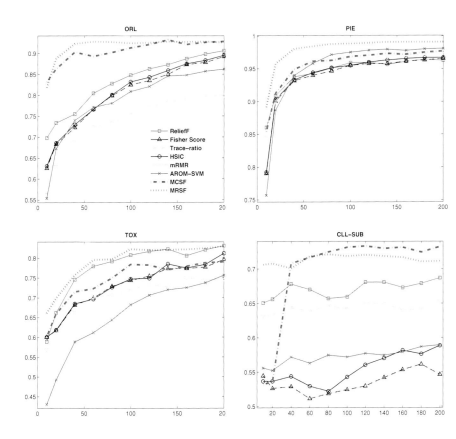

FIGURE 4.4: (**SEE COLOR INSERT**) Study of supervised cases: Plots for accuracy (y-axis) vs. different numbers of selected features (x-axis) on the six data sets. The higher the accuracy, the better.

TABLE 4.3: Supervised cases: Aggregated accuracy. The *p*-value in the parentheses is obtained from t-test.

Algorithm	ORL	PIE	TOX	CLL-SUB	AVE	WIN
ReliefF	0.83 (0.00)	0.94 (0.00)	0.77 (0.03)	0.67 (0.00)	0.80	0
Fisher Score	0.80 (0.00)	0.93 (0.00)	0.72 (0.00)	0.54 (0.00)	0.75	0
Trace-ratio	0.80 (0.00)	0.93 (0.00)	0.72 (0.00)	0.54 (0.00)	0.75	0
HSIC	0.80 (0.00)	0.94 (0.00)	0.73 (0.00)	0.55 (0.00)	0.75	0
mRMR	0.73 (0.00)	0.95 (0.00)	0.70 (0.00)	0.64 (0.00)	0.75	0
AROM-SVM	0.78 (0.00)	0.94 (0.02)	0.64 (0.00)	0.57 (0.00)	0.73	0
MCSF	0.90 (0.05)	0.95 (0.00)	0.74 (0.00)	0.69 (0.34)	0.82	0
MRSF	**0.91 (1.00)**	**0.98 (1.00)**	**0.79 (1.00)**	**0.71 (1.00)**	**0.85**	4

TABLE 4.4: Supervised cases: Averaged redundancy rate. The *p*-value in the parentheses is obtained from t-test.

Algorithm	ORL	PIE	TOX	CLL-SUB	AVE	WIN
ReliefF	0.92 (0.00)	0.36 (0.00)	0.34 (0.00)	0.59 (0.00)	0.55	0
Fisher Score	0.79 (0.00)	0.37 (0.00)	0.56 (0.00)	0.76 (0.00)	0.62	0
Trace-ratio	0.79 (0.00)	0.37 (0.00)	0.56 (0.00)	0.76 (0.00)	0.62	0
HSIC	0.79 (0.00)	0.37 (0.00)	0.56 (0.00)	0.76 (0.00)	0.62	0
mRMR	0.25 (0.29)	0.29 (0.00)	0.26 (0.00)	0.26 (0.00)	0.26	0
AROM-SVM	0.25 (0.44)	0.32 (0.00)	**0.15 (1.00)**	0.59 (0.00)	0.33	1
MCSF	0.26 (0.00)	0.24 (0.48)	0.30 (0.00)	0.44 (0.00)	0.31	0
MRSF	**0.25 (1.00)**	**0.24 (1.00)**	0.16 (0.00)	**0.21 (1.00)**	**0.21**	3

TABLE 4.5: Study of the unsupervised cases: Averaged residue scale, the lower the better.

Algorithm	ORL	PIE	TOX	CLL-SUB	AVE	WIN
Laplacian Score	112.80	208.97	178.69	127.67	157.03	0
SPEC-1	112.79	220.42	179.21	126.65	159.77	0
SPEC-3	122.51	201.25	176.15	120.74	155.16	0
Trace-Ratio	112.79	200.68	179.30	119.70	153.12	0
HSIC	112.79	200.64	179.24	119.79	153.12	0
MCSF	**91.03**	**183.04**	**166.23**	**107.25**	**136.89**	4
MRSF	91.19	187.05	167.07	108.96	138.57	0

rates. Since the two algorithms are able to remove redundant features, the observation is consistent with our expectation.

4.3.2 A Study of the Unsupervised Case

4.3.2.1 Residue Scale and Jaccard Score

Tables 4.5 and 4.6 present the averaged residue scale and Jaccard score achieved by different algorithms on the benchmark data sets, when the top n features are selected. The two measurements assess algorithms' capability of similarity preserving. The results show that among all the algorithms, MCSF and MRSF achieve better performance on all four data sets, indicating their strong capability of sample similarity preserving.

We observe that the performance of MRSF is inferior to that of MCSF. The reason is that MRSF optimizes $\|\mathbf{XWW}^\top\mathbf{X}^\top - \mathbf{K}\|_F^2$, while in residue scale and Jaccard score, $\mathbf{X_F}\mathbf{X_F}^\top$ is used to compute $\mathbf{K_F}$. It is possible that the performance of MRSF is underestimated by the two measurements, since MRSF may select features whose linear combination can produce a similarity matrix that well preserves the similarity specified by $\mathbf{K}$. To clearly show this, Table 4.7 lists the aggregated residue scale and Jaccard score of MRSF and MCSF, when $\mathbf{XWW}^\top\mathbf{X}^\top$ is used to compute $\mathbf{K_F}$ in the two measurements. Here the aggregated residue scale and Jaccard score are obtained by averaging the averaged residue scale and Jaccard score over four benchmark data sets. The results show that when the weight matrix $\mathbf{W}$ is taken into account, MRSF achieves better results than MCSF. This indicates that the features selected by MRSF also have strong capability of similarity preserving through their linear combinations. This fact is also verified by the good classification performance of the SVM classifier on the features selected by MRSF.

TABLE 4.6: Study of unsupervised cases: Averaged Jaccard score, the higher the better.

Algorithm	ORL	PIE	TOX	CLL-SUB	AVE	WIN
			$k_{NB} = 1$			
Laplacian Score	0.04	0.02	0.08	0.03	0.04	0
SPEC-1	0.04	0.03	0.09	0.02	0.05	0
SPEC-3	0.02	0.06	0.09	0.05	0.05	0
Trace-Ratio	0.06	0.04	0.13	0.06	0.07	0
HSIC	0.06	0.04	0.13	0.03	0.06	0
MCSF	0.53	0.26	**0.50**	**0.19**	**0.37**	2
MRSF	**0.60**	**0.35**	0.35	**0.19**	**0.37**	3
			$k_{NB} = 5$			
Laplacian Score	0.09	0.05	0.14	0.09	0.09	0
SPEC-1	0.09	0.05	0.14	0.11	0.10	0
SPEC-3	0.13	0.07	0.16	0.12	0.12	0
Trace-Ratio	0.08	0.07	0.15	0.12	0.11	0
HSIC	0.08	0.07	0.15	0.13	0.11	0
MCSF	**0.72**	0.27	**0.47**	**0.23**	0.42	3
MRSF	0.70	**0.44**	0.35	0.22	**0.43**	1

TABLE 4.7: The aggregated residue scale and Jaccard score of MCSF and MRSF when the weight matrix **W** of MRSF is considered in calculating the measurements.

Algorithm	Residue	JAC $k_{NB} = 1$	JAC $k_{NB} = 5$
MCSF	136.89	0.37	0.42
MRSF$_\mathbf{W}$	**91.45**	**0.63**	**0.53**

4.3.2.2 Redundancy Rate

Table 4.8 shows the averaged redundancy rates with the top n features selected by different algorithms on the benchmark data sets. The results show that the features selected by the MCSF and MRSF contain much less redundancy comparing with the other algorithms. This is expected, since those algorithms cannot remove redundant features.

TABLE 4.8: Study of unsupervised cases: Averaged redundancy rate, the lower the better.

Algorithm	ORL	PIE	TOX	CLL-SUB	AVE	WIN
Laplacian Score	0.86	0.75	0.46	0.65	0.68	0
SPEC-1	0.86	0.83	0.47	0.64	0.70	0
SPEC-3	0.90	0.68	0.41	0.51	0.63	0
Trace-Ratio	0.86	0.70	0.48	0.58	0.65	0
HSIC	0.86	0.70	0.48	0.58	0.65	0
MCSF	**0.28**	0.38	**0.16**	**0.15**	**0.24**	3
MRSF	**0.28**	**0.26**	0.22	0.29	0.26	2

4.4   Discussions

In this chapter, we studied the connections between spectral feature selection and a variety of exiting feature selection and feature extraction algorithms. The study provides us interesting insights into these existing algorithms, and enables us to develop more powerful dimensionality reduction approaches based on the presented spectral feature selection frameworks. We conducted experiments to study the performance of various spectral feature selection algorithms. The experiment results from both supervised and unsupervised learning settings showed that the multivariate formulations for spectral feature selection can select features containing less redundancy and producing superior learning performance.

Given a high-dimensional space, many approaches have been proposed to find a low-dimensional space, where the geometric structure of the data is preserved according to certain criteria. These methods in general fall into the category of dimensionality reduction via feature extraction, instead of feature selection. The representative algorithms in this category include Multidimensional Scaling (MDS) [35], ISOMAP [182], Locally Linear Embedding (LLE) [145], Laplacian Eigenmaps [13], Semidefinite Embedding (SDE) [191], Neighborhood Preserving Embedding (NPE) [75], and Structure Preserving Embedding (SPE) [155], to name a few. The difference between feature extraction and feature selection is that to reduce dimensionality, feature extraction generates a small set of new features by combining the original features, while feature selection selects a small set of original features exactly. By keeping the original features, feature selection improves the interpretability of learning models, which is preferred in many real applications, such as text mining and genetic analysis. Many frameworks have been proposed to unify the aforementioned *feature extraction* methods in various ways [148, 195, 198, 24, 176]. Comparing with these works, our multivariate formulations for spectral feature selection form a bridge connecting feature selection with feature extraction, and allow us to take full advantage of both techniques.

A data set with both very high dimensionality and huge numbers of samples proposes a serious challenge to feature selection. In the next chapter, we study how to how handle very large-scale data sets in spectral feature selection via distributed parallel processing.

Chapter 5

Large-Scale Spectral Feature Selection

Continual advances in computer-based technologies have enabled researchers and engineers to collect data at an increasingly fast pace. Business and scientific data from many fields, such as finance, genomics, and physics, are often measured in gigabytes (GB, 2^9 bytes), terabytes (TB, 2^{12} bytes), and sometimes even petabytes (PB, 2^{15} bytes). For instance, it is reported that in 2010, one of eBay's data warehouses reached 10PB and will grow to 20PB in 2011. Other business operators, such as Bank of America, WalMart, and Dell also reported their data warehouses to be in a PB range. The enormous proliferation of large-scale data sets brings new challenges to data mining techniques. Scalability and efficiency are two critical issues in large-scale applications [54, 31, 215, 66, 3, 139, 173, 193]. To address these challenges, existing data mining techniques need to be adapted and improved to handle large-scale data sets [16, 154, 101, 86, 194, 28, 61, 19].

Given a large-scale data set containing a huge number of samples and features, the scalability of a feature selection algorithm becomes extremely important [160, 65, 57]. Most existing feature selection algorithms are designed for handling data with a size under several gigabytes. Their efficiency may be significantly downgraded, if not totally unapplicable, when the data size reaches hundreds of gigabytes. Efficient distributed programming models and protocols, such as the Message Passing Interface (MPI) [163] and Google's MapReduce [1], have been proposed to facilitate programming on high performance computer grids [105] or clusters [10] to handle large-scale data problems.[1] However, most existing feature selection techniques are designed to run in a centralized computing environment. For instance, it is assumed that all data can be held in the memory or, at least, all data are stored in one central storage space. Therefore, these algorithms cannot benefit from advanced distributed parallel computing techniques for improving efficiency and scalability.

In this chapter, we show that the proposed spectral feature selection technique can be conveniently extended to handle large-scale data via applying mature distributed parallel computing techniques such MPI or MapReduce. The key idea is *data partition*, as shown in Figure 5.1. To fit spectral feature

---

[1]Both computer grid and computer cluster refer to a set of computers that are connected so that they can solve a problem together. The computer nodes of a grid are loosely coupled, while the computer nodes of a cluster are tightly coupled. Also the computer nodes in a cluster are homogenous, while the computer nodes in a grid can be heterogeneous.

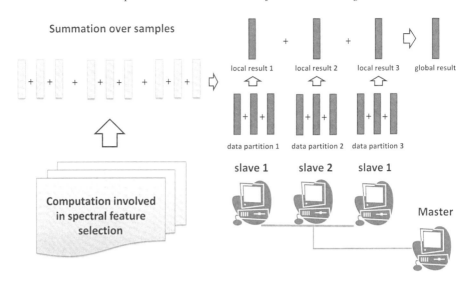

FIGURE 5.1: Data partition for large-scale spectral feature selection.

selection into a distributed computing environment, we first decompose the computation involved in feature evaluation into different types of summation computation over the samples. This allows us to distribute samples to the computer nodes of a grid (or cluster), so that different portions of the summation computation can be done in parallel to generate local results. These local results can then be aggregated to obtain a global result. It can be shown that when the sample size is huge, this computing scheme can result in a linear speedup as the number of computer nodes used for computation increases.

In the MPI framework, the computer nodes that generate the local results are called *slaves*, and the computer node that controls the slaves and aggregates the local results is called the *master*. Similarly, in the MapReduce framework, the functions that generate the local results (run in parallel) are called *mappers*, and the functions that aggregate the local results are called *reducers*. In this chapter, we show how spectral feature selection can be implemented using MPI for distributed parallel processing. This technique can also be implemented using MapReduce in a similar way.

In the following sections, we will first use linear regression as an example to illustrate how we can implement it in a distributed computing environment by partitioning data and distributing samples to computer nodes. We then show how to implement spectral feature selection in a distributed computing environment using MPI. We study both univariate and multivariate formulations for spectral feature selection. We also conduct complexity analysis to study the efficiency of the implementations.

5.1 Data Partitioning for Parallel Processing

It is shown in [32] that many existing machine learning models, such as Naive Bayes, logistic regression, support vector machine, and k-means, can be parallelized in four steps:

1. Decompose the training process into summation forms over samples.

2. Partition data and storing data segments on nodes of the cluster.

3. Compute local results in parallel on computer nodes of the cluster.

4. Calculate the global result by aggregating the local results.

Below we use standard linear regression as an example to show how this idea works. The objective of the standard linear regression is

$$\mathbf{w}^* = arg \min_{\mathbf{w}} \|\mathbf{y} - \mathbf{X}\mathbf{w}\|, \tag{5.1}$$

and its optimal solution is given by

$$\mathbf{w}^* = \left(\mathbf{X}^\top \mathbf{X}\right)^{-1} \mathbf{X}^\top \mathbf{y}. \tag{5.2}$$

In the above equation, we assume that each row of $\mathbf{X}$ is an instance, $\mathbf{X} = \{\mathbf{x}_1, \ldots, \mathbf{x}_n\}^\top$. To obtain the optimal solution, we need to compute $\mathbf{X}^\top \mathbf{X}$ and $\mathbf{X}^\top \mathbf{y}$. Let $\mathbf{A} = \mathbf{X}^\top \mathbf{X}$ and $\mathbf{b} = \mathbf{X}^\top \mathbf{y}$, and we can write $\mathbf{A}$ and $\mathbf{b}$ as two types of summation computation over the samples:

$$\mathbf{A} = \mathbf{X}^\top \mathbf{X} = \sum_{i=1}^n \mathbf{x}_i \mathbf{x}_i^\top$$

$$\mathbf{b} = \mathbf{X}^\top \mathbf{y} = \sum_{i=1}^n y_i \mathbf{x}_i. \tag{5.3}$$

As shown in Figure 5.2, assume our data are stored on three computer nodes (Slave 1, Slave 2, and Slave 3) of a cluster, and let P_1, P_2, and P_3 denote the index sets containing the indices of the instances stored on the three slaves, respectively. Equation (5.3) suggests that we can compute three local results of $\mathbf{A}$ on the three slaves as

$$\mathbf{A}_j = \sum_{i \in P_j} \mathbf{x}_i \mathbf{x}_i^\top, \; j = 1, 2, 3. \tag{5.4}$$

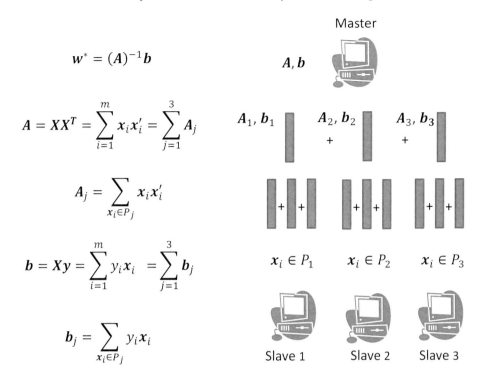

$$w^* = (A)^{-1}b$$

$$A = XX^T = \sum_{i=1}^{m} x_i x_i' = \sum_{j=1}^{3} A_j$$

$$A_j = \sum_{x_i \in P_j} x_i x_i'$$

$$b = Xy = \sum_{i=1}^{m} y_i x_i = \sum_{j=1}^{3} b_j$$

$$b_j = \sum_{x_i \in P_j} y_i x_i$$

FIGURE 5.2: Partitioning data for parallel processing.

Since the computations of $\mathbf{A}_1$, $\mathbf{A}_2$, and $\mathbf{A}_3$ are independent, they can be computed in parallel on each slave. After $\mathbf{A}_1$, $\mathbf{A}_2$, and $\mathbf{A}_3$ are obtained, they can be sent to the master. We can compute $\mathbf{A}$ on the master by $\mathbf{A} = \mathbf{A}_1 + \mathbf{A}_2 + \mathbf{A}_3$. Similarly, we can also compute $\mathbf{b}$ in parallel. After obtaining $\mathbf{A}$ and $\mathbf{b}$, the optimal $\mathbf{w}^*$ can be obtained by computing $\mathbf{w}^* = \mathbf{A}^{-1}\,\mathbf{b}$.

Let m be the number of features, n the number of samples, and p the number of slaves. Also denote $(\mathbf{X}_j, \mathbf{y}_j)$ as the data set containing the samples on the j-th slave. The time complexities for computing $\mathbf{A}_j$, $\mathbf{b}_j$, $\mathbf{A}$, $\mathbf{b}$, $\mathbf{A}^{-1}$, and $\mathbf{A}^{-1}\mathbf{b}$ are:

1. $\mathbf{A}_j$, $O_{CPU}\left(\frac{nm^2}{p}\right)$: $\mathbf{A}_j = \mathbf{X}_j^\top \mathbf{X}_j$, $\mathbf{X}_j \in \mathbb{R}^{\frac{n}{p} \times m}$.

2. $\mathbf{b}_j$, $O_{CPU}\left(\frac{nm}{p}\right)$: $\mathbf{b}_j = \mathbf{X}_j \mathbf{y}_j$, $\mathbf{X}_j \in \mathbb{R}^{\frac{n}{p} \times m}$, $\mathbf{y}_j \in \mathbb{R}^{\frac{n}{p} \times 1}$.

3. $\mathbf{A}$, $O_{CPU}\left(m^2 \log(p)\right) + O_{NET}\left(m^2 \log(p)\right)$: $\mathbf{A} = \sum_{j=1}^{p} \mathbf{A}_j$, $\mathbf{A}_j \in \mathbb{R}^{m \times m}$.

4. $\mathbf{b}$, $O_{CPU}\left(m \log(p)\right) + O_{NET}\left(m \log(p)\right)$: $\mathbf{b} = \sum_{j=1}^{p} \mathbf{b}_j$, $\mathbf{b}_j \in \mathbb{R}^{m}$.

5. $\mathbf{A}^{-1}$, $O_{CPU}\left(m^3\right)$: $\mathbf{A} \in \mathbb{R}^{m \times m}$.

6. $\mathbf{A}^{-1}\mathbf{b}$, $O_{CPU}\left(nm\right)$: $\mathbf{A}^{-1} \in \mathbb{R}^{m \times m}$, $\mathbf{b} \in \mathbb{R}^{m \times 1}$.

Here, $O_{CPU}\left(\cdot\right)$ denotes the computation cost spent on computing the solution. $O_{NET}\left(\cdot\right)$ denotes the communication cost spent on transforming data from the slaves to the master through the network. Usually, the time consumed by one network operation is much longer than that used by one computation operation, $time\left(O_{NET}\left(1\right)\right) \gg time\left(O_{CPU}\left(1\right)\right)$. Therefore, in time complexity analysis, we count the number of operations required for computation and network transmission separately. For computing $\mathbf{A}$ and $\mathbf{b}$, we need to send data from slaves to the master. Therefore, the time complexity for these two components contains both $O_{CPU}\left(\cdot\right)$ and $O_{NET}\left(\cdot\right)$. Here we assume that a tree-based [63] distributed computation scheme, e.g., MPI_REDUCE (see Section 5.2.0.5), is used for computing $\mathbf{A}$ and $\mathbf{b}$. And we will explain why $\log\left(p\right)$ appears here in Section 5.2.0.5. Based on the above analysis, the time complexity of the parallel regression process is

$$O_{CPU}\left(\frac{nm^2}{p} + m^3\right) + O_{NET}\left(m^2 \log\left(p\right)\right), \quad p = 3.$$

Assuming that $n \gg m$, $m \gg \log\left(p\right)$, and the network is fast enough, we have

$$O_{CPU}\left(\frac{nm^2}{p} + m^3\right) + O_{NET}\left(m^2 \log\left(p\right)\right) \approx O_{CPU}\left(\frac{nm^2}{p}\right), \quad p = 3.$$

This analysis shows that when sample size is large enough, the speedup of the regression process is linear. In the following sections, we show how similar processes can be used to parallelize spectral feature selection for handling large-scale data sets.

5.2 MPI for Distributed Parallel Computing

Before we try to parallelize spectral feature selection, we briefly introduce the message passing interface (MPI) standard.[2] MPI defines a standard interface for writing portable message-passing programs running on parallel machines. Figure 5.3 shows an example of how MPI works. Given a set of p computer nodes in the cluster, in most MPI applications, a set of p processes are created at the initialization step, and one process is created per computer node. These processes may execute different programs. Therefore, the MPI programming model is referred to as MPMD (Multiple Processes, Multiple Data) model to distinguish it from the SPMD (Single Process, Multiple

---

[2]www.mpi-forum.org.

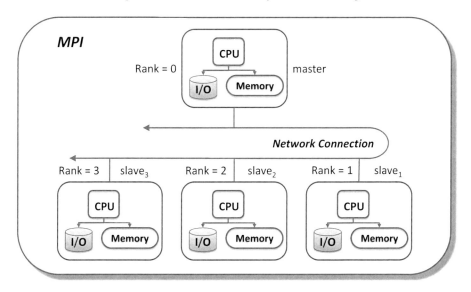

FIGURE 5.3: Message passing interface (MPI) for distributed computing.

Data) model. In the SPMD model, every computer node executes the same program. Therefore, compared with the SPMD model, the MPMD model has tremendous flexibility for handling complex problems. In an MPI-based application, one process may be assigned as the master (or root) and it coordinates other processes. The remaining processes are managed by the master and are called the slaves. In MPI, each computer node is associated with a number. The number is called the rank of the node. Usually the selected master node is numbered as rank = 0.

MPI defines a set of functions to facilitate the communication among the processes running on different computer nodes [163]. Below we introduce three MPI commands that will be used frequently in the following sections.

5.2.0.3 MPI_BCAST

MPI_BCAST(buffer, count, datatype, root, comm)

INOUT	buffer	starting address of buffer
IN	count	number of entries in buffer
IN	datatype	data type of buffer
IN	root	rank of broadcast root
IN	comm	communicator

MPI_BCAST broadcasts the buffer of the process with its rank = root to all other processes. When communication needs to be made, all processes call MPI_BCAST. After return, the contents of root's buffer are copied to all other processes' buffer. The first parameter of MPI_BCAST, buffer, has different roles for different processes. For the process with its rank = root, buffer is an input; for the processes with their rank ≠ root, buffer contains the output. Figure 5.4 shows how MPI_BCAST works. As shown in Figure 5.5, when the tree-based [63] distribution scheme is used for MPI_Bcast implementation, to broadcast a vector of length n to p computer nodes, the communication complexity is $O_{NET}(n \log_2(p))$.

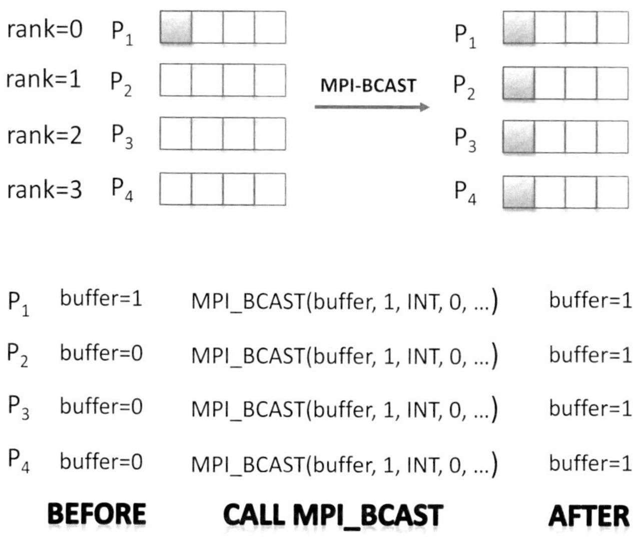

rank=0 P_1
rank=1 P_2 MPI-BCAST
rank=2 P_3
rank=3 P_4

P_1 P_2 P_3 P_4

P_1 buffer=1   MPI_BCAST(buffer, 1, INT, 0, ...)   buffer=1

P_2 buffer=0   MPI_BCAST(buffer, 1, INT, 0, ...)   buffer=1

P_3 buffer=0   MPI_BCAST(buffer, 1, INT, 0, ...)   buffer=1

P_4 buffer=0   MPI_BCAST(buffer, 1, INT, 0, ...)   buffer=1

BEFORE   **CALL MPI_BCAST**   **AFTER**

FIGURE 5.4: MPI_BCAST.

5.2.0.4 MPI_SCATTER

MPI_SCATTER(sendbuf, sendcount, sendtype, recvbuf, recvcount, recvtype, root, comm)

IN	sendbuf	address of send buffer
IN	sendcount	number of elements sent to each process
IN	sendtype	data type of send buffer elements
OUT	recvbuf	address of receive buffer
IN	recvcount	number of elements in receive buffer
IN	recvtype	data type of receive buffer elements
IN	root	rank of sending process
IN	comm	communicator

MPI_SCATTER splits the sendbuf of the process with rank = root into segments of length equals to sendcount, and sends each of the other processes (rank ≠ root) a segment. In the communication process, all processes call MPI_SCATTER. For the process with its rank = root, sendbuf is the input, and its length equals $p \times$ sendcount. For the processes with their rank ≠ root, recvbuf contains the output, and its length equals recvcount. Note sendcount

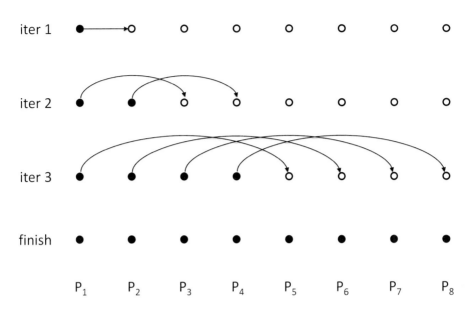

FIGURE 5.5: MPI_BCAST broadcasts data to p nodes in $\log_2(p)$ iterations.

and recvcount should be equal. Figure 5.6 illustrates how MPI_SCATTER works. To scatter a vector of length n to p computer nodes, the communication complexity is $O_{NET}(n)$. MPI_SCATTERV can be used, when data sent to different nodes have different length.

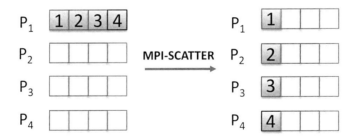

FIGURE 5.6: MPI_SCATTER.

5.2.0.5 MPI_REDUCE

MPI_REDUCE(sendbuf, recvbuf, count, datatype, op, root, comm)

IN	sendbuf	address of send buffer
OUT	recvbuf	address of receive buffer
IN	count	number of elements in send buffer
IN	datatype	data type of elements of send buffer
IN	op	reduce operation
IN	root	rank of root process
IN	comm	communicator

MPI_REDUCE combines the elements provided in sendbuf of each process using the operation op and returns the combined value in the recvbuf of the process whose rank is equal to root. Commonly used op operations supported in MPI include MPI_MAX, MPI_MIN, MPI_SUM, MPI_PROD (product), and some logical operations. In the communication process, all processes call MPI_REDUCE. For the process with its rank = root, recvbuf contains the output and its length is equal to count. For the processes with their rank $\neq$ root, sendbuf is the input, and its length is also equal to count. MPI_REDUCE applies element-wise operation on the inputs. For instance, assuming that there are three input vectors $\mathbf{x}_1$, $\mathbf{x}_2$, and $\mathbf{x}_3$, when op = MPI_MAX, the elements of the output vector $\mathbf{o}$ are computed by $o_i = \max(x_{1,i}, x_{2,i}, x_{3,i})$. As shown in Figure 5.8, when the tree-based [63] distribution scheme is used for MPI_REDUCE implementation, to reduce p vectors of length n, the communication complexity is $O_{NET}(n \log(p))$ and the computation complexity is $O_{CPU}(n \log(p))$.

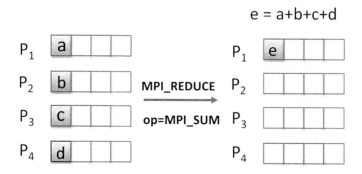

FIGURE 5.7: MPI_REDUCE.

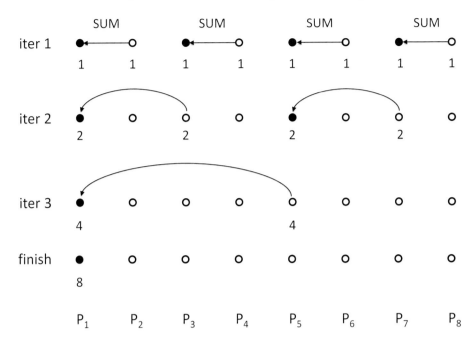

FIGURE 5.8: MPI_REDUCE (MPI_SUM) adds up data on p nodes in $\log_2(p)$ iterations.

5.3 Parallel Spectral Feature Selection

In this section, we study how to implement spectral feature selection algorithms in a distributed computing environment using MPI. The key idea here is to decompose the feature evaluation process into multiple steps, such that the majority of the computation of each steps can be written as summations over samples. This allows us to distribute samples to the computer nodes of a cluster, so that the computation strategy introduced in Section 5.1 can be utilized for parallel processing. To this end, we first list the major computation steps involved in spectral feature selection for both univariate and multivariate formulations.

5.3.1 Computation Steps of Univariate Formulations

Let $\mathbf{S}$ be the similarity matrix and $\mathbf{f}$ be a feature vector. According to Section 4.1, the major computation steps of univariate spectral feature selection formulations include:

1. Compute the similarity matrix $\mathbf{S}$.

2. Normalize $\mathbf{S}$ and $\mathbf{f}$ to obtain $\hat{\mathbf{S}}$ and $\hat{\mathbf{f}}$, respectively.

3. Compute feature scores, $\hat{\mathbf{f}}^{\top} \hat{\mathbf{S}} \, \hat{\mathbf{f}}$.

In real-world applications, we usually use a sparse similarity matrix. In a similarity matrix, for an instance $\mathbf{x}_i$, we keep $\mathbf{S}_{i,j}$ only if $\mathbf{x}_j$ (or $\mathbf{x}_i$) is in its k nearest neighbors of $\mathbf{x}_i$ or $(\mathbf{x}_j)$. The reason is that when the sample size is huge, the size of a dense similarity matrix will be tremendous. Assuming that the sample size is n, the size of the corresponding dense similarity matrix will be $4n(n+1)$ bytes,[3] assuming the matrix is in double precision, and each double precision float number occupies 8 bytes. From Figure 5.9, we can observe that when sample size n is 2 million, the size of the corresponding dense similarity matrix is about 14,901.17 GB.[4] Note that if the dimensionality of the data set is less than 2 million, which is almost always the case in a real-world application, the size of a dense similarity matrix will be even bigger than the original data set.

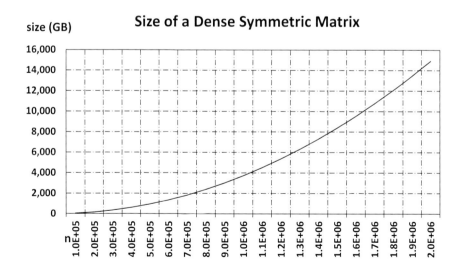

FIGURE 5.9: Size of a dense symmetric matrix as n increase.

---

[3]The similarity matrix is symmetric, we only need to store half of the matrix.
[4]$14901.17 \approx 8 \times \left(2 \times 10^6\right) \times \left(2 \times 10^6 + 1\right) \div \left(2^{30} \times 2\right)$.

In SPEC, for noise reduction, we apply spectral matrix function $\gamma(\cdot)$ to adjust the eigenvalues of the normalized similarity matrix (or the corresponding normalized Laplacian matrix) to penalize the high-frequency components[5] (see Section 2.4). It turns out that for a data set of very large scale, applying such an operation may be very expensive. First, the time complexity of computing a matrix-matrix multiplication is $O(n^3)$. When n is very large, this operation can be very expensive. Second, although our similarity matrix $\mathbf{S}$ is sparse, $\mathbf{S}^p$ can be dense. And this matrix may be too big to store. Alternatively, we can achieve noise reduction by only using the leading eigenvectors of the similarity matrix. When the similarity matrix is sparse, using the Lanczos method [142, 38] to calculate a few eigenpairs only requires roughly $O(n^2)$ operations, and the computation can also be parallelized.

5.3.2 Computation Steps of Multivariate Formulations

For spectral feature selection with a multivariate formulation, the major computation steps are different for the supervised and the unsupervised cases, so we discuss them separately.

- Unsupervised Case:

    1. Construct the similarity matrix $\mathbf{S}$.
    2. Compute its top k eigenpairs and the target matrix $\mathbf{Y}$.
    3. Solve the $L_{2,1}$ regularized multiple output regression problem

$$\arg \min_{\mathbf{W},\,\lambda} \|\mathbf{Y} - \mathbf{XW}\|_F^2 + \lambda \|\mathbf{W}\|_{2,1}$$
$$s.t. \; \mathbb{A} = \{i : \|\mathbf{w}^i\|_2 > 0\}, \; Card(\mathbb{A}) = l.$$

- Supervised Case:

    1. Compute the target matrix $\mathbf{Y}$.
    2. Solve the $L_{2,1}$ regularized multiple output regression problem

$$\arg \min_{\mathbf{W},\,\lambda} \|\mathbf{Y} - \mathbf{XW}\|_F^2 + \lambda \|\mathbf{W}\|_{2,1}$$
$$s.t. \; \mathbb{A} = \{i : \|\mathbf{w}^i\|_2 > 0\}, \; Card(\mathbb{A}) = l.$$

Similar to the univariate formulation case, we use a sparse similarity matrix in multivariate spectral feature selection for unsupervised learning.

In both univariate and multivariate spectral features, we need to compute the similarity matrix. In the next section, we study how to efficiently compute a sparse similarity matrix for a large-scale data set using a computer cluster.

---

[5]For normalized similarity matrix, the high-frequency components correspond to those eigenvectors having small eigenvalues, and for normalized Laplacian matrix, they correspond to the eigenvectors with large eigenvalues.

5.4   Computing the Similarity Matrix in Parallel

To construct a sparse similarity matrix $\mathbf{S}$, we may retain $\mathbf{S}_{i,j}$ only if $\mathbf{x}_j$ (or $\mathbf{x}_i$) is among the k-nearest neighbors of $\mathbf{x}_i$ (or $\mathbf{x}_j$). Typically k is a small number ($k \ll n$).

Suppose p computer nodes are allocated in a computer cluster for parallel spectral feature selection, and our data are partitioned in p parts and stored distributedly in the p computer nodes. As shown in Figure 5.10(a), we want to construct $\mathbf{S}$ in parallel and store a portion of it on each computer node. The advantages of this strategy are twofold. First, by splitting $\mathbf{S}$ into many parts and storing them distributedly, we can put the entire $\mathbf{S}$ in memory. This allows us to do computation efficiently without accessing the hard disk. Second, by storing $\mathbf{S}$ distributedly, we show that the computation related to constructing $\mathbf{S}$ and evaluating features can all be done in parallel efficiently.

5.4.1   Computing the Sample Similarity

Assume that we compute sample similarity using an RBF kernel defined as

$$K\left(\mathbf{x}_i, \mathbf{x}_j\right) = \exp\left(\|\mathbf{x}_i - \mathbf{x}_j\|^2\right).$$

Figure 5.10(b) illustrates how the first column of $\mathbf{S}$ can be computed in parallel on the p computer nodes of the cluster. The process contains the following two steps:

1. Node_1 broadcasts (MPI_Bcast) $\mathbf{x}_1$ and $\|\mathbf{x}_1\|^2$ to all the other computer nodes.

2. Node_t, $t = 1, \ldots, p$, computes similarity between $\mathbf{x}_1$ and the samples on the node_t

$$K\left(\mathbf{x}_1, \mathbf{x}_i\right) = \exp\left(\|\mathbf{x}_1 - \mathbf{x}_i\|^2\right), i \in Partition_t, \ t = 1, \ldots, p.$$

Since $\|\mathbf{x}_i - \mathbf{x}_j\|^2 = \|\mathbf{x}_i\|^2 + \|\mathbf{x}_j\|^2 - 2\mathbf{x}_i^\top \mathbf{x}_j$, we can accelerate the distance computation by precomputing $\|\mathbf{x}_i\|^2$ for all samples, and caching them on the computer nodes. In this process, broadcasting $\mathbf{x}_1$ and $\|\mathbf{x}_1\|^2$ requires $O_{NET}\left((m+1)\log(p)\right)$ for network transmission,[6] and the computation requires $O_{CPU}\left(m\frac{n}{p}\right)$ operations. By repeating this process for all samples, we can obtain the complete similarity matrix $\mathbf{S}$. The total cost is

$$O_{NET}\left((m+1)\, n \log(p)\right) + O_{CPU}\left(m\frac{n^2}{p}\right). \tag{5.5}$$

---

[6]Here, we assume that the tree-based distribution scheme is used for MPI_Bcast implementation [63].

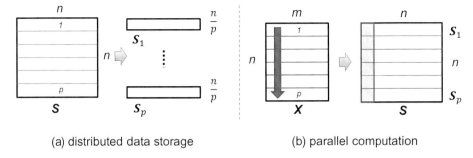

(a) distributed data storage　　　　　(b) parallel computation

FIGURE 5.10: The similarity matrix $\mathbf{S}$ is computed and stored in a distributed manner.

5.4.2　Inducing Sparsity

To construct a sparse similarity matrix efficiently, we can associate each row with a priority queue [96], which helps track the k largest elements in the row. Assuming that a binary heap is used for implementing the priority queue, the time complexity for obtaining the smallest element in the queue is $O(1)$, and for insertion and deletion are both $O(\log(l))$, where l is the size of the queue. Considering the computation involved in queue operations, so far, the cost for constructing $\mathbf{S}$ is

$$O_{NET}\left((m+1)\,n\log(p)\right) + O_{CPU}\left((m+\log(k))\frac{n^2}{p}\right). \tag{5.6}$$

5.4.3　Enforcing Symmetry

$\mathbf{S}$ should be symmetric. However, the $\mathbf{S}$ we obtained so far is not. To ensure that $\mathbf{S}$ is symmetric, we need to go through the following two steps:

1. Construct a list for each row of $\mathbf{S}$ that contains the k nonzero elements of the row. In the list, the elements are ordered by their column index in ascending order.

2. For each row of $\mathbf{S}$, $\mathbf{S}_{i,:}$, comparing it with all other rows, $\mathbf{S}_{j,:}$, $j \neq i$. Update the elements in $\mathbf{S}_{i,:}$ and $\mathbf{S}_{j,:}$ by $\mathbf{S}_{i,j} = \mathbf{S}_{j,i} = \max(\mathbf{S}_{i,j}, \mathbf{S}_{j,i})$.

The first step of the above process forms a list of lists (LIL) representation of the sparse similarity matrix $\mathbf{S}$ [137]. The computation for converting the content of the priority queues can be finished in $O_{CPU}\left(\frac{n}{p}k\log(k)\right)$ operations.

The second step makes $\mathbf{S}$ symmetric, e.g., if $\mathbf{S}_{j,i} = 0$ and $\mathbf{S}_{i,j} \neq 0$, then $\mathbf{S}_{j,i} = \max(\mathbf{S}_{i,j}, \mathbf{S}_{j,i}) = \mathbf{S}_{i,j}$. The time complexity of this step is

$$O_{NET}\left(\{k\log(p) + l\}\,n\right) + O_{CPU}\left(\frac{n^2}{p}\right),$$

where l is the maximal size of the neighborhood of a sample. Note that $l \geq k$, since for each row some of the zero elements may be set to nonzero after the symmetry enforcement process. Figure 5.11 shows how we can make $\mathbf{S}$ symmetric by updating its rows.

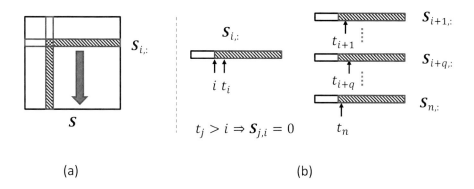

(a)   (b)

FIGURE 5.11: Update rows to make $\mathbf{S}$ symmetric.

First, as shown in Figure 5.11(a), for row $\mathbf{S}_{i,:}$, we only send its section $\mathbf{S}_{i,(i+1:n)}$ to the rows $\mathbf{S}_{i+1,:}, \ldots, \mathbf{S}_{n,:}$ for comparison. The reason is that $\mathbf{S}_{i,(1:i)}$ and $\mathbf{S}_{(1:i),i}$ have already been updated previously. Second, in the comparison process, we always maintain a pointer for each list, which points to the position t of the row. Here t is the smallest column index corresponding to a nonzero element of the row and is larger than $i - 1$, e.g., $\mathbf{S}_{j,t} > 0, t > i - 1$. These pointers help us find $\mathbf{S}_{j,i}$ in $O(1)$ operation. When $\mathbf{S}_{i,j} \neq 0$ and $\mathbf{S}_{j,i} = 0$, we update the row $\mathbf{S}_{j,:}$ by inserting $\mathbf{S}_{i,j}$ in $\mathbf{S}_{j,:}$ as $\mathbf{S}_{j,i}$. Similarly, if $\mathbf{S}_{i,j} = 0$ and $\mathbf{S}_{j,i} \neq 0$, we update $\mathbf{S}_{i,:}$ by inserting $\mathbf{S}_{j,i}$ in $\mathbf{S}_{i,:}$ as $\mathbf{S}_{i,j}$. After updating $\mathbf{S}_{j,i}$, for each row, if the t_j is equal to i, $t_j = i$, then the pointer is updated by being pointed to the next nonzero element in the list. Each computer node also sends its updates for $\mathbf{S}_{i,(i+1:n)}$ back to the computer node that holds $\mathbf{S}_{j,:}$ to update the original $\mathbf{S}_{j,:}$.

In $O_{NET}\left(\left(k \log\left(p\right) + t\right)n\right) + O_{CPU}\left(\frac{n^2}{p}\right)$, $O_{NET}\left(nk \log\left(p\right)\right)$ corresponds to the network transmission for broadcasting $\mathbf{S}_{i,(i+1,n)}$. $O_{NET}\left(nt\right)$ corresponds to the network transmission for sending the updated for $\mathbf{S}_{i,:}$ back to the computer node that contains $\mathbf{S}_{i,:}$ (via MPI_Scatter). And $O_{CPU}\left(\frac{n^2}{p}\right)$ corresponds to the computation required for updating the rows of $\mathbf{S}$. Considering the cost of making $\mathbf{S}$ symmetric, the total cost of constructing a sparse symmetric similarity matrix $\mathbf{S}$ is

$$O_{NET}\left(\left\{(m + k)\log\left(p\right) + t\right\}n\right) + O_{CPU}\left((m + \log\left(k\right))\frac{n^2}{p}\right). \qquad (5.7)$$

After obtaining the similarity matrix $\mathbf{S}$, we may also need to extract the top k eigenpairs of $\mathbf{S}$. This can be achieved by applying the implicit restarting Lanczos method [77]. The mechanism of this algorithm is beyond the scope of this book, and we refer readers to [38, 77] for details. It can be shown when p computer nodes are used for computation, the time complexity of a parallel implicitly restarted Lanczos method is

$$\left\{ O_{CPU}\left(u^3 + \left(\frac{nu}{p} + \frac{nt}{p} \right) \times (u - k) \right) \right.$$

$$\left. + O_{NET}\left\{ n\,(u - k)\log(p) \right\} \right\} \times iterations, \qquad (5.8)$$

where u is the total number of Lanczos vectors (Arnoldi length, $u > k$), t is the maximal neighborhood size of the samples, and *iteration* is the total number of restart iterations. Existing toolboxes, such as PARPACK[7] and ScaLAPACK,[8] can also be used to compute the eigenpairs of a symmetric matrix efficiently in parallel.

5.5 Parallelization of the Univariate Formulations

As discussed in Section 5.3.1, after obtaining the similarity matrix $\mathbf{S}$, there are two steps for spectral feature selection with a univariate formulation, including (1) normalizing $\mathbf{S}$ and $\mathbf{f}$ to obtain $\hat{\mathbf{S}}$ and $\hat{\mathbf{f}}$, and (2) computing feature scores via $\hat{\mathbf{f}}^\top \hat{\mathbf{S}}\,\hat{\mathbf{f}}$. It turns out that in a distributed computing environment it is usually beneficial to combine the two steps, since this will reduce the unnecessary network communication among computer nodes. Below we use the second feature evaluation criterion in SPEC, $\varphi_2\left(\cdot\right)$ as an example to show how a univariate spectral feature selection formulation can be parallelized.

Let $\mathbf{D}$ be the degree matrix of $\mathbf{S}$, and $\mathcal{L} = \mathbf{D}^{-\frac{1}{2}}\left(\mathbf{D} - \mathbf{S}\right)\mathbf{D}^{-\frac{1}{2}}$ be the normalized Laplacian matrix. If $\xi_1 = \frac{\mathbf{D}^{\frac{1}{2}}\mathbf{1}}{||\mathbf{D}^{\frac{1}{2}}\mathbf{1}||}$ and $\hat{\mathbf{f}} = \frac{\mathbf{D}^{\frac{1}{2}}\mathbf{f}}{||\mathbf{D}^{\frac{1}{2}}\mathbf{f}||}$, we have

$$\varphi_2(F) = \frac{\hat{\mathbf{f}}^\top \mathcal{L}\,\hat{\mathbf{f}}}{1 - \left(\hat{\mathbf{f}}^\top \xi_1\right)^2}.$$

---

[7]PARPACK: http://www.caam.rice.edu/~kristyn/parpack_home.html.
[8]ScaLAPACK: http://www.netlib.org/scalapack/.

Plugging $\mathcal{L}$, $\hat{\mathbf{f}}$, and ξ_1 in the above equation, we obtain

$$
\begin{aligned}
\varphi_2(F) &= \frac{1 - \frac{\mathbf{f}^\top \mathbf{S} \mathbf{f}}{\mathbf{f}^\top \mathbf{D} \mathbf{f}}}{1 - \left(\frac{\mathbf{f}^\top \mathbf{D} \mathbf{1}}{\sqrt{\mathbf{1}^\top \mathbf{D} \mathbf{1} \mathbf{f}^\top \mathbf{D} \mathbf{1}}}\right)^2} \\
&= \frac{(\mathbf{1}^\top \mathbf{D} \mathbf{1})(\mathbf{f}^\top \mathbf{D} \mathbf{f}) - (\mathbf{1}^\top \mathbf{D} \mathbf{1})(\mathbf{f}^\top \mathbf{S}\, \mathbf{f})}{(\mathbf{1}^\top \mathbf{D} \mathbf{1})(\mathbf{f}^\top \mathbf{D} \mathbf{f}) - (\mathbf{f}^\top \mathbf{D} \mathbf{1})^2}.
\end{aligned} \tag{5.9}
$$

The equation shows that to compute $\varphi_2(F)$, we need to obtain five intermediate results, including $\mathbf{D}$, $\mathbf{f}^\top \mathbf{D} \mathbf{f}$, $\mathbf{1}^\top \mathbf{D} \mathbf{1}$, $\mathbf{f}^\top \mathbf{D} \mathbf{1}$, and $\mathbf{f}^\top \mathbf{S}\, \mathbf{f}$. The first four intermediate results can be written directly into summation forms over samples and computed in parallel:

$$
d_i = \sum_{j=1}^{n} s_{i,j} \tag{5.10}
$$

$$
\mathbf{f}^\top \mathbf{D} \mathbf{f} = \sum_{i=1}^{n} f_i^2 d_i = \sum_{j=1}^{p} \sum_{i \in P_j} f_i^2\, d_i \tag{5.11}
$$

$$
\mathbf{1}^\top \mathbf{D} \mathbf{1} = \sum_{i=1}^{n} d_i = \sum_{j=1}^{p} \sum_{i \in P_j} d_i \tag{5.12}
$$

$$
\mathbf{f}^\top \mathbf{D} \mathbf{1} = \sum_{i=1}^{n} f_i d_i = \sum_{j=1}^{p} \sum_{i \in P_j} f_i\, d_i. \tag{5.13}
$$

In the above equations, d_i is the i-th diagonal element of the degree matrix $\mathbf{D}$, and f_i is the i-th element of the feature vector $\mathbf{f}$. Assuming that the data set is distributedly stored on p slaves, Figure 5.12 shows that we can obtain the four intermediate results in three steps:

1. Compute d_i on each slave using Equation (5.10) in parallel.

2. Compute $\sum_{i \in P_j} f_i^2 d_i$, $\sum_{i \in P_j} d_i$, and $\sum_{i \in P_j} f_i d_i$, $j = 1, \ldots, p$ on each slave in parallel.

3. Send local results from the p slaves to the master, and the master computing $\mathbf{1}^\top \mathbf{D} \mathbf{1}$, $\mathbf{1}^\top \mathbf{D} \mathbf{f}$, and $\mathbf{f}^\top \mathbf{D} \mathbf{f}$.

In the first two steps, there is no communication between the slaves and the master. In the third step, the slaves need to send out their local results, and the communication cost is $O_{NET}(3p)$ for one feature. Therefore, the total computation cost of the three steps is $O_{CPU}\left(n^2 + 6\frac{n}{p} + 3log(p)\right)$ for each feature. Note that in the process of computing feature scores for all the m features, the intermediate results for d_i and $\mathbf{1}^\top \mathbf{D} \mathbf{1}$ just need to be computed

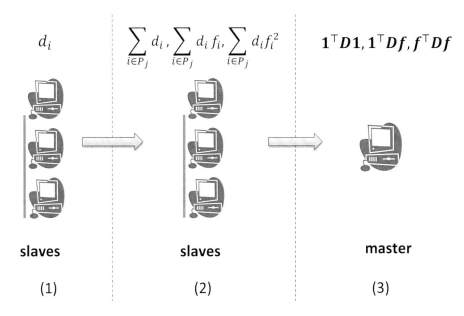

FIGURE 5.12: Parallel univariate spectral feature selection.

once. Therefore, to compute the first four intermediate results, $\mathbf{D}$, $\mathbf{f}^\top \mathbf{D} \mathbf{f}$, $\mathbf{1}^\top \mathbf{D} \mathbf{1}$, and $\mathbf{f}^\top \mathbf{D} \mathbf{1}$, for all m features, the total cost is:

$$
O_{NET}\left(2mp + p\right) + O_{CPU}\left(n^2 + \frac{n}{p} + 5m\frac{n}{p} + 2m\log\left(p\right) + \log\left(p\right)\right)
$$

$$
\approx \quad O_{NET}\left(mp\right) + O_{CPU}\left(n^2 + m\frac{n}{p} + m\log\left(p\right)\right). \tag{5.14}
$$

It turns out that computing $\mathbf{f}^\top \mathbf{S} \, \mathbf{f}$ is more complex than computing the other four intermediate results. This is because to compute $\mathbf{f}^\top \mathbf{S} \, \mathbf{f}$, a feature needs to see all the elements in $\mathbf{S}$, which are distributedly stored in the p slaves. Figure 5.13 shows an efficient way for computing $\mathbf{f}^\top \mathbf{S} \, \mathbf{f}$. Since the data set is distributedly stored in p slaves, a feature $\mathbf{f}$ is partitioned to p segments, and each slave holds a portion of the feature. Let $\mathbf{f} = \left(\mathbf{f}_1^\top, \ldots, \mathbf{f}_p^\top\right)^\top$, and we assume that $\mathbf{f}_i$ is stored in the i-th slave. The similarity matrix $\mathbf{S}$ is also distributedly stored in p slaves, and each slave holds $\frac{n}{p}$ rows of $\mathbf{S}$. We denote $\mathbf{S} = \left(\mathbf{S}_1^\top, \ldots, \mathbf{S}_p^\top\right)^\top$, and assume that $\mathbf{S}_j \in \mathbb{R}^{\frac{n}{p} \times n}$ is stored in the j-th slave.

Based on these notations, we can decompose the computation of $\mathbf{f}^\top \mathbf{S} \, \mathbf{f}$ as

$$
\begin{aligned}
\mathbf{f}^\top \mathbf{S} \, \mathbf{f} &= (\mathbf{f}_1^\top, \dots, \mathbf{f}_p^\top) \begin{pmatrix} \mathbf{S}_1 \\ \vdots \\ \mathbf{S}_p \end{pmatrix} \mathbf{f} \\
&= \left(\sum_{j=1}^p \mathbf{f}_j^\top \mathbf{S}_j \right) \mathbf{f} \\
&= \left((\mathbf{f}^\top \mathbf{S})_1, \dots, (\mathbf{f}^\top \mathbf{S})_p \right) \begin{pmatrix} \mathbf{f}_1 \\ \vdots \\ \mathbf{f}_p \end{pmatrix} \\
&= \sum_{j=1}^p (\mathbf{f}^\top \mathbf{S})_j \, \mathbf{f}_j .
\end{aligned}
\tag{5.15}
$$

In the above equations, $\mathbf{f}^\top \mathbf{S} \in \mathbb{R}^{1 \times n}$ is an n-dimensional row vector, and $(\mathbf{f}^\top \mathbf{S})_j \in \mathbb{R}^{1 \times \frac{n}{p}}$ is the j-th segment of $\mathbf{f}^\top \mathbf{S}$. $\mathbf{f}^\top \mathbf{S}$ is computed on the master using the local results obtained by the slaves. And $(\mathbf{f}^\top \mathbf{S})_j$ is sent from the master to the j-th slave for computing $(\mathbf{f}^\top \mathbf{S})_j \, \mathbf{f}_j$. Figure 5.13 shows how to compute $\mathbf{f}^\top \mathbf{S} \mathbf{f}$ in five steps.

1. Compute $\mathbf{f}_j^\top \mathbf{S}_j$ on the j-th slave. Here $\mathbf{f}_j^\top \mathbf{S}_j \in \mathbb{R}^{1 \times n}$ is a m-dimensional row vector. The cost of this step is $O_{CPU}\left(n\frac{n}{p}\right)$.

2. Slaves send $\mathbf{f}_j^\top \mathbf{S}_j$ to the master and compute $\mathbf{f}^\top \mathbf{S} = \sum_{j=1}^p \mathbf{f}_j^\top \mathbf{S}_j$ (via MPI_Reduce). The cost of this step is $O_{CPU}\left(n\log(p)\right) + O_{NET}\left(n\log(p)\right)$.

3. The master sends $\mathbf{f}^\top \mathbf{S}_j$ to the j-th slave (via MPI_Scatter). The cost is $O_{NET}\left(n\right)$.

4. $(\mathbf{f}^\top \mathbf{S})_j \, \mathbf{f}_j$ are computed by the slaves, and the cost is $O_{CPU}\left(\frac{n}{p}\right)$.

5. Slaves send the obtained $(\mathbf{f}^\top \mathbf{S})_j \, \mathbf{f}_j$ to the master to compute $\sum_{j=1}^p (\mathbf{f}^\top \mathbf{S})_j \, \mathbf{f}_j$ (via MPI_Reduce). The cost of this step is $O_{CPU}\left(\log(p)\right) + O_{NET}\left(\log(p)\right)$.

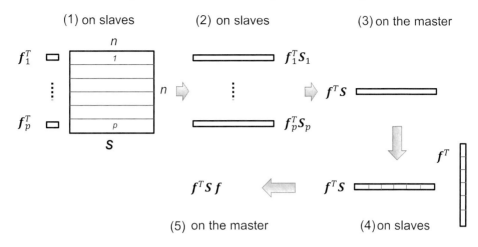

FIGURE 5.13: Parallel univariate spectral feature selection.

When m features are evaluated, the total cost is:

$$O_{NET} \left(mn \log(p) + mn + m \log(p) \right)$$
$$+ O_{CPU} \left(\frac{mn^2}{p} + mn \log(p) + \frac{mn}{p} + m \log(p) \right)$$
$$\approx O_{NET} \left(mn \log(p) \right) + O_{CPU} \left(\frac{mn^2}{p} + mn \log(p) \right). \qquad (5.16)$$

In Chapter 3, we study the multivariate formulations for spectral feature selection. In the next two sections, we show how to parallelize the multivariate formulations for large-scale spectral feature selection.

5.6 Parallel MRSF

Presented in Section 3.4, MRSF is a multivariate spectral feature selection framework based on sparse multiple output regression. Its key component is a multi-output regression with a sparse regularization on the weight matrix $\mathbf{W}$, which has the form

$$\arg \min_{\mathbf{W}, \lambda} \| \mathbf{Y} - \mathbf{X}\mathbf{W} \|_F^2 + \lambda \| \mathbf{W} \|_{2,1}$$
$$s.t. \quad \mathbb{A} = \{ i : \| \mathbf{w}^i \|_2 > 0 \}, \ Card(\mathbb{A}) = l. \qquad (5.17)$$

As we show in Sections 3.6 and 4.2, by defining $\mathbf{Y}$ in different ways, we can achieve different types of multivariate spectral feature selection. The problem defined in Equation (5.17) is a convex problem. In Section 3.4, we present an efficient solver, MRSF, for solving the problem, and the pseudo-code of the algorithm can be found below in Algorithm 7. It turns out that the major computational load of the algorithm comes from four key steps, which include:

1. Initialize the active set (Line 2).

2. Compute a tentative solution (Lines 4–10).

3. Obtain an optimal solution based on the current active set (Lines 11–12).

4. Check the global optimality of the solution obtained in Step 3 (Lines 13–18).

Algorithm 7: MRSF: Minimal redundance spectral feature selection (see Section 3.4)

Input: $\mathbf{X}$, $\mathbf{Y}$, l
Output: $\mathbf{W}$

1   $\mathbf{W}^{[1]} = \mathbf{0}$, $\lambda_1 = +\infty$, $i = 1$ and $\mathbf{R}^{[1]} = \mathbf{Y}$;

2   Compute the initial active set: $\mathbb{A}_1 = \arg\max_j \|\mathbf{f}_j^\top \mathbf{R}^{[1]}\|_2^2$;

3   **while** $i \leq l$ **do**

4   Compute the walking direction $\gamma_{\mathbb{A}_i}$: $\gamma_{\mathbb{A}_i} = \left(\mathbf{X}_{\mathbb{A}_i}^\top \mathbf{X}_{\mathbb{A}_i}\right)^{-1} \mathbf{X}_{\mathbb{A}_i}^\top \mathbf{R}^{[i]}$;

5   **for** *each* $j \notin \mathbb{A}_i$ *and an arbitrary* $t \in \mathbb{A}_i$ **do**

6   Compute the step size α_j in direction $\gamma_{\mathbb{A}_i}$ for $\mathbf{f}_j$ to enter $\mathbb{A}_i$.
$\|\mathbf{f}_j^\top \left(\mathbf{R}^{[i]} - \alpha_j \mathbf{X}_{\mathbb{A}_i} \gamma_{\mathbb{A}_i}\right)\|_2 = (1 - \alpha_j)\|\mathbf{f}_t^\top \mathbf{R}^{[i]}\|_2$;

7      $j^* = \arg\min_{j \notin \mathbb{A}_i} \alpha_j$;

8      $\hat{\mathbf{W}} = \left(\left(\mathbf{W}^{[i]} + \alpha_{j^*} \gamma_{\mathbb{A}_i}\right)^\top, \mathbf{0}\right)^\top$;

9      $\hat{\mathbb{A}} = \mathbb{A}_i \bigcup \{j^*\}$, $\lambda_i = (1 - \alpha_{j^*})\|\mathbf{f}_t^\top \mathbf{R}^{[i]}\|_2$;

10   Solve the smaller optimization problem,
$\min_{\tilde{\mathbf{W}}} \|\mathbf{Y} - \mathbf{X}_{\hat{\mathbb{A}}} \tilde{\mathbf{W}}\|_F^2 + \lambda_i \|\tilde{\mathbf{W}}\|_{2,1}$, using a general solver with $\hat{\mathbf{W}}$ as the starting point;

11     $\tilde{\mathbf{R}} = \mathbf{Y} - \mathbf{X}_{\hat{\mathbb{A}}} \tilde{\mathbf{W}}$;

12   **if** $\forall i \notin \hat{\mathbb{A}}$, $\|\mathbf{f}_i^\top \tilde{\mathbf{R}}\|_2 \leq \lambda_i$ **then**

13       $\mathbb{A}_{i+1} = \hat{\mathbb{A}}$, $\mathbf{W}^{[i+1]} = \tilde{\mathbf{W}}$, $\mathbf{R}^{[i+1]} = \tilde{\mathbf{R}}$, $i = i + 1$;

14   **else**

15       $\hat{\mathbb{A}} = \left\{i : \|\tilde{\mathbf{w}}^i\| \neq 0\right\} \bigcup \left\{j : \|\mathbf{f}_j^\top \tilde{\mathbf{R}}\|_2 > \lambda_i\right\}$;

16   Remove $\tilde{\mathbf{w}}^i$ from $\tilde{\mathbf{W}}$, if $\|\tilde{\mathbf{w}}^i\| = 0$,
$\hat{\mathbf{W}} = \left(\tilde{\mathbf{W}}^\top, \mathbf{0}, \ldots, \mathbf{0}\right)^\top$, **Goto** line 11;

17   Extend $\mathbf{W}^{[l]}$ to $\mathbf{W}$ by adding empty rows to $\mathbf{W}^{[l]}$;

18   **return** $\mathbf{W}^{[l]}$;

Below we study how to parallelize these key steps to improve the scalability and the efficiency of the original MRSF solver.

5.6.1 Initializing the Active Set

We initialize the active set by solving the problem

$$\mathbb{A}_1 = \arg\max_j \|\mathbf{f}_j^\top \mathbf{R}^{[0]}\|_2^2, \quad \mathbf{R}^{[0]} = \mathbf{Y}. \tag{5.18}$$

Assuming that $\mathbf{X}$ and $\mathbf{Y}$ are partitioned and stored in p slaves, we have $\mathbf{f} = \left(\mathbf{f}_1^\top, \ldots, \mathbf{f}_p^\top\right)^\top$, and $\mathbf{Y} = \left(\mathbf{Y}_1^\top, \ldots, \mathbf{Y}_p^\top\right)^\top$, where $\mathbf{f}_i$ and $\mathbf{Y}_i$ are the i-th partition of $\mathbf{f}$ and $\mathbf{Y}$ stored in the i-th slave, respectively. Using the above notations, we can rewrite $\mathbf{f}^\top \mathbf{Y}$ as

$$\mathbf{f}^\top \mathbf{Y} = \sum_{j=1}^{p} \mathbf{f}_j^\top \mathbf{Y}_j. \tag{5.19}$$

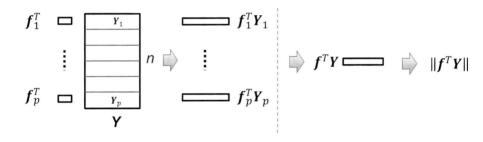

on slaves   on the master

FIGURE 5.14: Initializing the active set.

As illustrated in Figure 5.14, to compute $\|\mathbf{f}^\top \mathbf{Y}\|$, we first compute $\mathbf{f}_i^\top \mathbf{Y}_i$ on each slave in parallel, which results in p row vectors of C dimension. Here C is the number of columns of $\mathbf{Y}$. The time complexity of this step is $O_{CPU}\left(C\frac{n}{p}\right)$. We then aggregate $\mathbf{f}_j^\top \mathbf{Y}_j$, $j = 1, \ldots, p$ to the master and obtain $\mathbf{f}^\top \mathbf{Y} = \sum_{j=1}^{p} \mathbf{f}_i^\top \mathbf{Y}_j$ (via MPI_Reduce). The time complexity of this step is $O_{CPU}\left(C\log(p)\right) + O_{NET}\left(C\log(p)\right)$. Finally, we compute $\|\mathbf{f}^\top \mathbf{Y}\|$ on the master, and the time complexity is $O_{CPU}(C)$. We need to go through this process for all m features. Therefore, the total time complexity is

$$O_{CPU}\left(mC\left(\frac{n}{p} + \log(p)\right) + m\right) + O_{NET}\left(mC\log(p)\right), \tag{5.20}$$

where the additional $CPU(m)$ corresponds to the cost of finding the feature with the maximal $\|\mathbf{f}^\top \mathbf{Y}\|$ value. When $\frac{n}{p} \gg \log(p)$, and $O_{CPU}\left(\frac{n}{p}\right) \gg$

$O_{NET}\left(\log\left(p\right)\right)$, we have

$$O_{CPU}\left(mC\left(\frac{n}{p}+\log\left(p\right)\right)+m\right)+O_{NET}\left(mC\log\left(p\right)\right)$$

$$\approx\ O_{CPU}\left(mC\left(\frac{n}{p}\right)\right). \tag{5.21}$$

In this case, by using multiple slaves to construct the initial active set, we can achieve a linear speedup in terms of p.

5.6.2 Computing the Tentative Solution

After obtaining the active set of the i-th step, we need to compute a tentative solution based on the active set. The pseudo-code of this process is shown in Figure 5.15. It consists of three steps:

1. Compute the walking direction $\gamma_{\mathbb{A}_i}$.

2. Calculate the step size corresponding to each feature.

3. Construct the tentative solution based on the feature with the shortest step size.

Among the three substeps, the third substep can be computed on the master, and the other two can be computed on the slaves in parallel. Below, we show how the three substeps can be efficiently computed in detail.

4	Compute the walking direction $\gamma_{\mathbb{A}_i}$: $\gamma_{\mathbb{A}_i}=\left(\mathbf{X}_{\mathbb{A}_i}^{\top}\mathbf{X}_{\mathbb{A}_i}\right)^{-1}\mathbf{X}_{\mathbb{A}_i}^{\top}\mathbf{R}^{[i]}$;
5	**for** *each $j\notin\mathbb{A}_i$ and an arbitrary $t\in\mathbb{A}_i$* **do**
6	Compute the step size α_j in direction $\gamma_{\mathbb{A}_i}$ for $\mathbf{f}_j$ to enter $\mathbb{A}_i$. $\|\mathbf{f}_j^{\top}\left(\mathbf{R}^{[i]}-\alpha_j\mathbf{X}_{\mathbb{A}_i}\gamma_{\mathbb{A}_i}\right)\|_2=(1-\alpha_j)\|\mathbf{f}_t^{\top}\mathbf{R}^{[i]}\|_2$;
7	**end**
8	$j^{*}=\arg\min_{j\notin\mathbb{A}_i}\alpha_j$;
9	$\hat{\mathbf{W}}=\left(\left(\mathbf{W}^{[i]}+\alpha_{j^{*}}\gamma_{\mathbb{A}_i}\right)^{\top},\mathbf{0}\right)^{\top}$;
10	$\hat{\mathbb{A}}=\mathbb{A}_i\bigcup\{j^{*}\},\ \lambda_i=(1-\alpha_{j^{*}})\|\mathbf{f}_t^{\top}\mathbf{R}^{[i]}\|_2$;

FIGURE 5.15: Computing the tentative solution as in Algorithm 7.

5.6.2.1 Computing the Walking Direction

In the first step of computing the tentative solution, we need to compute the walking direction $\gamma_{\mathbb{A}_i}$, where $\gamma_{\mathbb{A}_i}\in\mathbb{R}^{k\times C}$ is the solution to the multi-output regression $\mathbf{X}_{\mathbb{A}_i}\gamma_{\mathbb{A}_i}=\mathbf{R}^{[i]}$. It can be computed in a similar way as in Section 5.1. In the i-th step, there are i features in the active set. Therefore, $\mathbf{X}_{\mathbb{A}_i}^{\top}\mathbf{X}_{\mathbb{A}_i}$ is an $i\times i$ matrix. The time complexity for computing $\mathbf{X}_{\mathbb{A}_i}^{\top}\mathbf{X}_{\mathbb{A}_i}$

is $O_{CPU}\left(i^2\frac{n}{p} + i^2\log(p)\right) + O_{NET}\left(i^2\log(p)\right)$. Similarly, we can show that the time complexity for computing $\mathbf{X}_{\mathbb{A}_i}^\top\mathbf{R}^{[i]}$ is $O_{CPU}\left(Ck\frac{n}{p} + Ck\log(p)\right) + O_{NET}\left(Ck\log(p)\right)$, where C is the number of columns of $\mathbf{R}^{[i]}$. After obtaining $\mathbf{X}_{\mathbb{A}_i}^\top\mathbf{X}_{\mathbb{A}_i}$ and $\mathbf{X}_{\mathbb{A}_i}^\top\mathbf{R}^{[i]}$, $\left(\mathbf{X}_{\mathbb{A}_i}^\top\mathbf{X}_{\mathbb{A}_i}\right)^{-1}\mathbf{X}_{\mathbb{A}_i}^\top\mathbf{R}^{[i]}$ can be computed on the master, and the time complexity is $O_{CPU}\left(i^3 + k^2C\right)$. In the above process, for $\mathbf{X}_{\mathbb{A}_i}^\top\mathbf{X}_{\mathbb{A}_i}$ and $\mathbf{X}_{\mathbb{A}_i}^\top\mathbf{R}^{[i]}$, p local results are computed on the slaves, and the global result is obtained on the master by aggregating the local results (via MPI_Reduce). $\left(\mathbf{X}_{\mathbb{A}_i}^\top\mathbf{X}_{\mathbb{A}_i}\right)^{-1}\mathbf{X}_{\mathbb{A}_i}^\top\mathbf{R}^{[i]}$ is also computed on the master. Assuming $\frac{n}{p}\gg C\log(p)$, and $\frac{n}{p}\gg i$, the total time complexity of this step is

$$O_{CPU}\left(\left(i^2 + Ci\right)\frac{n}{p}\right) + O_{NET}\left(\left(i^2 + Ci\right)\log(p)\right). \tag{5.22}$$

The above equation shows that when i is small, and the network is fast enough, the time complexity is dominated by $O_{CPU}\left(\left(i^2 + Ci\right)\frac{n}{p}\right)$. In this case, the speedup ratio of the computation is linear in terms of p.

5.6.2.2 Calculating the Step Size

In the second step of computing the tentative solution, we need to compute the step size α_j corresponding to each feature $\mathbf{f}_j$. α_j defines the minimal length we need to proceed in the direction of $\gamma_{\mathbb{A}_i}$ until $\mathbf{f}_j$ enters the active set.[9] To compute α_j, we need to solve the equation

$$\|\mathbf{f}_j^\top\left(\mathbf{R}^{[i]} - \alpha_j\mathbf{X}_{\mathbb{A}_i}\gamma_{\mathbb{A}_i}\right)\|_2 = (1 - \alpha_j)\|\mathbf{f}_t^\top\mathbf{R}^{[i]}\|_2.$$

As shown in Figure 5.16, α_j can be computed in four substeps.

In the first substep, we compute three row vectors: $\mathbf{f}_j^\top\mathbf{R}^{[i]}$, $\mathbf{f}_j^\top\mathbf{X}_{\mathbb{A}_i}$, and $\mathbf{f}_t^\top\mathbf{R}^{[i]}$, where $\mathbf{f}_j^\top\mathbf{R}^{[i]}, \mathbf{f}_t^\top\mathbf{R}^{[i]} \in \mathbb{R}^{1\times C}$, and $\mathbf{f}_j^\top\mathbf{X}_{\mathbb{A}_i} \in \mathbb{R}^{1\times i}$. Each of the three vectors can be computed in parallel in a similar way as we show in Section 5.6.1. The time complexity of computing $\mathbf{f}_j^\top\mathbf{R}^{[i]}$ and $\mathbf{f}_j^\top\mathbf{X}_{\mathbb{A}_i}$ is $O_{CPU}\left((C + i)\frac{n}{p} + (C + i)\log(p)\right) + O_{NET}\left((C + i)\log(p)\right)$. Similarly, the time complexity of computing $\mathbf{f}_t^\top\mathbf{R}^{[i]}$ is $O_{CPU}\left(C\frac{n}{p} + C\log(p)\right) + O_{NET}\left(C\log(p)\right)$. After the first step, $\mathbf{f}_j^\top\mathbf{R}^{[i]}$, $\mathbf{f}_j^\top\mathbf{X}_{\mathbb{A}_i}$, and $\mathbf{f}_t^\top\mathbf{R}^{[i]}$ are all obtained on the master.

In the second substep, we compute $\mathbf{f}_j^\top\mathbf{X}_{\mathbb{A}_i}\gamma_{\mathbb{A}_i}$ on the master, which requires $O_{CPU}(iC)$ operations, and results in a C dimensional vector.

In the third substep, we compute $\|\mathbf{f}_t^\top\mathbf{R}^{[i]}\|$. The computation is done by the master. And the time complexity is $O_{CPU}(C)$.

---

[9] A feature enters the active set when it has the same amount of correlation to the residual as the features in the active set.

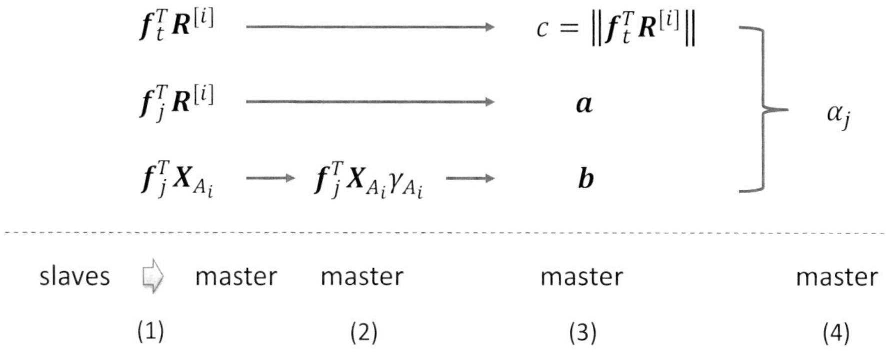

FIGURE 5.16: Computing the step size α_j in four substeps. The step 1 accounts for the major computational load for calculating α_j, and is parallelized.

In the fourth substep, we compute α_j. Let $c = \|\mathbf{f}_t^\top \mathbf{R}^{[i]}\|$, $\mathbf{a}^\top = \mathbf{f}_t^\top \mathbf{R}^{[i]}$, and $\mathbf{b}^\top = \mathbf{f}_j^\top \mathbf{X}_{\mathbb{A}_i} \gamma_{\mathbb{A}_i}$. α_j can be obtained by solving the problem

$$x\alpha^2 - 2y\alpha + z = 0, \quad 0 \le \alpha \le 1,$$
$$\text{where } x = \mathbf{b}^\top \mathbf{b} - c^2,$$
$$y = \mathbf{a}^\top \mathbf{b} - c^2,$$
$$z = \mathbf{a}^\top \mathbf{a} - c^2. \tag{5.23}$$

The time complexity of solving this problem is $O_{CPU}(C)$.

If we assume that $\frac{n}{p} \gg C \log(p)$, $\frac{n}{p} \gg i$, and $m \gg i$, the time complexity of computing the step size for all $m - i$ features is

$$O_{CPU}\left(m(C+i)\frac{n}{p}\right) + O_{NET}\left(m(C+i)\log(p)\right). \tag{5.24}$$

Note that c in Equation (5.23) can be shared by all features, and just needs to be computed once.

The above analysis shows that the substep 1 accounts for the major computational load for calculating α_j. Since the majority of the computation is done by the slaves, when i is small and the network is fast enough, we can achieve linear speedup in terms of p.

5.6.2.3 Constructing the Tentative Solution

In the third step of computing the tentative solution, we need to update the weight matrix $\hat{\mathbf{W}}$, the active set, and λ. The computation is done on the master and the time complexity is $O_{CPU}(\log(m) + iC)$.

5.6.2.4 Time Complexity for Computing a Tentative Solution

Assuming that $m \gg i$, based on the above analysis, the total time complexity for computing a tentative solution according to $\mathbb{A}_i$ is

$$O_{CPU}\left(m\left(C+i\right)\frac{n}{p}\right) + O_{NET}\left(m\left(C+i\right)\log\left(p\right)\right). \tag{5.25}$$

It shows that when $m \gg i$, the computation in the second step (calculating the step size) dominates the computational load. And when n is large enough, increasing the number of slaves leads to linear speedup in terms of p.

5.6.3 Computing the Optimal Solution

After obtaining the tentative solution, we need to compute a solution that is optimal on the current active set with the updated regularization parameter λ. This corresponds to solving a smaller optimization problem defined as

$$\min_{\tilde{\mathbf{W}}} \|\mathbf{Y} - \mathbf{X}_{\hat{\mathbb{A}}}\tilde{\mathbf{W}}\|_F^2 + \lambda\|\tilde{\mathbf{W}}\|_{2,1}. \tag{5.26}$$

As shown in Section 3.3, this problem can be solved efficiently by either the coordinate gradient descent method or the accelerated gradient descent method. In the following, we use the accelerated gradient descent method as an example to illustrate how the method can be parallelized for solving the problem specified in Equation (5.26).

Algorithm 8 contains the pseudo-code of the accelerated gradient descent method. It defines an iterative process to compute the optimal solution of Equation (5.26). In each iteration, three steps are taken to compute $\mathbf{W}_j$, the weight matrix of the j-th iteration:

1. Compute β_j and $\mathbf{S}_j$.

2. Calculate the minimizer of the model function, $\mathcal{M}_{\mathbf{S}_j,\lambda}(\mathbf{W})$.

3. Update L_j and α_{j+1}.

Since $\mathbf{W}_0$ is stored on the master and is small, we can compute Steps 1 and 3 on the master. Below we show how the second step can be decomposed and accomplished in parallel.

In the second step, we need to compute the minimizer of the model function $\mathcal{M}_{\mathbf{S}_j,\lambda}(\mathbf{W})$. As shown in Section 3.3, this boils down to computing the matrix $\mathbf{V}$, which is defined as

$$\mathbf{V} = \mathbf{S}_j - \frac{1}{L_j}\mathbf{X}_{\mathbb{A}}^{\top}\left(\mathbf{X}_{\mathbb{A}}\mathbf{S}_j - \mathbf{Y}\right). \tag{5.27}$$

And the weight matrix $\mathbf{W}$ can be derived from $\mathbf{V}$ using the equation

$$\mathbf{w}^i = \begin{cases} \mathbf{v}^i\left(1 - \dfrac{\rho}{\|\mathbf{v}^i\|}\right), & \text{when } \|\mathbf{v}^i\|_2 > \rho \\ \mathbf{0}, & \text{when } \|\mathbf{v}^i\|_2 \leq \rho \end{cases}. \tag{5.28}$$

Algorithm 8: Accelerated gradient descent method (see Section 3.3.2)

Input: $\mathbf{X}_{\mathbb{A}}$, $\mathbf{Y}$, λ, $\mathbf{W}_0$, $L_0 > 0$, M

Output: $\mathbf{W}_{M+1}$

1   $\mathbf{W}_1 = \mathbf{W}_0$, $\alpha_{-1} = 0$, $\alpha_0 = 1$, $L = L_0$;

2   **for** $j = 1 \ldots M$ **do**

3     $\beta_j = \frac{\alpha_{j-2}-1}{\alpha_{j-1}}$, $\mathbf{S}_j = \beta_j (\mathbf{W}_j - \mathbf{W}_{j-1})$;

4   **for** $L = L_{j-1}, 2L_{j-1}, 4L_{j-1}, \ldots$ **do**

5       $\mathbf{W}_{j+1} = \arg\min_{\mathbf{W}} \mathcal{M}_{\mathbf{S}_j,\lambda}(\mathbf{W})$;

6   **if** $\frac{1}{2} \|\mathbf{Y} - \mathbf{X}_{\mathbb{A}} \mathbf{W}_{j+1}\|_F^2 + \lambda \|\mathbf{W}_{j+1}\|_{2,1} \leq \mathcal{M}_{\mathbf{S}_j,\lambda}(\mathbf{W}_{j+1})$ **then**

7   **break**;

8     $L_j = L$, $\alpha_{j+1} = \frac{1+\sqrt{1+4\alpha_i^2}}{2}$;

9   **return** $\mathbf{W}_{M+1}$;

In the above equation, ρ is defined as: $\rho = \frac{\lambda}{L_j}$. The equations show that the major computational load in the second step comes from computing $\mathbf{V}$. Since $\mathbf{S}$, $\mathbf{V}$, and $\mathbf{W}$ are all of small size, once we obtain $\mathbf{V}$, we can easily obtain $\mathbf{W}$ on the master. Below, we demonstrate how to compute $\mathbf{V}$ in parallel.

To compute $\mathbf{V}$, we need to compute two components including $\mathbf{X}_{\mathbb{A}}^{\top}\mathbf{X}_{\mathbb{A}} \in \mathbb{R}^{i \times i}$ and $\mathbf{X}_{\mathbb{A}}^{\top}\mathbf{Y} \in \mathbb{R}^{i \times C}$. Assuming that $\mathbf{X}_{\mathbb{A}}$ and $\mathbf{Y}$ are both partitioned into p parts, $\mathbf{X}_{\mathbb{A},i}$, $\mathbf{Y}_i$, $i = 1, \ldots, p$, and each part is stored on a slave, the computation of $\mathbf{X}_{\mathbb{A}}^{\top}\mathbf{X}_{\mathbb{A}}$ and $\mathbf{X}_{\mathbb{A}}^{\top}\mathbf{Y}$ can be decomposed and done in parallel as

$$\mathbf{X}_{\mathbb{A}}^{\top}\mathbf{X}_{\mathbb{A}} = \sum_{i=1}^{p} \mathbf{X}_{\mathbb{A},i}^{\top}\mathbf{X}_{\mathbb{A},i} \tag{5.29}$$

$$\mathbf{X}_{\mathbb{A}}^{\top}\mathbf{Y} = \sum_{i=1}^{p} \mathbf{X}_{\mathbb{A},i}^{\top}\mathbf{Y}_i. \tag{5.30}$$

The decomposition suggests that we can compute $\mathbf{X}_{\mathbb{A},i}^{\top}\mathbf{X}_{\mathbb{A},i} \in \mathbb{R}^{i \times i}$ and $\mathbf{X}_{\mathbb{A},i}^{\top}\mathbf{Y}_i \in \mathbb{R}^{i \times C}$ on the i-th slave and aggregate the local results on the master (via MPI_Reduce) to obtain $\mathbf{X}_{\mathbb{A}}^{\top}\mathbf{X}_{\mathbb{A}}$ and $\mathbf{X}_{\mathbb{A}}^{\top}\mathbf{Y}$. The time complexity of computing $\mathbf{X}_{\mathbb{A}}^{\top}\mathbf{X}_{\mathbb{A}}$ and $\mathbf{X}_{\mathbb{A}}^{\top}\mathbf{Y}$ is

$$O_{CPU}\left(\left(i^2 + iC\right)\frac{n}{p} + \left(i^2 + iC\right)\log(p)\right) + O_{NET}\left(\left(i^2 + iC\right)\log(p)\right). \tag{5.31}$$

After obtaining $\mathbf{X}_{\mathbb{A}}^{\top}\mathbf{X}_{\mathbb{A}}$ and $\mathbf{X}_{\mathbb{A}}^{\top}\mathbf{Y}$, $\mathbf{V}$ can be computed on the master as

$$\mathbf{V} = \mathbf{S}_j - \frac{1}{L_j}\mathbf{X}_{\mathbb{A}}^{\top}(\mathbf{X}_{\mathbb{A}}\mathbf{S}_j - \mathbf{Y}) = \mathbf{S}_j - \frac{1}{L_j}\left(\mathbf{X}_{\mathbb{A}}^{\top}\mathbf{X}_{\mathbb{A}}\mathbf{S}_j - \mathbf{X}_{\mathbb{A}}^{\top}\mathbf{Y}\right). \tag{5.32}$$

And the corresponding time complexity is $O_{CPU}\left(i^2 C\right)$. Based on $\mathbf{V}$, we can obtain $\mathbf{W}$ using Equation (5.28), and the time complexity is $O_{CPU}(iC)$.

After obtaining $\mathbf{W}_{j+1}$, we need to check whether the current L is valid by requiring

$$\frac{1}{2}\|\mathbf{Y} - \mathbf{X}_{\mathbb{A}}\mathbf{W}_{j+1}\|_F^2 + \lambda\|\mathbf{W}_{j+1}\|_{2,1} \le \mathcal{M}_{\mathbf{S}_j,\lambda}(\mathbf{W}_{j+1}).$$

We can show that

$$\frac{1}{2}\|\mathbf{Y} - \mathbf{X}_{\mathbb{A}}\mathbf{W}_{j+1}\|_F^2 + \lambda\|\mathbf{W}_{j+1}\|_{2,1} \qquad (5.33)$$
$$= \frac{1}{2}\mathrm{Trace}\left(\mathbf{Y}^\top\mathbf{Y}\right) + \frac{1}{2}\mathrm{Trace}\left(\mathbf{W}_{j+1}^\top\mathbf{X}_{\mathbb{A}}^\top\mathbf{X}_{\mathbb{A}}\mathbf{W}_{j+1}\right)$$
$$- \mathrm{Trace}\left(\mathbf{W}_{j+1}^\top\mathbf{X}_{\mathbb{A}}^\top\mathbf{Y}\right) + \lambda\|\mathbf{W}_{j+1}\|_{2,1};$$

and

$$\mathcal{M}_{\mathbf{S}_j,\lambda}(\mathbf{W}) = \frac{1}{2}\|\mathbf{X}_{\mathbb{A}}\mathbf{S}_j - \mathbf{Y}\|_F^2 + \mathrm{Trace}\left((\mathbf{X}_{\mathbb{A}}\mathbf{S}_j - \mathbf{Y})^\top\mathbf{X}_{\mathbb{A}}(\mathbf{S}_j - \mathbf{W})\right)$$
$$+ \lambda\|\mathbf{W}_{j+1}\|_{2,1} + \frac{L_j}{2}\mathrm{Trace}\left((\mathbf{S}_j - \mathbf{W}_{j+1})^\top(\mathbf{S}_j - \mathbf{W}_{j+1})\right)$$
$$= \frac{1}{2}\mathrm{Trace}\left(\mathbf{Y}^\top\mathbf{Y}\right) + \frac{1}{2}\mathrm{Trace}\left(\mathbf{S}_j^\top\mathbf{X}_{\mathbb{A}}^\top\mathbf{X}_{\mathbb{A}}\mathbf{S}_j\right) - \mathrm{Trace}\left(\mathbf{S}_j^\top\mathbf{X}_{\mathbb{A}}^\top\mathbf{Y}\right)$$
$$+ \mathrm{Trace}\left(\mathbf{S}_j^\top\mathbf{X}_{\mathbb{A}}^\top\mathbf{X}_{\mathbb{A}}(\mathbf{S}_j - \mathbf{W})\right) - \mathrm{Trace}\left(\mathbf{Y}^\top\mathbf{X}_{\mathbb{A}}(\mathbf{S}_j - \mathbf{W})\right)$$
$$+ \lambda\|\mathbf{W}_{j+1}\|_{2,1} + \frac{L_j}{2}\mathrm{Trace}\left((\mathbf{S}_j - \mathbf{W}_{j+1})^\top(\mathbf{S}_j - \mathbf{W}_{j+1})\right).$$

The above two equations show that in the validation process, except $\mathbf{Y}^\top\mathbf{Y}$, all the computations involving $\mathbf{Y}$ and $\mathbf{X}_{\mathbb{A}}$ are in the form of $\mathbf{X}_{\mathbb{A}}^\top\mathbf{X}_{\mathbb{A}}$ or $\mathbf{X}_{\mathbb{A}}^\top\mathbf{Y}$, which have already been computed on the master in the last step. Since $\mathbf{Y}^\top\mathbf{Y}$ appear in both $\frac{1}{2}\|\mathbf{Y} - \mathbf{X}_{\mathbb{A}}\mathbf{W}_{j+1}\|_F^2 + \lambda\|\mathbf{W}_{j+1}\|_{2,1}$ and $\mathcal{M}_{\mathbf{S}_j,\lambda}(\mathbf{W})$, and can be canceled, we do not need to compute it in the validation process. The time complexity of the validation step is $O_{CPU}\left(i^2C + iC^2\right)$.

After the validation step, we need to send $\tilde{\mathbf{W}} = \mathbf{W}_{M+1}$ back to the slaves (via MPI_Bcast) for computing $\tilde{\mathbf{R}}_i$, $i = 1,\ldots,p$, which is the residue corresponding to $\tilde{\mathbf{W}}$, and will be used in the next step. Since $\tilde{\mathbf{R}}_i = \mathbf{Y}_i - \mathbf{X}_{\hat{\mathbb{A}},i}\tilde{\mathbf{W}}$, the time complexity for computing it is

$$O_{CPU}\left(iC\frac{n}{p}\right) + O_{NET}\left(iC\log(p)\right). \qquad (5.34)$$

In summary, assuming that $\frac{n}{p} \gg \log(p)$, the total time complexity of computing the optimal solution based on the current active set is

$$O_{CPU}\left(Ml_L\left(i^2 + iC\right)\frac{n}{p}\right) + O_{NET}\left(Ml_L\left(i^2 + iC\right)\log(p)\right), \qquad (5.35)$$

where M is the maximal number of iterations specified in Algorithm 8, and l_L is the averaged number of tries for searching the proper L in the validation process. The analysis shows that when i and C are small and $\frac{n}{p}$ is large, we can obtain near linear speedup in terms of p.

5.6.4 Checking the Global Optimality

Finally, we need to check whether the obtained $\tilde{\mathbf{W}}$ is globally optimal. The pseudo-code of this step is presented in Figure 5.17.

```
13   if  ∀i ∉ Â, ‖fᵢᵀR̃‖₂ ≤ λᵢ then
14   │    Aᵢ₊₁ = Â, W^[i+1] = W̃, R^[i+1] = R̃, i = i + 1;
15   else
16   │    Â = {i : ‖w̃ⁱ‖ ≠ 0} ∪ {j : ‖fⱼᵀR̃‖₂ > λⱼ};
17   │    Remove w̃ⁱ from W̃, if ‖w̃ⁱ‖ = 0, Ŵ = (W̃ᵀ, 0, . . . , 0)ᵀ.  Goto line 11;
18   end
```

FIGURE 5.17: Checking the global optimality.

In this step, we need to compute the correlation between each unselected feature $\mathbf{f}_i$ and the current residual $\tilde{\mathbf{R}}$, then check whether the correlation is larger than λ. Assuming there are features with correlations larger than λ, we want to pick the feature with the largest correlation and add it to the active set. In this process, computing $\mathbf{f}_i^\top \tilde{\mathbf{R}}$ is the most expensive part. Its computation can be decomposed and done in parallel as described in Section 5.6.1. We can show that the time complexity of this step is

$$O_{CPU}\left(C\left(m - i\right)\frac{n}{p} + C\left(m - i\right)\log\left(p\right)\right) + O_{NET}\left(C\left(m - i\right)\log\left(p\right)\right). \quad (5.36)$$

When $\frac{n}{p} \gg \log\left(p\right)$, this can be simplified to

$$O_{CPU}\left(C\left(m - i\right)\frac{n}{p}\right) + O_{NET}\left(C\left(m - i\right)\log\left(p\right)\right). \quad (5.37)$$

5.6.5 Summary

Tables 5.1 and 5.2 summarize the time complexity of the four key steps listed on page 129, and the computations that can be parallelized in these steps, respectively. In the analysis, we assume that $\frac{n}{p}, m \gg l, C, p$.

The first step is performed just once at the very beginning. The second step will be done l times, where l is the number of selected features. The third and the fourth steps will be done $l \times l_V$ times, where l_V is the averaged number of backtraces for adjusting the active set $\hat{A}$, when the solution obtained on $\hat{A}$ is not globally optimal. When these factors are considered, we can obtain the

TABLE 5.1: The time complexity of each step.

Step	Time Complexity
1	$O_{CPU}\left(mC\frac{n}{p}\right) + O_{NET}\left(mC\log(p)\right)$
2	$O_{CPU}\left(m(C+i)\frac{n}{p}\right) + O_{NET}\left(m(C+i)\log(p)\right)$
3	$O_{CPU}\left(Ml_L(i^2+iC)\frac{n}{p}\right) + O_{NET}\left(Ml_L(i^2+iC)\log(p)\right)$
4	$O_{CPU}\left(C(m-i)\frac{n}{p}\right) + O_{NET}\left(C(m-i)\log(p)\right)$

TABLE 5.2: Parallel computation involved in each step.

Step	Parallel Computation
1	$\mathbf{f}_j^\top \mathbf{Y}$
2	$\mathbf{X}_{\mathbb{A}}^\top \mathbf{X}_{\mathbb{A}}, \quad \mathbf{X}_{\mathbb{A}}^\top \mathbf{R}^{[i]}, \quad \mathbf{f}_j^\top \mathbf{R}^{[i]}, \quad \mathbf{f}_j^\top \mathbf{X}_{\mathbb{A}_i}, \quad \mathbf{f}_t^\top \mathbf{R}^{[i]}$
3	$\mathbf{X}_{\hat{\mathbb{A}}}^\top \mathbf{X}_{\hat{\mathbb{A}}}, \quad \mathbf{X}_{\hat{\mathbb{A}}}^\top \mathbf{Y}, \quad \mathbf{Y} - \mathbf{X}_{\hat{\mathbb{A}}}\tilde{\mathbf{W}}$
4	$\mathbf{f}_j^\top \tilde{\mathbf{R}}$

total time complexity of parallel MRSF as

$$O_{CPU}\left(mC\frac{n}{p} + \sum_{i=1}^{l} m(C+i)\frac{n}{p} + \sum_{i=1}^{l} Ml_L l_V (i^2+iC)\frac{n}{p}\right.$$
$$\left. + \sum_{i=1}^{l} l_V C(m-i)\frac{n}{p}\right)$$
$$= O_{CPU}\left(mC\frac{n}{p} + ml(C+l)\frac{n}{p} + Ml_L l_V l^2(l+C)\frac{n}{p} + Cl_V l(m-l)\frac{n}{p}\right)$$
$$= O_{CPU}\left(\left(ml(Cl_V + l) + Ml_L l_V l^2(l+C)\right)\frac{n}{p}\right).$$

$$O_{NET}\left(\left(mC + \sum_{i=1}^{l} m\left(C + i\right) + \sum_{i=1}^{l} Ml_L l_V \left(i^2 + iC\right)\right.\right.$$

$$\left.\left. + \sum_{i=1}^{l} l_V C \left(m - i\right)\right) \log\left(p\right)\right)$$

$$= O_{NET}\left(\left(mC + ml\left(C + l\right) + Ml_L l_V l^2 \left(l + C\right) + Cl_V l \left(m - l\right)\right) \log\left(p\right)\right)$$

$$= O_{NET}\left(\left(ml\left(Cl_V + l\right) + Ml_L l_V l^2 \left(l + C\right)\right) \log\left(p\right)\right).$$

Total time complexity

$$O_{CPU}\left(\left(ml\left(Cl_V + l\right) + Ml_L l_V l^2 \left(l + C\right)\right)\frac{n}{p}\right)$$

$$+ O_{NET}\left(\left(ml\left(Cl_V + l\right) + Ml_L l_V l^2 \left(l + C\right)\right) \log\left(p\right)\right). \quad (5.38)$$

The decription of the variables in Equation (5.38) can be found in Table 5.3.

TABLE 5.3: Description of the variables in Equation (5.38).

Variable	Description
m	number of features
n	number of samples
p	number of slaves
l	number of selected features
C	number of columns of $\mathbf{Y}$
M	number of accelerate gradient iterations
l_V	number of backtrace for adjusting $\hat{\mathbf{A}}$
l_L	number of iterations for searching L

5.7 Parallel MCSF

Presented in Section 3.5, MCSF is a multivariate spectral feature selection framework based on matrix comparison. In MCSF, we want to select a set of

k features such that the linear kernel constructed on the features is close to the given sample similarity matrix $\mathbf{S}$,

$$\min_{\mathcal{A}} \|\mathbf{S} - \mathbf{X}_{\mathcal{A}}\mathbf{X}_{\mathcal{A}}^{\top}\|, \tag{5.39}$$

$$\text{where } \mathbf{X}_{\mathcal{A}} = (\mathbf{f}_{i_1}, \dots, \mathbf{f}_{i_l}), \; i_j \in \mathcal{A}, \; j = 1, \dots, k.$$

Assuming that features have been normalized to have unit norm, we showed in Section 3.5 that MCSF needs to run k iterations to select k features. And in each iteration, it selects a feature using the criterion

$$\arg\max_{j \notin \mathbb{A}_i} \mathbf{f}_j^{\top} \mathbf{R}_i \mathbf{f}_j, \tag{5.40}$$

where $\mathbf{R}_i = \mathbf{S} - \mathbf{X}_{\mathbb{A}_i}\mathbf{X}_{\mathbb{A}_i}^{\top}$ is the residual matrix in the i-th iteration.

It turns out that for a large-scale problem, we cannot use Equation (5.40) to select features. The reason is that the residual matrix $\mathbf{R}_i$ may not be sparse. When the sample size is large, we may not be able to store it, even on the hard disk. To address this problem we can rewrite the computation specified in Equation (5.40) as

$$
\begin{aligned}
\arg\max_{j \notin \mathbb{A}_i} \mathbf{f}_j^{\top} \mathbf{R}_i \mathbf{f}_j &= \arg\max_{j \notin \mathbb{A}_i} \mathbf{f}_j^{\top} \left(\mathbf{S} - \mathbf{X}_{\mathbb{A}_i}\mathbf{X}_{\mathbb{A}_i}^{\top} \right) \mathbf{f}_j \\
&= \arg\max_{j \notin \mathbb{A}_i} \left(\mathbf{f}_j^{\top} \mathbf{S} \mathbf{f}_j - \mathbf{f}_j^{\top} \mathbf{X}_{\mathbb{A}_i}\mathbf{X}_{\mathbb{A}_i}^{\top} \mathbf{f}_j \right).
\end{aligned} \tag{5.41}
$$

In the first iteration, $\mathbb{A}_1 = \emptyset$, and we select the first feature by using the criterion

$$\arg\max_{j=1,\dots,m} \mathbf{f}_j^{\top} \mathbf{S} \mathbf{f}_j. \tag{5.42}$$

Assume that i features have been selected. Let the i-th selected feature be $\mathbf{f}^{[i]}$, and the score of the j-th feature $\mathbf{f}_j$ in the i-th iteration be $sc_i(j)$. We can show that the score of $\mathbf{f}_j$ in the $(i+1)$-th iteration is

$$
\begin{aligned}
sc_{i+1}(j) &= \mathbf{f}_j^{\top} \left(\mathbf{S} - \mathbf{X}_{\mathbb{A}_i}\mathbf{X}_{\mathbb{A}_i}^{\top} \right) \mathbf{f}_j \\
&= \mathbf{f}_j^{\top} \left(\mathbf{S} - \mathbf{X}_{\mathbb{A}_{i-1}}\mathbf{X}_{\mathbb{A}_{i-1}}^{\top} - \mathbf{f}^{[i]}\mathbf{f}^{[i]\top} \right) \mathbf{f}_j \\
&= \mathbf{f}_j^{\top} \left(\mathbf{S} - \mathbf{X}_{\mathbb{A}_{i-1}}\mathbf{X}_{\mathbb{A}_{i-1}}^{\top} \right) \mathbf{f}_j - \mathbf{f}_j^{\top} \mathbf{f}^{[i]}\mathbf{f}^{[i]\top} \mathbf{f}_j \\
&= sc_i(j) - \mathbf{f}_j^{\top} \mathbf{f}^{[i]}\mathbf{f}^{[i]\top} \mathbf{f}_j.
\end{aligned}
$$

Therefore, given $sc_i(j)$, $sc_{i+1}(j)$ can be computed as

$$sc_{i+1}(j) = sc_i(j) - \mathbf{f}_j^{\top} \mathbf{f}^{[i]}\mathbf{f}^{[i]\top} \mathbf{f}_j. \tag{5.43}$$

Equation (5.43) shows that after selecting the first feature, in each of the remaining iterations, we can update feature scores by subtracting $\mathbf{f}_j^{\top} \mathbf{f}^{[i]}\mathbf{f}^{[i]\top} \mathbf{f}_j$ from their current score. We then select the feature with the largest score, and continue with the next iteration.

As shown in Section 5.5, $\mathbf{f}_j^\top \mathbf{S} \mathbf{f}_j$ can be computed in parallel, and the time complexity is

$$O_{CPU}\left(\frac{mn^2}{p} + mn\log(p)\right) + O_{NET}\left(mn\log(p)\right). \qquad (5.44)$$

Similarly, after the first step, we can parallelize the computation of each iteration specified in Equation (5.43), which has the time complexity of

$$O_{CPU}\left(\frac{mn}{p} + m\log(p)\right) + O_{NET}\left(m\log(p)\right). \qquad (5.45)$$

Therefore, for selecting $l+1$ features, the total time complexity is

$$O_{CPU}\left((n+l)\left(\frac{mn}{p} + m\log(p)\right)\right) + O_{NET}\left((n+l)\,m\log(p)\right). \qquad (5.46)$$

The above equation shows that when $n \gg l$, the major computational load of parallel MCSF comes from the first iteration of the algorithm. Also, when $\frac{n}{p} \gg \log(p)$, and the network is fast enough, we can obtain near linear speedup as the number of computer nodes p increases.

5.8 Discussions

In this chapter, we discuss how different univariate and multivariate formulations for spectral feature selection can be implemented in a distributed computing environment. The key is to decompose the computation involved in these formulations into various summation forms over the samples. The decomposition allows us to parallelize the computation by computing local results in parallel on the computer nodes of a cluster. And the global results can be efficiently obtained by aggregating the local results. Our analysis suggests that the technique presented in this chapter can effectively improve the scalability and the efficiency of spectral feature selection algorithms. In most cases, the technique provides a near linear speedup, as the number of computer nodes used for computation increases.

When we face the small sample problem, if the number of features is larger, we will not have enough information to reliably estimate the relevance of features. The small sample problem is a very challenging problem in feature selection [143, 93, 42, 41, 159, 125]. Using multiple knowledge sources available for feature selection provides a promising way of handling this problem. In the next chapter, we study how to use multiple knowledge sources in spectral feature selection to achieve multi-source feature selection.

Chapter 6

Multi-Source Spectral Feature Selection

One challenging problem in many feature selection applications is the small-sample problem [143, 93, 42, 41, 159, 125], where the dimensionality of data is extremely high, while the sample size is very small. For instance, a typical cDNA microarray data [88]) used in modern genetic analysis usually contains more than 30,000 features (the oligonucleotide probes), but the sample size is often less than 100. With so few samples, many irrelevant features can easily gain their statistical relevance due to randomness [159]. With a data set of this kind, most existing feature selection algorithms become unreliable by selecting many irrelevant features. For example, in cancer study based on cDNA microarray, researchers found that traditional feature selection algorithms offer limited or inaccurate selection of biological features [118, 159]. Fold change[1] is a popular method used in gene selection.

To study its actual performance when sample size is small, we obtain a microarray data set from Gene Expression Omnibus (GEO) [11] with the reference id GSE2403. We randomly partition samples into positive and negative groups with 10 samples in each group. We then apply the fold change measurement on the split sample to identify significantly regulated genes. We repeat this process 10 times, and the number of significantly regulated genes identified each time is shown in Figure 6.1. On average, we identify 12.7 significantly regulated genes on each random split. We also apply the t-test [123] on the original split,[2] and identify 16 significantly regulated genes, which is only a little bit larger than the average number obtained on the random splits. This example shows that when sample size is small (20), and the number of features is very large (11,362), many features can be identified as significant on an arbitrary split of the samples. This implies that on the original split, some

---

[1]The ratio between the positive sample mean, μ_+, and the negative sample mean, μ_-, of the expression of a gene. When $\mu_+ \leq \mu_-$, the ratio is computed as: μ_+/μ_- and the gene is called up-regulated. Otherwise, it is computed as μ_-/μ_+ and the gene is called down-regulated. To improve reliability, we usually apply the t-test [123] to verify whether the positive and the negative sample means are statistically different. When the p-value computed from the t-test is small enough, e.g., ≤ 0.05, and the fold change is large enough, e.g., ≥ 2, we say the gene is significantly regulated.

[2]The data are split into the positive and the negative sample sets using the class label information.

of the significant features identified by fold change may gain their statistical significance by sheer randomness.

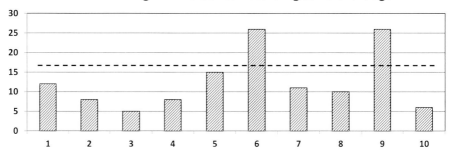

FIGURE 6.1: Significantly regulated genes identified by fold change when samples are randomly split into positive and negative groups. The dash line stands for the number of significantly regulated genes identified using the original split.

To improve the reliability of statistical analysis, we need to increase sample size. However, in many real applications, it is impossible for us to increase the size considerably, since the process of acquiring additional samples can be very costly. One way to address this problem is to include additional information sources to enhance our understanding of the data in hand. For instance, the recent developments in bioinformatics have made various knowledge sources available, including the KEGG pathway repository [87], the Gene Ontology database [25] and the NCI Gene-Cancer database [151], etc. Recent work has also revealed the existence of a class of small noncoding RNA (ribonucleic acid) species known as microRNAs, which are surprisingly informative for identifying cancerous tissues [118]. The availability of these various knowledge sources presents unprecedented opportunities to advance research by solving previously unsolvable problems. However, most feature selection algorithms are designed to handle learning tasks with a single data source, and cannot benefit from any additional knowledge sources.

To address this limitation, in this chapter, we discuss novel multi-source feature selection algorithms for integrating different types of knowledge in the feature selection process. In different domains, the relationships among knowledge sources can be very different. To facilitate our study, we focus on genetic analysis based on microarray data. We show that using different types of knowledge such as gene annotation and biological network can improve the reliability of gene relevance estimation. In genetic analysis, different types of knowledge describe genes or samples from different perspectives and have heterogenous representations. One major challenge in multi-source feature selection is how to address the heterogeneity in different types of knowledge sources. In the following, we first categorize different types of knowledge that can be used in multi-source feature selection, which helps us identify the common characters of the knowledge from the same category, to facilitate us in handling the heterogeneity of knowledge representations. We then describe two multi-source feature selection algorithms. One is based on the combination of similarity matrices, and the other on rank aggregation. Both algorithms can effectively integrate multiple knowledge sources with heterogeneous representations.

6.1 Categorization of Different Types of Knowledge

In order to handle different types of knowledge properly in multi-source feature selection, we first study how to categorize different types of knowledge for feature selection. To facilitate analysis, we fix our domain in genetic analysis, where genes correspond to features.

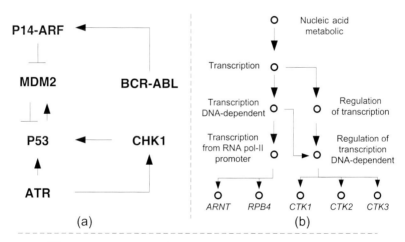

FIGURE 6.2: Knowledge of genes (features): (a) metabolic pathway, (b) gene ontology annotation, and (c) gene sequence.

Categorically, there are two types of knowledge: knowledge about features, and knowledge about samples. The knowledge about features usually contains information about the properties of features and their relationships. Figure 6.2 presents three different types of knowledge about features (genes) that can be used in genetic analysis: (a) metabolic pathway, which depicts a series of biochemical reactions occurring in cells and reflects how genes interact with one another to accomplish a specific function; (b) gene ontology (GO) annotation [25], which uses a controlled vocabulary to describe the characteristics of genes; and (c) gene sequence, which describes the order of the nucleotide bases of genes. The figure shows that the three types of knowledge have heterogenous representations. The nature of the knowledge determines how it can be used in feature selection. According to the way knowledge is used in feature selection, we further divide different types of knowledge into three categories:

1. Knowledge about feature similarity: $\mathcal{K}_{SIM}^{FEA}$.

   For instance, with gene sequence information, gene similarities can be obtained by applying a sequence alignment algorithm.

2. Knowledge of feature functions: $\mathcal{K}_{FUN}^{FEA}$.

   For instance, in a metabolic pathway, a set of genes act together to accomplish a biological function. The functions of genes are also provided in gene ontology annotation.

3. Knowledge of feature interaction: $\mathcal{K}_{INT}^{FEA}$.

   For instance, in the BioGRID [169], over 198K genetic interactions related to different types of biological processes are recorded.

The knowledge of features is accumulated and cross-examined by human researchers via multiple independent experiments. Therefore, it is relatively reliable, and independent of any specific experiment.

The knowledge of samples is usually about sample categories, $\mathcal{K}_{CAT}^{SAM}$, or their similarity, $\mathcal{K}_{SIM}^{SAM}$. Samples can be categorized by either a flat structure, as shown in Figure 6.3(a), which forms the standard class label, or a hierarchical structure, as shown in Figure 6.3(b). The similarity among samples, depicted by the pairwise sample similarity matrix, can be derived from a given auxiliary data set. Auxiliary data refers to the data containing additional information of the same set of samples in the target data. The target and the auxiliary data depict the same set of samples, while using different measurements. Auxiliary data may help us get a better understanding of the geometric pattern of the samples. For example, as shown in Figure 6.3(c), for gene selection, the microRNA microarray can serve as auxiliary data, which measure the microRNA expression of samples. cDNA microarray (messenger-RNA microarray) and microRNA microarray are collected from the same set of samples. Compared with cDNA microarray, microRNA microarray contains the expression of only several hundred microRNA and is found to be surprisingly informative in separating tissues of cancer from noncancer, as well as tissues of different types of cancers [78]. Using microRNA microarray as auxiliary data helps improve our understanding about how cancerous samples cluster together. Compared with knowledge about features, knowledge about samples is obtained from an individual experiment. Therefore, it is more specific.

Table 6.1 summarizes different categories of knowledge that can be used for feature selection in genetic analysis. Some types of knowledge may fall

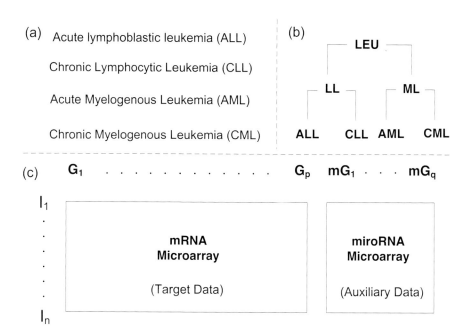

FIGURE 6.3: Knowledge of samples: (a) the class label information, (b) a sample hierarchy, and (c) an example of the auxiliary data.

TABLE 6.1: Categories of different types of knowledge for gene selection.

Knowledge	Sample	$\mathcal{K}_{CAT}^{SAM}$ - Category	Class Label, Sample Hierarchy
		$\mathcal{K}_{SIM}^{SAM}$ - Similarity	miRNA Expression Profile, mRNA Expression Profile
	Feature	$\mathcal{K}_{SIM}^{FEA}$ - Similarity	Gene Sequence, Gene Ontology Annotation, Gene Lineage, Gene Locus
		$\mathcal{K}_{FUN}^{FEA}$ - Function	Gene Ontology Annotation, Metabolic Pathway, Gene-Disease Association
		$\mathcal{K}_{INT}^{FEA}$ - Interaction	Metabolic Pathway, Protein-Protein Interaction

into more than one category. For instance, gene ontology annotation can be used for obtaining the knowledge of both gene similarities and gene functions: gene similarities can be obtained by comparing the annotation terms shared among genes; and knowledge of gene function can be identified by checking the annotation terms related to gene functions. Different types of knowledge describe features or samples from different perspectives. The categorization of different types of knowledge helps us identify their common characters and allows us to develop common approaches to analyze the knowledge from the same category.

6.2   A Framework Based on Combining Similarity Matrices

Given multiple knowledge sources carrying information about features and samples, we need to exploit them effectively in feature selection. The heterogeneity of knowledge representations necessitates a common way to represent knowledge that meets the following requirements: (1) information can be easily extracted for both features and samples; (2) information can be combined for integration; and (3) information can be effectively used for feature selection. In this section, we use the similarity among samples as the common representation. We show: (1) given relationships among features, we can obtain the similarity among samples; (2) upon obtaining sample similarity matrices from various knowledge sources, we can combine them to form a global sample similarity matrix; and (3) using the obtained global sample similarity matrix we can select features using spectral feature selection algorithms.

The high level idea of this multi-source feature selection approach is shown in Figure 6.4 as three steps:

(1) Knowledge Conversion — knowledge understandable for human beings may not be directly applicable in a learning model. Therefore, the first step is to extract knowledge for learning. Assume we have L different knowledge sources $\mathcal{K}_1, \ldots, \mathcal{K}_L$. For the i-th knowledge source, we can apply a conversion operator $c_i(\cdot)$ to extract a local specification of the sample similarity matrix, $\mathbf{S}_i$. This allows us to formalize the knowledge conversion step as

$$\mathbf{S}_i = c_i(\mathcal{K}_i), \ i = 1, \ldots, L. \tag{6.1}$$

(2) Knowledge Integration — Given multiple local sample similarity matrices, we can obtain a global similarity matrix by linearly combining local similarity matrices [228],

$$\mathbf{S}_{global} = \sum_{i=1}^{L} a_i \mathbf{S}_i, \tag{6.2}$$

where α_i is the combination coefficient, which can be assigned by domain

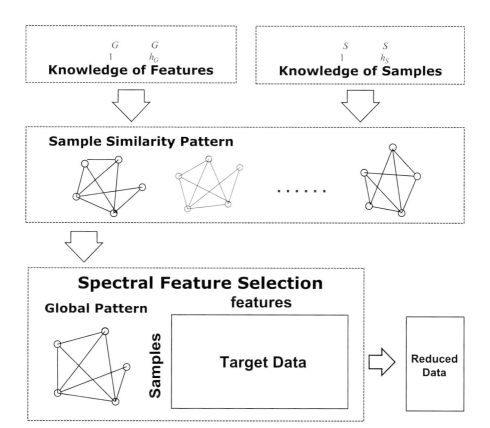

FIGURE 6.4: The framework of multi-source spectral feature selection.

experts according to their domain knowledge [228]. If the label information is available, α_i can also be learned automatically via convex optimization, which is related to kernel learning. The study of kernel learning goes beyond the scope of this book, and we refer readers to the literature for a comprehensive introduction [99, 206].

(3) Feature Selection — after the $\mathbf{S}_{global}$ is obtained, it can be used in a spectral feature selection algorithm for feature selection. Since $\mathbf{S}_{global}$ is constructed using multiple knowledge sources, the feature selection conducted in this step forms a type of multi-source feature selection.

Since Step 1 is source-dependent, we discuss next how to define the conversion operators $c(\cdot)$ to extract local sample similarity from different knowledge sources with heterogeneous representations.

6.2.1 Knowledge Conversion

The conversion from $\mathcal{K}_{CAT}^{SAM}$ (the knowledge of sample category, e.g., class label) to $\mathcal{K}_{SIM}^{SAM}$ (the knowledge of sample similarity, e.g., sample similarity matrix), $\mathcal{K}_{CAT}^{SAM} \rightarrow \mathcal{K}_{SIM}^{SAM}$, is straightforward. For example, given the class label $\mathbf{y}$, we can use the following equation to obtain the sample similarity matrix $\mathbf{S}$:

$$\mathbf{S}_{ij}^{FIS} = \left\{ \begin{array}{ll} \frac{1}{n_l}, & y_i = y_j = l \\ 0, & otherwise \end{array} \right. .$$

As we show in Chapter 4, by applying $\mathbf{S}_{ij}^{FIS}$ in the spectral feature selection framework SPEC, we obtain the Fisher score feature selection algorithm. Below, we discuss how to perform conversions from other knowledge sources to the knowledge of sample similarity:

- $\mathcal{K}_{SIM}^{FEA}$, knowledge of feature similarity
  - $\rightarrow \mathcal{K}_{SIM}^{SAM}$, knowledge of sample similarity.

- $\mathcal{K}_{FUN}^{FEA}$, knowledge of feature function
  - $\rightarrow \mathcal{K}_{SIM}^{SAM}$, knowledge of sample similarity.

- $\mathcal{K}_{INT}^{FEA}$, knowledge of feature interaction
  - $\rightarrow \mathcal{K}_{SIM}^{SAM}$, knowledge of sample similarity.

Figure 6.5 illustrates how to convert $\mathcal{K}_{SIM}^{FEA}$ and $\mathcal{K}_{FUN}^{FEA}$ to $\mathcal{K}_{SIM}^{SAM}$. The idea is to use $\mathcal{K}_{SIM}^{FEA}$ and $\mathcal{K}_{FUN}^{FEA}$ to influence the computation of the pairwise sample similarity. When $\mathcal{K}_{SIM}^{FEA}$ is given, we can use it to compute the feature covariance, which then can be used in Mahalanobis distance [122] to derive the pairwised sample similarity. When $\mathcal{K}_{FUN}^{FEA}$ is given, we can use it to filter the data, and then compute the pairwised sample similarity using the filtered data. Below we show how to convert $\mathcal{K}_{SIM}^{FEA}$, $\mathcal{K}_{FUN}^{FEA}$, and $\mathcal{K}_{INT}^{FEA}$ to $\mathcal{K}_{SIM}^{SAM}$ in detail.

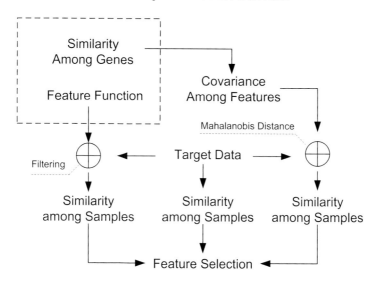

FIGURE 6.5: Converting $\mathcal{K}_{SIM}^{FEA}$ and $\mathcal{K}_{FUN}^{FEA}$ to $\mathcal{K}_{SIM}^{SAM}$.

6.2.1.1 $\quad \mathcal{K}_{SIM}^{FEA} \to \mathcal{K}_{SIM}^{SAM}$

Given similarities among features, feature covariance can be constructed and used in calculating the pairwise sample similarity via Mahalanobis distance [122] as

$$\|\mathbf{x} - \mathbf{y}\|_M^2 = (\mathbf{x} - \mathbf{y})^T \mathbf{C}^{-1} (\mathbf{x} - \mathbf{y}), \tag{6.3}$$

where $\mathbf{x}, \mathbf{y} \in \mathbb{R}^m$ are two samples with m features $F_1, \ldots, F_m$, and $\mathbf{C} \in \mathbb{R}^{m \times m}$ is the covariance matrix. In comparison with the standard Euclidean distance, Mahalanobis distance provides a better way to determine the similarities among samples by considering the probability distribution of the underlying model. The ellipsoid best representing the probability distribution can be estimated from $\mathbf{C}$ [72]. In real-world applications, $\mathbf{C}$ is usually estimated using the equation

$$\mathbf{C} = \frac{1}{n-1} \sum_{k=1}^{n} (\mathbf{x}_k - \bar{\mathbf{x}})(\mathbf{x}_k - \bar{\mathbf{x}})^\top, \tag{6.4}$$

where $\mathbf{x}_1, \ldots, \mathbf{x}_n$ are the n samples of the data, and $\bar{\mathbf{x}}$ is their mean. Let $\mathbf{I} - \frac{1}{n}\mathbf{1}\mathbf{1}^\top$ be the projection matrix [59] that centralizes the data to have zero mean. It has the properties

$$\left(\mathbf{x}_1 - \bar{\mathbf{x}}, \ldots, \mathbf{x}_n - \bar{\mathbf{x}}\right) = \mathbf{X}\left(\mathbf{I} - \frac{1}{n}\mathbf{1}\mathbf{1}^\top\right), \tag{6.5}$$

$$\left(\mathbf{I} - \frac{1}{n}\mathbf{1}\mathbf{1}^\top\right)^\top = \left(\mathbf{I} - \frac{1}{n}\mathbf{1}\mathbf{1}^\top\right), \tag{6.6}$$

$$\left(\mathbf{I} - \frac{1}{n}\mathbf{1}\mathbf{1}^\top\right)\left(\mathbf{I} - \frac{1}{n}\mathbf{1}\mathbf{1}^\top\right) = \left(\mathbf{I} - \frac{1}{n}\mathbf{1}\mathbf{1}^\top\right). \tag{6.7}$$

Hence, we can also write Equation (6.4) in the form

$$\mathbf{C} = \frac{1}{n-1}\mathbf{X}\left(\mathbf{I} - \frac{1}{n}\mathbf{1}\mathbf{1}^\top\right)\mathbf{X}^\top. \tag{6.8}$$

Although Equation (6.4) specifies an unbiased estimator of the covariance matrix, when sample size is small, its estimation can be poor [97]. In addition, the covariance matrix can also be obtained from our knowledge of feature similarities, providing another (maybe more stable and reliable) way for estimating $\mathbf{C}$. For instance, in genetic analysis, the similarities among genes (features) are usually specified by: graphs (or kernels), e.g., biological pathway and protein-protein interaction; or they can be derived from gene descriptions, e.g., gene annotation [25]. The similarities among features are usually described by a similarity matrix of *features*, $\mathbf{S}_{FEA}$. And $\mathbf{S}_{FEA,(i,j)}$ presents the similarity between features $\mathbf{f}_i$ and $\mathbf{f}_j$. Given $\mathbf{S}_{FEA}$, we can calculate an embedding [14] for the features, which can be then used in Equation (6.8) to construct $\mathbf{C}$. Below we study how to compute $\mathbf{C}$ from $\mathbf{S}_{FEA}$ in detail.

Given a feature similarity matrix $\mathbf{S}_{FEA}$, we first construct a commute time embedding [188]. The commute time embedding preserves commute distance that measures the expected time that takes for a random walk to travel from one vertex to another and back [117]. It has been shown effective in preserving similarities in the embedding space. Let $\mathbf{L} = \mathbf{D} - \mathbf{S}$ and $\mathbf{L} = \mathbf{U}\boldsymbol{\Sigma}\mathbf{U}^\top$ be the SVD of L, the embedding of the features is given by $\mathbf{X}_{FEA} = (\Sigma^+)^{\frac{1}{2}} U^T$, where each column of $\mathbf{X}_{FEA}$ corresponds to a feature vector $\mathbf{f}_i$. By transposing $\mathbf{X}_{FEA}$, we obtain the explicit expression of features: $X_{EM}^W = U(\Sigma^+)^{\frac{1}{2}}$. By substituting X_{EM}^W in Equation (6.8), we can obtain the covariance matrix $\mathbf{C}$. We use the following proposition to summarize how to compute $\mathbf{C}$ from $\mathbf{S}_{FEA}$.

Proposition 1 *Given a feature similarity matrix* $\mathbf{S}$ *depicting similarity among features, using commute time embedding, the covariance matrix* $\mathbf{C}$ *is given by*

$$\mathbf{C} = \mathbf{U}\left(\boldsymbol{\Sigma}^+ - \frac{1}{l}(\boldsymbol{\Sigma}^+)^{\frac{1}{2}}\mathbf{1}\mathbf{1}^\top(\boldsymbol{\Sigma}^+)^{\frac{1}{2}}\right)\mathbf{U}^\top, \ \mathbf{L} = \mathbf{D} - \mathbf{S}, \ \mathbf{L} = \mathbf{U}\boldsymbol{\Sigma}\mathbf{U}^\top. \tag{6.9}$$

6.2.1.2 $\mathcal{K}_{FUN}^{FEA}, \mathcal{K}_{INT}^{FEA} \to \mathcal{K}_{SIM}^{SAM}$

In real-world applications, some particular feature functions or certain types of feature interactions may be of interests according to a specific research purpose. For example, in gene selection for cancer study, genes with certain types of functions or genes participating in certain types of biological processes (e.g., genetic interactions) are of special interest to biologists.

Given $\mathcal{K}_{FUN}^{FEA}$ or $\mathcal{K}_{INT}^{FEA}$, and $\mathbb{F}$, a set of feature functions, or $\mathbb{I}$, a set of feature interactions, data can be filtered by the features associated with $\mathbb{F}$, or $\mathbb{I}$:

$$\mathbf{X}_{\mathbb{F}} = \Pi_{\mathbf{F}_{\mathbb{F}}}(\mathbf{X}), \qquad \mathbf{X}_{\mathbb{I}} = \Pi_{\mathbf{F}_{\mathbb{I}}}(\mathbf{X}). \tag{6.10}$$

Here $\mathbf{F}_{\mathbb{F}}$ and $\mathbf{F}_{\mathbb{I}}$ are the features related to $\mathbb{F}$ and $\mathbb{I}$, respectively, and $\Pi(\cdot)$ is the projection operator. Using the filtered data $X_{\mathbb{F}}$ or $X_{\mathbb{I}}$, we can obtain a pairwise sample similarity matrix $\mathbf{S}$ through any similarity measure. Since all features in $\mathbf{F}_{\mathbb{F}}$ (or $\mathbf{F}_{\mathbb{I}}$) are related to the feature functions (or feature interactions) of interest, sample similarity matrix $\mathbf{S}$ should reflect the distribution under the influence of the functions (or the interactions). In case that the functions (or the interactions) are closely related to the target concept under study, the distribution will give us an insight of the target concept, and help us to select relevant features. Using features that are known to have a particular function or participate in a particular interaction as the seeds (or a initial set of selected features), we can select features that perform the same function or participate in the same interaction.

6.2.2 MSFS: The Framework

The above discussion paves the way to a framework for Multi-Source Feature Selection based on spectral feature selection: *MSFS*. The detail of the framework can be found in Algorithm 1, which consists of three major steps: (1) obtaining local sample similarity from each data source (Lines 1–3); (2) combining local sample similarity to construct a global sample similarity (Line 4); and (3) using the global sample similarity in a spectral feature selection algorithm to select features (Line 5).

Algorithm 9: *MSFS: Multi-Source Feature Selection*

Input: $\mathcal{K}_1 \ldots \mathcal{K}_L$ and X
Output: $List_F$ - the selected feature list
1 **forall the** $\mathcal{K}_i \in (\mathcal{K}_1 \ldots \mathcal{K}_L)$ **do**
2 $\quad\lfloor$ construct $\mathbf{S}_i$, the local sample similarity;
3 obtain global sample similarity $\mathbf{S}$ from $\mathbf{S}_1, \ldots, \mathbf{S}_L$;
4 feed $\mathbf{S}$ in to SPEC to select feature and form $List_F$;
5 **return** $List_F$;

6.3 A Framework Based on Rank Aggregation

One limitation of MSFS is that it replies on combining sample similarity, which restricts its flexibility in handling small-sample data. To address this limitation we propose in [226] a general approach to systematically integrate different types of knowledge for Knowledge-Oriented multi-source feature selection, named KOFS. Figure 6.6 presents the major steps in the approach.

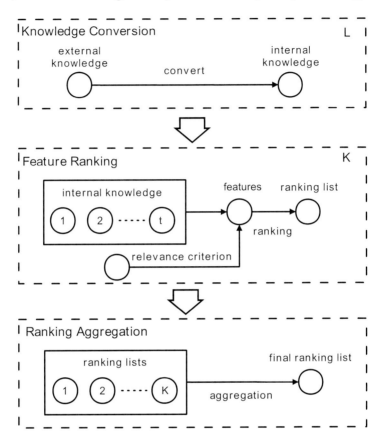

FIGURE 6.6: KOFS, a framework for knowledge-oriented multi-source feature selection.

Step 1: Knowledge conversion — Knowledge understandable for human beings may not be directly applicable in a learning model. Therefore, the first step is to convert different types of human or external knowledge to certain types of internal knowledge that can be used by gene selection algorithms. Assume we have L different external knowledge sources $\mathcal{K}_1^{ext}, \ldots, \mathcal{K}_L^{ext}$. For the ith external knowledge source, we can apply a conversion operator $c_i(\cdot)$ to convert the external knowledge $\mathcal{K}_i^{ext}$ to the corresponding internal knowledge $\mathcal{K}_i^{int}$, and this allows us to formalize knowledge conversion with the following equation:

$$\mathcal{K}_i^{int} = c_i\left(\mathcal{K}_i^{ext}\right), \ i = 1, \ldots, L. \tag{6.11}$$

Step 2: Feature ranking — Assume K sets of internal knowledge

$KNOW_1, \ldots, KNOW_K$ is used to rank features, where $KNOW_i$ is defined as $KNOW_i = \left\{ \mathcal{K}_{i_1}^{int} \ldots \mathcal{K}_{i_{t_i}}^{int} \right\}$. Let $\mathcal{C}_i$ be a relevance criterion, $\mathbb{F} = \{F_1, \ldots, F_M\}$ be a set of M features, and $\mathcal{R}_i(\cdot)$ be a feature ranking function. The task of feature ranking is to use the internal knowledge with the given criterion to rank the relevance of the features in $\mathbb{F}$. This can be formulated as

$$R_i^{rank} = \mathcal{R}(KNOW_i, \mathcal{C}_i, \mathbb{F}). \qquad (6.12)$$

Step 3: **Rank aggregation** — After obtained the K ranking lists, they need to be integrated to generate the final ranking to estimate the relevance of features. Let $\mathcal{A}(\cdot)$ be an aggregating operator for ranking lists and $\mathcal{C}$ be an aggregation criterion, we use $\mathcal{A}(\cdot)$ to aggregate the K ranking lists. This can be formulated as

$$R_F^{rank} = \mathcal{A}\left(R_1^{rank}, \ldots, R_K^{rank}, \mathcal{C}\right). \qquad (6.13)$$

The final feature ranking list can be obtained by considering the ranking lists from all internal knowledge sources in either a supervised or an unsupervised fashion, depending upon how $\mathcal{C}$ is specified.

KOFS and MSFS are different in the following ways:

1. KOFS explicitly defines the concepts of external and internal knowledge, and organizes different types of knowledge into well-defined categories, while this is not the case for MSFS.

2. In KOFS, the coefficient combination can be automatically learned, while this problem is not addressed in MSFS.

3. KOFS is based on combining ranking lists, while MSFS relies on combining sample similarity, which restricts the model flexibility.

4. MSFS forms a special case of KOFS, if we specify sample similarity, $\mathcal{K}_{SIM}^{SAM}$, as the only representation for internal knowledge in KOFS, and converge all other representations to it.

6.3.1 Handling Knowledge in KOFS

Different types of external knowledge and internal knowledge need to be handled properly in KOFS. In Section 6.1, we studied how to categorize different types of external knowledge sources. Below we define different types of the internal knowledge that can be used with KOFS. We also show how to convert different types of external knowledge to corresponding internal knowledge.

6.3.1.1 Internal Knowledge

While defining internal knowledge, the following two issues should be considered. First, the definition should ensure that certain types of external knowledge can be easily converted to its form. Second, it can be effectively used to rank features. Based on these two considerations, in KOFS, we use the following types of knowledge:

- Knowledge about samples:
  - sample category, $\mathcal{K}_{CAT}^{int,SAM}$
  - sample geometric pattern, $\mathcal{K}_{SIM}^{int,SAM}$
- Knowledge about features:
  - feature relation, $\mathcal{K}_{REL}^{int,FEA}$
  - feature function, $\mathcal{K}_{FUN}^{int,FEA}$

Here feature relation can refer to either the similarity among features or the interaction among features, since both types of knowledge provides us with the information about the relationship among the features. Later on, we will show how to propagate feature relevance on the network derived from $\mathcal{K}_{REL}^{int,FEA}$. KOFS is not restricted to the four types of internal knowledge defined above. As long as new knowledge can be used to rank features, it can be treated as a type of internal knowledge. This ensures the extendability of KOFS. In real-world applications, we found that most available external knowledge in feature selection for genetic analysis can be conveniently converted to one of the four types of internal knowledge. Next we show how to convert various types of external knowledge to internal knowledge.

6.3.1.2 Knowledge Conversion

Table 6.2 contains the information of how different types of external knowledge can be mapped to their corresponding internal knowledge.

TABLE 6.2: The conversion of different types of external knowledge to internal knowledge.

External Knowledge	Internal Knowledge
$\mathcal{K}_{SIM}^{ext,SAM}$, $\mathcal{K}_{FUN}^{ext,FEA}$, $\mathcal{K}_{SIM}^{ext,FEA}$, $\mathcal{K}_{INT}^{ext,FEA}$	$\mathcal{K}_{SIM}^{int,SAM}$
$\mathcal{K}_{SIM}^{ext,FEA}$, $\mathcal{K}_{INT}^{ext,FEA}$	$\mathcal{K}_{REL}^{int,FEA}$
$\mathcal{K}_{FUN}^{ext,FEA}$	$\mathcal{K}_{FUN}^{int,FEA}$
$\mathcal{K}_{CAT}^{ext,SAM}$	$\mathcal{K}_{CAT}^{int,SAM}$

The conversions of $\mathcal{K}_{SIM}^{ext,SAM} \to \mathcal{K}_{SIM}^{int,SAM}$, $\mathcal{K}_{CAT}^{ext,SAM} \to \mathcal{K}_{CAT}^{int,SAM}$, $\mathcal{K}_{SIM}^{ext,FEA} \to \mathcal{K}_{REL}^{int,FEA}$, $\mathcal{K}_{INT}^{ext,FEA} \to \mathcal{K}_{REL}^{int,FEA}$, and $\mathcal{K}_{FUN}^{ext,FEA} \to \mathcal{K}_{FUN}^{int,FEA}$ are straightforward. For example, $\mathcal{K}_{SIM}^{ext,FEA}$, the similarity among features, and $\mathcal{K}_{INT}^{ext,FEA}$, the interaction among features, can be directly used to construct feature relation graphs, corresponding to $\mathcal{K}_{REL}^{int,FEA}$. Also, we have studied the conversion of $\mathcal{K}_{SIM}^{ext,FEA} \rightarrow \mathcal{K}_{SIM}^{int,SAM}$ and $\mathcal{K}_{FUN}^{ext,FEA} \rightarrow \mathcal{K}_{SIM}^{int,SAM}$ in Section 6.2.1. Below, we show how to use different types of internal knowledge to rank features.

6.3.2 Ranking Using Internal Knowledge

Now that we have the various types of internal knowledge ready, we can study how to use them to rank features as well as how to combine various ranking lists to obtain a final list.

The internal knowledge can be used to rank features in various ways. Selecting features using $\mathcal{K}_{CAT}^{int,SAM}$, corresponding to traditional supervised feature selection algorithms, has been well studied. Given $\mathcal{K}_{SIM}^{int,SAM}$, features can also be ranked via spectral feature selection algorithms. Below we show how to rank features using the other two types of internal knowledge.

6.3.2.1 Relevance Propagation with $\mathcal{K}_{REL}^{int,FEA}$

Given $\mathcal{K}_{REL}^{int,FEA}$, the knowledge of feature relation, we can derive a graph $\mathbb{G}$ to depict the knowledge. Given a set of features $\mathbb{F} = \{F_1, \ldots, F_t\}$, which are known to be relevant, we can propagate their relevance on the graph to nearby nodes. Assuming $\mathcal{K}_{REL}^{int,FEA}$ is built from $\mathcal{K}_{SIM}^{ext,FEA}$, the knowledge of feature similarity, relevance propagation corresponds to the hypothesis that if a feature is relevant, the features, which are similar to it, may also be relevant. We can formulate the idea using the concept from random walk theory [117]. Assume $\mathbf{S}_F$ is the similarity matrix corresponding to $\mathbb{G}$, which is derived from $\mathcal{K}_{REL}^{int,FEA}$. The transition probability matrix is defined as

$$
\begin{aligned}
P_F &= \mathbf{D}_F^{-1}\mathbf{S}_F, \\
\mathbf{D}_F &= \text{diag}\left(d_1^F, \ldots, d_M^F\right), \\
d_i^F &= \sum_k \mathbf{S}_F(i,k).
\end{aligned}
$$

Assuming $\mathbf{r}$ is the vector containing the initial relevance of features, the final relevance of features is given by

$$
\begin{aligned}
\mathbf{r}^* &= \mathbf{r} + \ldots + (\lambda P_F)^k \mathbf{r} + \ldots + (\lambda P_F)^\infty \mathbf{r} \\
&= (\mathbf{I} - \lambda P_F)^{-1} \mathbf{r}. \quad (6.14)
\end{aligned}
$$

In the above equation, $(\lambda P_F)^k \mathbf{r}$ corresponds to the relevance gained by genes after k steps of propagation, and $0 < \lambda < 1$ is the decay parameter, which is used to reduce the magnitude of the relevance when it is propagated from one node to another node. After obtained $\mathbf{r}^*$, features can be ranked according to their corresponding value in $\mathbf{r}^*$.

6.3.2.2 Relevance Voting with $\mathcal{K}_{FUN}^{int,FEA}$

The functions of features are usually depicted by a controlled vocabulary. In this case, the terms can be regarded as the hyper features of the original features. Let F_i be the i-th feature in the feature list, its function can be obtained from $\mathcal{K}_{FUN}^{int,FEA}$, which is described by a vector $\mathbf{v}_i = (v_{i,1}, \ldots, v_{i,T})$. Here T is the total number of functions. And $v_{i,j} = 1$, if and only if the feature i is related to the function j, otherwise $v_{i,j} = 0$. Assuming we know the relevance of all the functions, which is described by a vector $\mathbf{r}^{\text{fun}} = \left(r_1^{\text{fun}}, \ldots, r_T^{\text{fun}}\right)$, the relevance of F_i can be obtained by the following equation:

$$r_i = \sum_{l=1}^{T} v_{i,\,l} \times r_l^{\text{fun}}. \tag{6.15}$$

The equation sums the relevance of all the functions related to the feature as its relevance score. $\mathbf{r}_{\text{fun}}$ can either be assigned by researchers according to their research purpose or learned automatically. In Section 6.4, we show an example on how to learn the relevance of feature functions from the data automatically.

6.3.3   Aggregating Feature Ranking Lists

Using different types of knowledge, we can obtain multiple lists that rank features in different ways. Aggregating these rankings has been studied as rank aggregation in both machine learning and information retrieval [149]. In this section, we propose a probabilistic model for rank aggregation. While existing rank aggregation algorithms treat different ranking lists equally in the combination process, e.g., the methods presented in [149], the proposed method is able to automatically learn a set of combination coefficients according to the importance of different ranking lists. This is achieved by maximizing the relevance likelihood of the features in a given feature set. When the set only contains features that are known to be relevant, the model achieves rank aggregation in a supervised way. When the set contains all features, it combines ranking lists in an unsupervised way.

Let F_i denote the i-th feature, $1 \leq i \leq M$, and its rank in ranking list l be $r_{l,i}$. We define the probability of F_i to be relevant according to its rank in the ranking list l as

$$P(r_{l,i}) = \frac{1}{B} \exp\left(\frac{1}{r_{l,i}}\right), B = \sum_{j=1}^{M} \exp\left(\frac{1}{j}\right).$$

In the equation, B is the normalization factor for the distribution. For defining the probability, the exponential function $\exp(\cdot)$ is adopted to emphasize the top ranked features. Given L ranking lists $R_1, \ldots, R_L$, let the prior probability of picking the l-th ranking list, R_l, to rank features as π_l with $\pi_1 + \ldots + \pi_L = 1$. π_l reflects the reliability of R_l. To construct a mixture model [15], for each feature F_i, we introduce an L-dimensional latent variable $\mathbf{z}_i = \{z_{i,1}, \ldots, z_{i,L}\}$ indicating which ranking list is used to rank F_i. That is, if F_i's rank is taken from its rank in R_l, then $z_{i,l} = 1$, and all other elements in $\mathbf{z}_i$ are set to

0. Based on these definitions, we can formulate the joint likelihood of the relevance of a feature set $\mathbf{G} = \{F_1, \ldots, F_K\}$ as

$$p(F_1, \ldots, F_K, Z | R_1, \cdots, R_L, \Theta) = \prod_{i=1}^{K} \prod_{l=1}^{L} \pi_l^{z_{i,l}} P(r_{l,i})^{z_{i,l}}. \qquad (6.16)$$

In Equation (6.16), Z is the set of latent variables, $Z = (z_{i,l})_{K \times L}$ $=(\mathbf{z}_1, \ldots, \mathbf{z}_K)$. $\boldsymbol{\pi} = \{\pi_1, \ldots, \pi_L\}$ can be obtained by maximizing the joint likelihood specified in Equation (6.16) with an EM algorithm.

6.3.3.1   An EM Algorithm for Computing π

Expectation maximization (EM) is a standard iterative approach for finding the maximum likelihood estimates of parameters in a probabilistic model [15]. The probabilistic model specified in Equation 6.16 can be solved by the EM approach in the following way:

E Step. Assuming that $\boldsymbol{\pi}$ is known, the posterior distribution of Z takes the form

$$P(Z | R_1, \cdots, R_L, \mathbf{G}) \propto P(Z) P(\mathbf{G} | K_1, \cdots, K_L, Z)$$

$$= \prod_{i=1}^{N} \prod_{l=1}^{L} \pi_l^{z_{i,l}} \prod_{i=1}^{N} \prod_{l=1}^{L} \mathcal{N}\left(t_i | m_{i,c}^{(l)}, \left(\sigma_{i,c}^{(l)}\right)^2\right)^{z_{i,l}}$$

$$= \prod_{i=1}^{K} \prod_{l=1}^{L} \{\pi_l P(r_{l,i})\}^{z_{i,l}}.$$

Using standard techniques, we can show that $\gamma_{i,l}$, the responsibility of L_l for F_i, is given by

$$\gamma_{i,l} = E(z_{i,l}) = \frac{\pi_l P(r_{l,i})}{\sum\limits_{j=1}^{L} \pi_j P(r_{l,i})}. \qquad (6.17)$$

$\gamma_{i,l}$ can be used to determine the expectation of the complete log likelihood, which defines the Q function [15] as

$$Q\left(\Theta, \Theta^{\text{old}}\right) = E_z\left(\ln P\left(\mathbf{G}, Z | \Theta\right)\right)$$

$$= \sum_{i=1}^{K} \sum_{l=1}^{L} \gamma_{i,l} \{\ln \pi_l + \ln P(r_{l,i})\}.$$

M Step. Assuming that Z is known, we can find the Θ by maximizing the Q function under the constraint of $\pi_1 + \ldots + \pi_L = 1$. And this leads to the equation for updating π_i as

$$\pi_l^{new} - \frac{1}{K} \sum_{i=1}^{K} \gamma_{i,l}. \qquad (6.18)$$

The algorithm is guaranteed to converge as shown in [15]. After obtained π, the probability of F_i to be relevant can be calculated by marginalizing the joint probability $P(F_i, R_l)$:

$$
\begin{aligned}
P(F_i) &= \sum_{l=1}^{L} P(F_i, R_l) = \sum_{l=1}^{L} P(F_i|R_l) P(R_l) \\
&= \sum_{l=1}^{L} P(r_{l,i}) P(R_l) = \sum_{l=1}^{L} P(r_{l,i}) \pi_l. \quad (6.19)
\end{aligned}
$$

The final feature ranking list can be obtained by ranking the obtained relevance likelihood of features.

6.4 Experimental Results

We empirically evaluate the effect of multi-source feature selection in the domain of genetic analysis. As we mentioned in Section 6.3, if we specify sample similarity, $\mathcal{K}_{SIM}^{SAM}$, as the only representation for internal knowledge in KOFS, MSFS actually forms a special case of KOFS. Therefore, the KOFS framework forms a more general case than the MSFS framework. Hence, in this section we focus on evaluating the performance of the KOFS framework for multi-source feature selection.

6.4.1 Data and Knowledge Sources

6.4.1.1 Pediatric ALL Data

The data is obtained from the Gene Expression Omnibus (GEO).[3] The data contain the expression profiling of 4,670 genes in bone marrow from 18 pediatric patients with acute lymphoblastic leukemia (ALL): 10 B-cell ALL, 5 T-cell ALL, and 3 B-cell ALL with the MLL/AF4 chromosomal rearrangement. Each bone marrow is measured twice, resulting in 36 samples. The data provide insight into the pathogenesis of childhood acute lymphoblastic leukemia.

6.4.1.2 Knowledge Sources

Five different knowledge sources are used in the experiments:

1. Sample category:

   Patients are assigned to one of the three classes, B-ALL, T-ALL, or MLL/AF4. The sample category information forms one type of $\mathcal{K}_{CAT}^{ext,SAM}$.

---

[3]http://www.ncbi.nlm.nih.gov/geo. Access ID: GSE2604.

2. Gene expression:

   The expression profiles of genes are used to obtain sample pairwise similarity with Mahalanobis distance, forming one type of $\mathcal{K}_{SIM}^{ext,FEA}$.

3. Metabolic pathway:

   The 208 Homo sapiens metabolic pathways are obtained from the KEGG pathway repository [87]. Six ALL-related pathways, including B-CELL RECEPTOR pathway and T-CELL RECEPTOR pathway are selected by the biologist. These pathways form one type of the $\mathcal{K}_{FUN}^{ext,FEA}$ (gene function), and the genes involved in these pathways are used to filter data for calculating $\mathcal{K}_{SIM}^{int,SAM}$.

4. Cancer-gene annotation:

   The cancer gene annotation data are obtained from three knowledge sources: IPA gene annotation,[4] NCI Gene-Cancer database [151], and Cancer Gene Census project.[5] The cancer gene annotation data form one type of $\mathcal{K}_{FUN}^{ext,FEA}$, which is used to construct both $\mathcal{K}_{SIM}^{int,SAM}$ and $\mathcal{K}_{FUN}^{int,FEA}$.

5. Gene ontology (GO):

   We obtain the GO annotations for genes from the Gene Ontology Database [25]. The information forms one type of $\mathcal{K}_{FUN}^{ext,FEA}$ and one type of $\mathcal{K}_{SIM}^{ext,FEA}$ (gene similarity). $\mathcal{K}_{SIM}^{ext,FEA}$ is extracted from GO annotation using an information content based measure proposed in [135]. The obtained $\mathcal{K}_{SIM}^{ext,FEA}$ is used to construct $\mathcal{K}_{SIM}^{int,SAM}$ with Mahalanobis distance and $\mathcal{K}_{REL}^{int,FEA}$ for relevance propagation.

6.4.2 Experiment Setup

By using different types of knowledge, and their combinations we can obtain eight ranking lists. Detailed information of how these lists are obtained can be found in Tables 6.3 and 6.4. Among the eight lists, SPEC (φ_2) and Fisher score correspond to using the traditional unsupervised and supervised feature selection algorithms on microarray data to select genes, respectively. The other six ranking lists correspond to using one or two types of external knowledge to select genes. The eight lists are used as baselines in the experiment for comparison. For GO-REL-VOTE and GO-CAN-MAH, the relevance of a GO term is determined by M_{can}/M_{all}, where M_{all} denotes the number of the genes associated with the term and M_{can} denotes the number of the cancer-related genes associated to the term.

---

[4]http://www.ingenuity.com/.
[5]http://www.sanger.ac.uk/genetics/CGP/Census/.

The eight ranking lists are aggregated in three ways:

1. $KOFS_{Borda}$:

   Rank aggregation with Borda count [46].

2. $KOFS_{Prob}$:

   Rank aggregation using the probabilistic model proposed in Section 6.3.3 with all genes.

3. $KOFS_{Prob-SUP}$:

   Rank aggregation using the probabilistic model proposed in Section 6.3.3 with only the acute lymphoblastic leukemia (ALL)-related genes.

The Borda count [46] is a representative rank aggregation algorithm based on majority voting. It is used as a baseline in the experiment for comparison.

6.4.3   Performance Evaluation

To evaluate the performance of different methods, we use four evaluation criteria: (1) **Accuracy**: accuracy of 1NN achieved on the top ranked genes provided by different algorithms; (2) $\textbf{Sim}_{anno}$: the similarity between selected genes and the known ALL-related genes according to GO annotation; (3) $\textbf{Hit}_{canc}$; and (4) $\textbf{HIT}_{leu}$. The last two are the counts of known cancer-related genes and ALL-related genes in the top ranked genes provided by methods.

Among the four, **Accuracy** is the standard criterion for evaluating the statistical relevance of the selected genes. For genes that are related to the biological process inducing different phenotypes, their expression patterns should be different on samples of different phenotypes. Therefore, using these genes in classification or clustering should result in high accuracy. However, due to the small sample problem in cDNA microarray analysis, genes that result in high accuracy may not be biologically relevant. The next three criteria, $\textbf{Sim}_{anno}$, $\textbf{Hit}_{canc}$, and $\textbf{HIT}_{leu}$, are designed to provide evidence of how many selected genes are biologically relevant according to literature. They form "evidence criteria" for performance evaluation. The hypothesis is that if a gene list results in high accuracy and contains many genes that are biologically relevant according to literature, it indicates that (1) the corresponding algorithm can select biologically relevant genes; and (2) other genes in the list may also be biologically relevant. Achieving high values on the three evidence criteria with low accuracy indicates that genes do not show a discriminative expression pattern with different phenotypes. Therefore, it requires high value on both accuracy and evidence criteria to confirm the biological relevance of a gene list. In the following, we compare ranking lists obtained using the traditional gene selection algorithms, using one or two types of knowledge, and using multiple types of knowledge.

TABLE 6.3: The details of how ranking lists are generated. SPEC and Fisher score correspond to traditional unsupervised and supervised gene selection algorithms based on microarray data, respectively.

Knowledge Sources	External Knw.	Internal Knw.	Ranking Criterion	Ranking Method
cDNA Expression	$\mathcal{K}_{SIM}^{ext,SAM}$	$\mathcal{K}_{SIM}^{int,SAM}$	Similarity Preserving	SPEC
Sample Category	$\mathcal{K}_{CAT}^{ext,SAM}$	$\mathcal{K}_{CAT}^{int,SAM}$	Supervised Gene Selection	Fisher score
Metabolic Pathway	$\mathcal{K}_{FUN}^{ext,FEA}$	$\mathcal{K}_{SIM}^{int,SAM}$	Similarity Preserving	Pathway-FILT
Gene Ontology	$\mathcal{K}_{FUN}^{ext,FEA}$	$\mathcal{K}_{FUN}^{int,FEA}$	Functional Relevance Voting	GO-REL-VOTE
Gene Ontology	$\mathcal{K}_{SIM}^{ext,FEA}$	$\mathcal{K}_{SIM}^{int,SAM}$	Similarity Preserving	GO-MAH
Gene Ontology, Cancer-Gene	$\mathcal{K}_{SIM}^{ext,FEA}, \mathcal{K}_{FUN}^{ext,FEA}$	$\mathcal{K}_{SIM}^{int,SAM}$	Similarity Preserving	GO-CAN-MAH
Gene Ontology, Cancer-Gene	$\mathcal{K}_{SIM}^{ext,FEA}, \mathcal{K}_{FUN}^{ext,FEA}$	$\mathcal{K}_{REL}^{int,FEA}, \mathcal{K}_{FUN}^{int,FEA}$	Relevance Propagation	GO-REL-PROP
Cancer-Gene	$\mathcal{K}_{FUN}^{ext,FEA}$	$\mathcal{K}_{SIM}^{int,SAM}$	Similarity Preserving	Leukemia-FILT

TABLE 6.4: The conversion of different types of external knowledge to internal knowledge.

Ranking Method	Knowledge Conversion
SPEC	The whole gene expression data are used to construct $\mathcal{K}_{SIM}^{ext,SAM}$ with Mahalanobis distance.
Fisher score	$\mathcal{K}_{CAT}^{ext,SAM}$, the label information, is used as $\mathcal{K}_{CAT}^{int,SAM}$ in supervised gene selection.
Pathway-FILT	Genes in the selected pathways ($\mathcal{K}_{FUN}^{ext,FEA}$) are used to filter the data, based on which $\mathcal{K}_{SIM}^{int,SAM}$ is obtained.
GO-REL-VOTE	GO terms ($\mathcal{K}_{FUN}^{ext,FEA}$) are used as $\mathcal{K}_{FUN}^{int,FEA}$, and are weighed according to their relevance for ranking genes.
GO-MAH	GO based gene similarity ($\mathcal{K}_{SIM}^{ext,FEA}$) in Mahalanobis distance to extract $\mathcal{K}_{SIM}^{int,SAM}$. See Section 6.2.1.1
GO-CAN-MAH	Similar to GO-MAH, but only cancer-related GO terms are used to calculate gene similarity ($\mathcal{K}_{SIM}^{ext,FEA}$).
GO-REL-PROP	Relevance ($\mathcal{K}_{FUN}^{int,FEA}$) is propagated on the graph ($\mathcal{K}_{REL}^{ext,FEA}$) constructed from gene similarity ($\mathcal{K}_{SIM}^{ext,FEA}$).
Leukemia-FILT	Use genes of ALL-related functions ($\mathcal{K}_{FUN}^{ext,FEA}$) to filter data. $\mathcal{K}_{SIM}^{ext,SAM}$ is obtained on the filtered data.

6.4.4   Empirical Findings

Table 6.5 contains the results obtained from methods using different types of knowledge.

First, in terms of accuracy, the gene lists obtained from the Fisher Score, $\text{KOFS}_{\text{Borda}}$, $\text{KOFS}_{\text{Prob}}$, and $\text{KOFS}_{\text{Prob-SUP}}$ achieve good performance. High accuracy indicates that the genes in these lists are statistically relevant, since they can separate samples from different phenotypes. We also notice that compared with SPEC, GO-MAH achieved higher accuracy. Both SPEC and GO-MAH use Mahalanobis distance, but GO-MAH uses the gene covariance learned from GO-based gene similarity. This suggests that the strategy proposed in Section 6.2.1 is effective.

Second, in terms of the three evidence criteria (Sim_{anno}, HIT_{canc}, and HIT_{leu}), the two methods using $\mathcal{K}_{FUN}^{int,FEA}$ (GO-REL-VOTE and GO-REL-PROP), and the two methods of KOFS ($\text{KOFS}_{\text{Prob}}$ and $\text{KOFS}_{\text{Prob-SUP}}$) achieve good performance, while the Fisher score and the other ranking methods do not perform well. This is reasonable, since in Sim_{anno}, HIT_{canc}, and HIT_{leu} we actually use $\mathcal{K}_{FUN}^{int,FEA}$ to evaluate genes. As GO-REL-VOTE and GO-REL-PROP are provided with $\mathcal{K}_{FUN}^{int,FEA}$, it is understandable that they can achieve better performance. We notice that by using only the terms related to cancer for learning gene similarity, GO-CAN-MAH achieves a better performance than GO-MAH according to the three evidence criteria. For the methods of KOFS, the two methods using the probabilistic model proposed in Section 6.3.3 achieve good performance. Compared with $\text{KOFS}_{\text{Prob}}$, $\text{KOFS}_{\text{Prob-SUP}}$ achieves better performance with the evidence criteria. This clearly suggests that the label information used in $\text{KOFS}_{\text{Prob-SUP}}$ helps. Both $\text{KOFS}_{\text{Prob}}$ and GO-REL-PROP generate gene lists that have strong support from evidence criteria. However, in terms of accuracy, GO-REL-PROP's performance is about 20% lower than that of $\text{KOFS}_{\text{Prob}}$. To intuitively observe the expression pattern of genes in each list, we apply cluster analysis on the genes selected by the two algorithms. The obtained heatmaps are presented in Figure 6.7. Results show that although many genes selected by the GO-REL-PROP are reported to be leukemia related in other studies, most of these genes do not show discriminative expression patterns on the current data. When clustering data using these genes, samples of different phenotypes are mixed up. The fact suggests that these genes may not be related to the current study. As compared with GO-REL-PROP, we observe that the genes selected by $\text{KOFS}_{\text{Prob}}$ show discriminative expression patterns and lead to good clustering performance.

Last, considering both accuracy and evidence criteria, the experiment results in Table 6.5 show that the traditional algorithms and the algorithms using just one or two types of knowledge can only achieve either high statistical relevance, or strong support for evidence criteria, but not both. Compared with these algorithms, the algorithms derived from KOFS can achieve a high performance with both types of criteria. The results clearly demonstrate the

TABLE 6.5: Performance comparison for gene ranking lists generated by different methods.

Ranking Methods	ACC-10	ACC-30	ACC-50	ACC Ave	Sim_{anno}	HIT_{canc}	HIT_{leu}
SPEC	0.64	0.66	0.83	0.71	797	2	0
Fisher score	**0.97**	**0.97**	**0.97**	**0.97**	823	8	2
Pathway-FILT	0.61	0.81	0.89	0.77	807	4	0
GO-REL-VOTE	0.56	0.69	0.83	0.70	**7686**	**26**	**8**
GO-MAH	0.69	0.80	0.86	0.78	759	3	0
GO-CAN-MAH	0.62	0.83	0.86	0.77	2996	5	1
GO-REL-PROP	0.70	0.78	0.86	0.78	**7688**	**22**	**15**
Leukemia-FILT	0.55	0.62	0.64	0.60	687	4	1
KOFS$_{Borda}$	**0.91**	**0.95**	**0.97**	**0.95**	1723	6	2
KOFS$_{Prob}$	**0.97**	**0.94**	**0.94**	**0.95**	6954	**21**	**12**
KOFS$_{Prob-SUP}$	**0.94**	**0.91**	**0.91**	**0.92**	**7766**	**25**	**17**

Note: Bold numbers indicate good performance. ACC-10, ACC-30, and ACC-50 correspond to the accuracy achieved on the top 10, 30, and 50 genes provided by different algorithms, respectively. ACC-AVE is the averaged accuracy achieved by genes using the top 10, 30, and 50 genes provided by the algorithms. Sim_{anno} is the functional similarity between selected genes and known ALL related genes according to GO annotation. Hit_{canc} and HIT_{leu} are the hit ratios of known cancer and leukemia related genes, respectively. To confirm the biological relevance of a gene list requires both high accuracy and strong supports from evidence criteria.

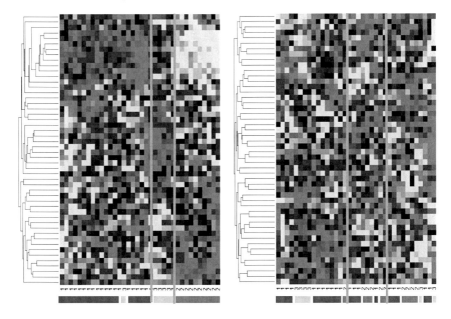

FIGURE 6.7: (**SEE COLOR INSERT**) Cluster analysis on the genes selected by $KOFS_{Prob}$ (left) and GO-REL-PROP (right), respectively. The color lines on the bottom of the figure correspond to the samples from patients of B-cell ALL (blue), T-cell ALL (red), and B-cell ALL with the MLL/AF4 chromosomal rearrangement (green), respectively.

efficacy of the proposed integrative approach for identifying biologically relevant genes.

6.4.5 Discussion of Biological Relevance

In order to more closely examine the biological relevance of the selected genes, we perform some further study, in which our biologist collaborators examine the top 50 genes selected by $KOFS_{Prob-SUP}$. The information of relevant genes is summarized in Table 6.6. The upper part of the table contains the genes whose relevance to leukemia has been confirmed by the literature. The lower part of the table contains the genes, whose relevance is unknown but cannot be ruled out. Analysis of these genes may yield the discovery of new leukemia-related genes. 17 leukemia-relevant genes are selected by $KOFS_{Prob-SUP}$. This list involves several crucial genes, such as USP33, LMO1, TIMP1, TIMP2 and STAT5B, which play important roles in the leukemia-related tumorigenesis and may lead to different subtypes of acute lymphoblastic leukemia (ALL). For instance, USP33 is reported to be consistently over-expressed in B-ALL samples but not in T-ALL samples [138]. LMO1 is mapped to an area of consistent chromosomal translocation in chromosome 11, disrupting it in T-cell ALL. The LMO1 gene family is also defined as a class of T-cell oncogenes [181]. TIMP1 and TIMP2, members of Tissue Inhibitor of Metallo-Proteinases, are found to be related to the infiltration of ALL leukemia cells into extramedullary organs [175]. STAT5B is a member of the Signal Transducers and Activator of Transcription (STAT). The dysregulation of the signaling pathways mediated by this protein may be the cause of the ALL and other human cancers [209]. Twelve genes are found to be possibly leukemia or cancer related due to the following reasons: (1) their functions are related to tumorigensis and cell cycle control (e.g., PPARA, TIMP4, and CDK4); (2) they have cAMP-dependence (PRKACA and PRKAR1A); (3) they are transcription factors (BRD8 and NCOR1), whose expressions are closely related to other known ALL genes mentioned above; (4) they are known to have high expression in leukemia (e.g., SIVA). Recent research results reveal a role of SIVA inactivation in leukemia-related tumorigenesis, presumably through enhancing NF-kappaB-mediated anti-apoptotic activity [64]. The study of these genes may help identify new biomarkers that are crucial to leukemia tumorigenesis.

6.5 Discussions

In gene selection research, various types of knowledge can be used to assist gene selection. For instance, the authors in [4] propose using different types of knowledge about genes to calculate gene similarity, which is then used to identify genes that are closest to the given example genes. In [172] the authors focus on using gene sets, which are groups of genes that share common biological functions, chromosomal locations, or regulations to interpret the gene selection outputs. In [136], gene annotation is used for choosing the optimal gene ranking criterion. In [7], protein interaction, gene-disease association, and gene function annotation are used for choosing cancer-related genes. Gene selection approaches using gene regulatory network and gene ontology are also studied in [104] and [140, 168], respectively. Since most existing work is designed for specific research purposes, they can only handle one or limited types of knowledge of the same category. For instance, the models proposed in [172, 4, 7] can only handle knowledge about genes (features), but not knowledge about samples. To address this limitation, we present an integrative approach in this chapter to systematically incorporate different types of knowledge in feature selection.

In this chapter, we investigate a novel problem arising from the need to select features on one data source given multiple additional information sources. We extend the proposed spectral feature selection frameworks to achieve multi-source feature selection based on similarity combination (MSFS), which is further extended to achieve knowledge-oriented multi-source feature se-

TABLE 6.6: The biologically relevant genes in the top 50 gene list provided by KOFS$_{\text{Prob-sup}}$. The upper part contains 17 genes which are known to be leukemia related according to literature. The lower part contains 12 genes whose biological relevance cannot be ruled out according to their biological functions or roles in pediatric ALL.

Rank	Gen Symbol	Gene Name	Related Cancers
		Genes Known to Be Leukemia Related (17)	
1	LMO1	LIM domain only 1 (rhombotin 1)	leukemia
2	CBFA2T3	core-binding factor, runt domain, α subunit 2; translocated to, 3	leukemia, breast cancer, + 2 more
4	TYROBP	TYRO protein tyrosine kinase binding protein	leukemia
5	STAT5B	signal transducer and activator of transcription 5B	leukemia, breast cancer, + 2 more
6	IGFBP3	insulin-like growth factor binding protein 3	leukemia, breast cancer, + 4 more
7	JUN	jun oncogene	leukemia, breast cancer, + 4 more
8	USP33	ubiquitin specific peptidase 33	leukemia
9	GSN	gelsolin (amyloidosis, Finnish type)	leukemia, bladder tumours
10	BTG1	B-cell translocation gene 1, anti-proliferative	leukemia, ovarian carcinomas
11	TFRC	transferrin receptor (p90, CD71)	leukemia, breast cancer, + 2 more
13	PTK2	PTK2 protein tyrosine kinase 2	leukemia, lung cancer, + 2 more
15	PDE7A	phosphodiesterase 7A	leukemia
16	TIMP1	TIMP metallopeptidase inhibitor 1	leukemia, bladder cancer, + 11 more
17	AKT1	v-akt murine thymoma viral oncogene homolog 1	leukemia, prostate cancer, + 4 more
19	FLT1	fms-related tyrosine kinase 1	leukemia, breast cancer, + 4 more
47	CEBPD	CCAAT/enhancer binding protein (C/EBP), delta	leukemia
48	TIMP2	TIMP metallopeptidase inhibitor 2	leukemia, bladder cancer, + 6 more
		Potential Leukemia-Related Genes (12)	
18	TIMP4	TIMP metallopeptidase inhibitor 4	breast cancer, glioma
23	TYK2	tyrosine kinase 2	fibrosarcoma
25	CDK4	cyclin-dependent kinase 4	retinoblastoma, melanoma, glioma
31	SERPINF2	serpin peptidase inhibitor, clade F, member 2	pituitary tumor
32	PRKACA	protein kinase, cAMP-dependent, catalytic, alpha	prostate cancer, breast cancer
34	NCOR1	nuclear receptor co-repressor 1	
36	SIVA1	SIVA1, apoptosis-inducing factor	pancreatic cancer
38	BRD8	bromodomain containing 8	
40	CAPN7	calpain 7	
43	SPATA2	spermatogenesis associated 2	
49	PRKAR1A	protein kinase, cAMP-dependent, regulatory, type I, alpha	adrenocortical cancer, myxoma,
50	PPARA	peroxisome proliferator-activated receptor alpha	colorectal cancer, bladder cancer

lection (KOFS) through rank aggregation. We design and conduct extensive experiments to objectively and systematically evaluate the KOFS framework, in comparison with existing representative single-source feature selection methods. The affirmative results demonstrate that using multiple knowledge sources can help improve feature selection of the target data. As multi-source data become more common, feature selection using multi-source data will be in high demand in many real applications.

References

[1] Jeffrey Dean and Sanjay Ghemawat, System and method for efficient large-scale data processing, January 2010.

[2] Daniel J. Abadi, Wolfgang Lindner, Samuel Madden, and Jorg Schuler. An integration framework for sensor networks and data stream management systems. In *Proceedings of the Thirtieth International Conference on Very Large Data Bases*, 2004.

[3] Jean-Marc Adamo. *Data Mining for Association Rules and Sequential Patterns: Sequential and Parallel Algorithms*. Springer, 2000.

[4] Stein Aerts, Diether Lambrechts, Sunit Maity, Peter Van Loo, Bert Coessens, Frederik De Smet, Leon-Charles Tranchevent, Bart De Moor, Peter Marynen, Bassem Hassan, Peter Carmeliet, and Yves Moreau. Gene prioritization through genomic data fusion. *Nature Biotechnology*, 24:537–545, 2006.

[5] Uri Alon. *An Introduction to Systems Biology: Design Principles of Biological Circuits*. Chapman & Hall/CRC, 2006.

[6] Annalisa Appice, Michelangelo Ceci, Simon Rawles, and Peter Flach. Redundant feature elimination for multi-class problems. In *Proceedings of the Twenty-First International Conference on Machine Learning (ICML)*, 2004.

[7] Ramon Aragues, Chris Sander, and Baldo Oliva. Predicting cancer involvement of genes from heterogeneous data. *BMC Bioinformatics*, 9:172, 2008.

[8] A. Argyriou, T. Evgeniou, and Massimiliano Pontil. Convex multi-task feature learning. *Machine Learning*, 73(3):243–272, 2008.

[9] F. Bach. Consistency of the group lasso and multiple kernel learning. *Journal of Machine Learning Research*, 9:1179–1225, 2008.

[10] Mark Baker, editor. *Cluster Computing White Paper*. http://arxiv.org, 2000.

[11] T. Barrett and R. Edgar. Gene expression omnibus: microarray data storage, submission, retrieval, and analysis. *Methods in Enzymology*, 411:352–369, 2006.

[12] A. Beck and M. Teboulle. A fast iterative shrinkage-thresholding algorithm for linear inverse problems. *SIAM Journal on Imaging Sciences*, 2:183–202, 2009.

[13] M. Belkin and P. Niyogi. Laplacian eigenmaps for dimensionality reduction and data representation. *Advances in Neural Information Processing Systems*, 15, 2003.

[14] Yoshua Bengio, Olivier Delalleau, Nicolas Le Roux, Jean-François Paiement, Pascal Vincent, and Marie Ouimet. Learning eigenfunctions links spectral embedding and kernel PCA. *Neural Computation*, 16(10):2197–2219, 2004.

[15] Christopher M. Bishop. *Pattern Recognition and Machine Learning*. Springer, 2006.

[16] P. Biswanath, Joshua S. Herbach, Sugato Basu, and Roberto J. Bayardo. Planet: Massively parallel learning of tree ensembles with mapreduce. In *35th International Conference on Very Large Data Bases (VLDB)*, 2009.

[17] Turker Biyikoglu, Josef Leydold, and Peter F. Stadler. *Laplacian Eigenvectors of Graphs*. Springer, 2007.

[18] Stephen Boyd and Lieven Vandenberghe. *Convex Optimization*. Cambridge University Press, 2004.

[19] Joseph Bradley, Aapo Kyrola, Daniel Bickson, and Carlos Guestrin. Parallel coordinate descent for L1-regularized loss minimization. In *The 28th International Conference on Machine Learning*, 2011.

[20] P. S. Bradley and O. L. Mangasarian. Feature selection via concave minimization and support vector machines. In *Proceedings of Fifteenth International Conference on Machine Learning*, pages 82–90, 1998.

[21] Martin D. Buhmann. *Radial Basis Functions: Theory and Implementations*. Cambridge University Press, 2003.

[22] C.J.C. Burges. A tutorial on support vector machines for pattern recognition. *Journal of Data Mining and Knowledge Discovery*, 2, 121–167, 1998.

[23] Stewart C Bushong. *Magnetic Resonance Imaging: Physical and Biological Principles*. Mosby, 2003.

[24] Deng Cai, Xiaofei He, and Jiawei Han. Spectral regression: A unified approach for sparse subspace learning. In *Proceedings of International Conference on Data Mining (ICDM)*, 2007.

[25] Evelyn Camon, Michele Magrane, Daniel Barrell, Vivian Lee, Emily Dimmer, John Maslen, David Binns, Nicola Harte, Rodrigo Lopez, and Rolf Apweiler. The gene ontology annotation (GOA) database: Sharing knowledge in uniprot with gene ontology. *Nucleic Acids Research*, 32:262–266, 2004.

[26] G. C. Cawley, N. L. C. Talbot, and M. Girolami. Sparse multinomial logistic regression via Bayesian l1 regularisation. In *Advances in Neural Information Processing Systems*, 2007.

[27] Chih-Chung Chang and Chih-Jen Lin. *LIBSVM: A Library for Support Vector Machines*, 2001. Software available at http://www.csie.ntu.edu.tw/ cjlin/libsvm.

[28] Edward Chang, Kaihua Zhu, Hao Wang, Hongjie Bai, Jian Li, Zhihuan Qiu, and Hang Cui. Parallelizing support vector machines on distributed computers. In *Advances in Neural Information Processing Systems 20*, pages 257–264, 2008.

[29] Kai-Wei Chang, Cho-Jui Hsieh, and Chih-Jen Lin. Coordinate descent method for large-scale l2-loss linear support vector machines. *Journal of Machine Learning Research*, 9:1369–1398, 2008.

[30] O. Chapelle, B. Schölkopf, and A. Zien, editors. *Semi-Supervised Learning*. MIT Press, 2006.

[31] Jaturon Chattratichat, John Darlington, Moustafa Ghanem, Yike Guo, Harald Huning, Martin Kohler, Janjao Sutiwaraphun, Hing Wing To, and Dan Yang. Large-scale data mining: Challenges and responses. In *The Third ACM SIGKDD International Conference of Knowledge Discovery and Data Mining (KDD)*, 1997.

[32] Cheng-Tao Chu, Sang Kyun Kim, Yi-An Lin, YuanYuan Yu, Gary Bradski, Andrew Ng, and Kunle Olukotun. Map-reduce for machine learning on multicore. In *Proceedings of Neural Information Processing Systems Conference (NIPS)*, 2007.

[33] F. Chung. *Spectral Graph Theory*. American Mathematical Society, 1997.

[34] C. Cortes and V. Vapnik. Support vector networks. *Machine Learning*, 20:273–297, 1995.

[35] T. Cox and M. Cox. *Multidimensional Scaling*. Chapman & Hall, 2001.

[36] Nello Cristianini and John Shawe-Taylor. *An Introduction to Support Vector Machines and Other Kernel-Based Learning Methods*. Cambridge University Press, 2000.

[37] M. Dash, K. Choi, P. Scheuermann, and H. Liu. Feature selection for clustering – A filter solution. In *Proceedings of International Conference on Data Mining (ICDM)*, 2002.

[38] James W. Demmel. *Applied Numerical Linear Algebra*. SIAM, 1997.

[39] I. S. Dhillon, Y. Guan, and B. Kulis. A unified view of kernel k-means, spectral clustering and graph partitioning. Technical report, Department of Computer Sciences, University of Texas at Austin, 2005.

[40] C. Ding and H. Peng. Minimum redundancy feature selection from microarray gene expression data. In *Proceedings of the Computational Systems Bioinformatics Conference (CSB '03)*, pages 523–529, 2003.

[41] E. Dougherty. Feature-selection overfitting with small-sample classifier design. *IEEE Intelligent Systems*, 20(6):64–66, November/December 2005.

[42] E. R. Dougherty. Small sample issue for microarray-based classification. *Comparative and Functional Genomics*, 2:28–34, 2001.

[43] R. Duangsoithong. Relevant and redundant feature analysis with ensemble classification. In *Proceedings of the Seventh International Conference on Advances in Pattern Recognition (ICAPR '09)*, 2009.

[44] J. Duchi and Y. Singer. Online and batch learning using forward backward splitting. *Journal of Machine Learning Research*, 10:2899–2934, 2009.

[45] R. O. Duda, P. E. Hart, and D. G. Stork. *Pattern Classification*. John Wiley & Sons, second edition, 2001.

[46] C. Dwork, R. Kumar, M. Naor, and D. R. Sivakumar. Aggregation methods for the web. In *Proceedings of the 10th International World Wide Web Conference*, 2001.

[47] Jennifer G. Dy and Carla E. Brodley. Feature selection for unsupervised learning. *Journal of Machine Learning Research*, 5:845–889, 2004.

[48] B. Efron, T. Hastie, I. Johnstone, and R. Tibshirani. Least angle regression. *Annals of Statistics*, 32:407–49, 2004.

[49] Ronen Feldman and James Sanger. *The Text Mining Handbook: Advanced Approaches in Analyzing Unstructured Data*. Cambridge University Press, 2007.

[50] F. J. Ferri, P. Pudil, M. Hatef, and J. Kittler. Comparative study of techniques for large-scale feature selection. In *Pattern Recognition in Practice IV: Multiple Paradigms, Comparative Studies and Hybrid Systems*, pages 403–413. Elsevier, 1994.

[51] R. A. Fisher. The use of multiple measurements in taxonomic problems. *Annals of Eugenics*, 7(2):179–188, 1936.

[52] George Forman. An extensive empirical study of feature selection metrics for text classification. *Journal of Machine Learning Research*, 3:1289–1305, 2003.

[53] A. Frank and A. Asuncion. UCI machine learning repository, 2010.

[54] Alex A. Freitas and Simon H. Lavington. *Mining Very Large Databases with Parallel Processing*. Springer, 1997.

[55] T. S. Furey, N. Cristianini, N. Duffy, D. W. Bednarski, M. Schummer, and D. Haussler. Support vector machine classification and validation of cancer tissue samples using microarray expression data. *Bioinformatics*, 16:906–914, 2000.

[56] Evgeniy Gabrilovich and Shaul Markovitch. Text categorization with many redundant features: Using aggressive feature selection to make SVMS competitive with c4.5. In *Proceedings of the Twenty-First International Conference on Machine Learning (ICML'04)*, 2004.

[57] Daniel J. Garcia, Lawrence O. Hall, Dmitry B. Goldgof, and Kurt Kramer. A parallel feature selection algorithm from random subsets. In *International Workshop on Parallel Data Mining in Conjunction with ECML/PKDD*, 2006.

[58] Chris Godsil and Gordon F. Royle. *Algebraic Graph Theory*. Springer, 2001.

[59] G. H. Golub and C. F. Van Loan. *Matrix Computations*. The Johns Hopkins University Press, third edition, 1996.

[60] R. Gonzalez and R. Woods. *Digital Image Processing*. Addison-Wesley, 2nd edition, 1993.

[61] Hans Peter Graf, Eric Cosatto, Leon Bottou, Igor Dourdanovic, and Vladimir Vapnik. Parallel support vector machines: The cascade SVM. In *Advances in Neural Information Processing Systems, 17*, 2005.

[62] A. Gretton, O. Bousquet, A. Smola, and B. Scholkopf. Measuring statistical dependence with Hilbert-Schmidt norms. In *Proceedings of International Conference on Algorithmic Learning Theory*, pages 63–78, 2005.

[63] W. Gropp, E. Lusk, and A. Skjellum. *Using MPI: Portable Parallel Programming with the Message-Passing Interface*. MIT Press, 1999.

[64] R. Gudi, J. Barkinge, S. Hawkins, F. Chu, S. Manicassamy, Z. Sun, J. S. Duke-Cohan, and K. V. Prasad. Siva-1 negatively regulates nf-kappab activity: Effect on t-cell receptor-mediated activation-induced cell death (aicd). *Oncogene*, 8:3458–62, 2006.

[65] Alberto Guillen, Antti Sorjamaa, Yoan Miche, Amaury Lendasse, and Ignacio Rojas. Efficient parallel feature selection for steganography problems. In *Bio-Inspired Systems: Computational and Ambient Intelligence*, volume 5517/2009, pages 1224–1231, 2009.

[66] Yike Guo and Robert Grossman, editors. *High Performance Data Mining: Scaling Algorithms, Applications, and Systems*. Springer, 2000.

[67] I. Guyon and A. Elisseeff. An introduction to variable and feature selection. *Journal of Machine Learning Research*, 3:1157–1182, 2003.

[68] I. Guyon, J. Weston, S. Barnhill, and V. Vapnik. Gene selection for cancer classification using support vector machines. *Machine Learning*, 46(1–3):389–422, 2002.

[69] M. A. Hall. Correlation Based Feature Selection for Machine Learning. PhD thesis, Department of Computer Science, University of Waikato, 1999.

[70] M.A. Hall. Correlation-based feature selection for discrete and numeric class machine learning. In *Proceedings of Seventeenth International Conference on Machine Learning (ICML-00)*. Morgan Kaufmann, 2000.

[71] J. Han and M. Kamber. *Data Mining: Concepts and Techniques*. Morgan Kaufmann, 2001.

[72] T. Hastie, R. Tibshirani, and J. Friedman. *The Elements of Statistical Learning*. Springer, 2001.

[73] Trevor Hastie, Saharon Rosset, Robert Tibshirani, and Ji Zhu. The entire regularization path for the support vector machine. *Journal of Machine Learning Research*, 5:1391–1415, 2004.

[74] X. He, D. Cai, and P. Niyogi. Laplacian score for feature selection. In Y. Weiss, B. Schölkopf, and J. Platt, editors, *Advances in Neural Information Processing Systems 18*, Cambridge, MA, 2005. MIT Press.

[75] X. He, D. Cai, S. Yan, and H. J. Zhang. Neighborhood preserving embedding. In *International Conference on Computer Vision (ICCV)*, 2005.

[76] Thibault Helleputte and Pierre Dupont. Partially supervised feature selection with regularized linear models. In *Proceedings of the 26th Annual International Conference on Machine Learning (ICML 2009)*, 2009.

[77] Leslie Hogben, editor. *Handbook of Linear Algebra*. CRC Press, 2006.

[78] J. C. Huang, T. Babak, T. W. Corson, G. Chua, S. Khan, B. L. Gallie, T. R. Hughes, B. J. Blencowe, B. J. Frey, and Q. D. Morris. Using expression profiling data to identify human microRNA targets. *Nature Methods*, 4:1045–1049, 2007.

[79] Kaizhu Huang, Irwin King, and Michael R. Lyu. Direct zero-norm optimization for feature selection. In *Proceedings of The Eighth IEEE International Conference on Data Mining*, 2008.

[80] Inaki Inza, Pedro Larranaga, Rosa Blanco, and Antonio J. Cerrolaza. Filter versus wrapper gene selection approaches in DNA microarray domains. *Artificial Intelligence in Medicine*, 31:91–103, 2004.

[81] Paul Jaccard. Étude comparative de la distribution florale dans une portion des Alpes et des Jura. *Bulletin de la Société Vaudoise des Sciences Naturelles*, 37:547–579, 1901.

[82] A. Jain and D. Zongker. Feature selection: Evaluation, application, and small sample performance. *IEEE Transaction on Pattern Analysis and Machine Intelligence*, 19(2):153–158, 1997.

[83] R. Jin and H. Liu. Robust feature construction for support vector machines. In *Proceedings of the 21th International Conference on Machine Learning (ICML-04)*, July, 2004, Bannf, Canada, 2004.

[84] T. Joachims. Text categorization with support vector machines: Learning with many relevant features. In C. Nedellec and C. Rouveirol, editors, *Proceedings of 10th European Conference on Machine Learning*, pages 137–142, Chemnitz, Germany, 1998. Springer.

[85] I. T. Jolliffe. *Principal Component Analysis*. Springer, second edition, 2002.

[86] M. Joshi, G. Karypis, and V. Kumar. Scalparc: A new scalable and efficient parallel classification algorithm for mining large datasets. In *International Parallel Processing Symposium (IPPS)*, pages 573–579, 1998.

[87] M. Kanehisa and S. Goto. Kegg: Kyoto encyclopedia of genes and genomes. *Nucleic Acids Research*, 28:27–30, 2000.

[88] Fumiaki Katagiri and Jane Glazebrook. Overview of mRNA expression profiling using DNA microarrays. *Current Protocols in Molecular Biology*, 22.4:s85, 2009.

[89] M. J. Kearns and U. V. Vazirani. *An Introduction to Computational Learning Theory*. MIT Press, 1994.

[90] K. Kira and L. A. Rendell. A practical approach to feature selection. In Sleeman and P. Edwards, editors, *Proceedings of the Ninth International Conference on Machine Learning (ICML-92)*, pages 249–256. Morgan Kaufmann, 1992.

[91] R. Kohavi and G. H. John. Wrappers for feature subset selection. *Artificial Intelligence*, 97(1–2):273–324, 1997.

[92] R. Kohavi and G. H. John. *The Wrapper Approach*, pages 33–50. In Liu and Motoda [107], 1998. Second Printing, 2001.

[93] R. Kohavi and D. Sommerfield. Feature subset selection using the wrapper method: Overfitting and dynamic search space topology. In *Proceedings: First International Conference on Knowledge Discovery & Data Mining*, pages 192–197, Montreal, Canada, 1995. Morgan Kaufmann.

[94] I. Kononenko. Estimating attributes: Analysis and extension of RELIEF. In F. Bergadano and L. De Raedt, editors, *Proceedings of the European Conference on Machine Learning, April 6–8*, pages 171–182, Catania, Italy, 1994. Springer-Verlag.

[95] M. Kowalski. Sparse regression using mixed norms. *Applied and Computational Harmonic Analysis*, 27:303–324, 2009.

[96] R. Kruse, C. L. Tondo, and B. Leung. Data structures & program design in C. Prentice Hall, 1996.

[97] Bor-Chen Kuo and D.A. Landgrebe. A covariance estimator for small sample size classification problems and its application to feature extraction. *IEEE Transactions on Geoscience and Remote Sensing*, 40:814–819, 2002.

[98] Carmen Lai, Marcel J. T. Reinders, Laura J. van't Veer, and Lodewyk F. A. Wessels. A comparison of univariate and multivariate gene selection techniques for classification of cancer datasets. *BMC Bioinformatics*, 7:235, 2006.

[99] Gert R. G. Lanckriet, Nello Cristianini, Peter Bartlett, Laurent El Ghaoui, and Michael I. Jordan. Learning the kernel matrix with semidefinite programming. *Journal of Machine Learning Research*, 5:27–72, 2004.

[100] Thomas K. Landauer, Peter W. Foltz, and Darrell Laham. An introduction to latent semantic analysis. *Discourse Processes*, 25:259–284, 1998.

[101] A. Lazarevic. The distributed boosting algorithm. In *SIGKDD Conference on Knowledge Discovery and Data Mining (KDD)*, 2001.

[102] W. Lee, S. J. Stolfo, and K. W. Mok. Adaptive intrusion detection: A data mining approach. *AI Review*, 14(6):533–567, 2000.

[103] E. Leopold and J. Kindermann Text categorization with support vector machines. How to represent texts in input space? *Machine Learning*, 46:423–444, 2002.

[104] Caiyan Li and Hongzhe Li. Network-constrained regularization and variable selection for analysis of genomic data. *Bioinformatics*, 24(9):1175–1182, May 2008.

[105] Maozhen Li and A. Baker Mark. *The Grid: Core Technologies*. Wiley, 2005.

[106] T. Li, C. Zhang, and M. Ogihara. A comparative study of feature selection and multiclass classification methods for tissue classification based on gene expression. *Bioinformatics*, 20:2429–2437, 2004.

[107] H. Liu and H. Motoda, editors. *Feature Extraction, Construction and Selection: A Data Mining Perspective*. Kluwer Academic Publishers, 1998. Second Printing, 2001.

[108] H. Liu and H. Motoda. *Feature Selection for Knowledge Discovery and Data Mining*. Kluwer Academic Publishers, 1998.

[109] H. Liu and H. Motoda, editors. *Computational Methods of Feature Selection*. Chapman & Hall/CRC Press, 2007.

[110] H. Liu and R. Setiono. Feature selection and classification: A probabilistic wrapper model. Technical report, Department of Information Systems and Computer Science National University of Singapore, 1995.

[111] H. Liu and R. Setiono. Feature selection and classification — a probabilistic wrapper approach. In T. Tanaka, S. Ohsuga, and M. Ali, editors, *Proceedings of the Ninth International Conference on Industrial and Engineering Applications of AI and ES*, pages 419–424, Fukuoka, Japan, 1996.

[112] H. Liu and R. Setiono. A probabilistic approach to feature selection — a filter solution. In L. Saitta, editor, *Proceedings of International Conference on Machine Learning (ICML-96), July 3-6, 1996*, pages 319–327, Bari, Italy, 1996. Morgan Kaufmann.

[113] H. Liu and L. Yu. Toward integrating feature selection algorithms for classification and clustering. *IEEE Transactions on Knowledge and Data Engineering*, 17:491–502, 2005.

[114] Huiqing Liu, Jinyan Li, and Limsoon Wong. A comparative study on feature selection and classification methods using gene expression profiles and proteomic patterns. *Genome Informatics*, 13:51–60, 2002.

[115] Jun Liu, Shuiwang Ji, and Jieping Ye. Multi-task feature learning via efficient L2,L-norm minimization. In *The Twenty-Fifth Conference on Uncertainty in Artificial Intelligence (UAI 2009)*, 2009.

[116] Jun Liu and Jieping Ye. Efficient L1-Lq norm regularization. Technical report, Arizona State University, 2010.

[117] L. Lovasz. Random walks on graphs: A survey. *Combinatorics, Paul Erdos is Eighty*, 2:353–397, 1993.

[118] J. Lu, G. Getz, E. A. Miska, E. Alvarez-Saavedra, J. Lamb, D. Peck, A. Sweet-Cordero, B. L. Ebert, R. H. Mak, A. Ferrando, J. R. Downing, T. Jacks, H. R. Horvitz, and T. R. Golub. MicroRNA expression profiles classify human cancers. *Nature*, 435:834–838, 2005.

[119] Bin Luo, Richard C. Wilson, and Edwin R. Hancock. Spectral embedding of graphs. *Pattern Recognition*, 36:2213–2230, 2003.

[120] Shuangge Ma. Empirical study of supervised gene screening. *BMC Bioinformatics*, 7:537, 2006.

[121] Shuangge Ma and Jian Huang. Penalized feature selection and classification in bioinformatics. *Briefings in Bioinformatics*, 9(5):392–403, Sept. 2008.

[122] P. C. Mahalanobis. On the generalized distance in statistics. *Proceedings of the National Institute of Science of India*, 12:49–55, 1936.

[123] W. Mendenhall and T. Sincich. *Statistics for Engineering and the Sciences*. Prentice Hall, fourth edition, 1995.

[124] Piet Van Mieghem. *Graph Spectra for Complex Networks*. Cambridge University Press, 2011.

[125] Carl Murie, Owen Woody, Anna Lee, and Robert Nadon. Comparison of small n statistical tests of differential expression applied to microarrays. *BMC Bioinformatics*, 10(1):45, Feb. 2009.

[126] S. Negahban, P. Ravikumar, M. Wainwright, and B. Yu. A unified framework for high-dimensional analysis of m-estimators with decomposable regularizers. In *Advances in Neural Information Processing Systems (NIPS)*, pages 1348–1356, 2009.

[127] Y. Nesterov. Gradient methods for minimizing composite objective function. In *CORE Discussion Papers*, 2007, 06. University Catholique de Louvain, Center for Operations Research and Econometrics (CORE), 2007.

[128] A. Ng, M. Jordan, and Y. Weiss. On spectral clustering: Analysis and an algorithm. In *Proceedings of 14th Advances in Neural Information Processing Systems (NIPS)*, 849–856, 2001.

[129] Andrew Y. Ng, Alice X. Zheng, and Michael I. Jordan. Link analysis, eigenvectors and stability. In *International Joint Conference on Artificial Intelligence*, 2001.

[130] Feiping Nie, Feiping Nie, Shiming Xiang, Yangqing Jia, Changshui Zhang, and Shuicheng Yan. Trace ratio criterion for feature selection. In *Proceedings of the 23rd National Conference on Artificial Intelligence (AAAI)*, 2008.

[131] Jorge Nocedal and Stephen Wright. *Numerical Optimization*. Springer, second edition, 2000.

[132] G. Obozinski, B. Taskar, and M. I. Jordan. Joint covariate selection for grouped classification. Technical report, Statistics Department, University of California at Berkeley, 2007.

[133] G. Obozinski, M. J. Wainwright, and M. I. Jordan. Highdimensional union support recovery in multivariate regression. In *Neural Information Processing Systems*, 2008.

[134] Arzucan Ozgur, Thuy Vu, Gunes Erkan, and Dragomir R. Radev. Identifying gene-disease associations using centrality on a literature mined gene-interaction network. *Bioinformatics*, 24:i277–i285, 2008.

[135] Catia Pesquita, Daniel Faria, Hugo Bastos, Antonio E. N. Ferreira, Andre O. Falcao, and Francisco M. Couto. Metrics for GO based protein semantic similarity: A systematic evaluation. *BMC Bioinformatics*, 9:S4, 2008.

[136] John H. Phan, Qiqin Yi Goen, Andrew N. Young, and May D. Wang. Improving the efficiency of biomarker identification using biological knowledge. In *Pacific Symposium on Biocomputing*, pages 427–438, 2009.

[137] Sergio Pissanetzky. *Sparse Matrix Technology*. Academic Press, 1984.

[138] C. D. Pitta, L. Tombolan, M. Campo Dell'Orto, and B. Accordi. A leukemia-enriched CDNA microarray platform identifies new transcripts with relevance to the biology of pediatric acute lymphoblastic leukemia. *Haematologica*, 90:890–898, 2005.

[139] F. Provost and U. Fayyad. A survey of methods for scaling up inductive algorithms. *Data Mining and Knowledge Discovery*, 3:131–169, 1999.

[140] Jianlong Qi and Jian Tang. Gene ontology driven feature selection from microarray gene expression data. In *Computational Intelligence and Bioinformatics and Computational Biology*, 2006.

[141] J. R. Quinlan. *C4.5: Programs for Machine Learning*. Morgan Kaufmann, 1993.

[142] Richard J. Radke. A MATLAB implementation of the implicitly restarted arnoldi method for solving large-scale eigenvalue problems. Master's thesis, Department of Computational and Applied Mathematics, Rice University, 1996.

[143] Sarunas J. Raudys and Anil K. Jain. Small sample size effects in statistical pattern recognition: Recommendations for practitioners. *IEEE Transa Pattern Anal. Mach. Intell.*, 13:252–264, 1991.

[144] V. Roth and B. Fischer. The group-lasso for generalized linear models: Uniqueness of solutions and efficient algorithms. In *International Conference on Machine Learning*, pages 848–855, 2008.

[145] S. T. Roweis and L. K. Saul. Nonlinear dimensionality reduction by locally linear embedding. *Science*, 290:2323–2326, 2000.

[146] Yvan Saeys, Thomas Abeel, and Yves Van de Peer. Robust feature selection using ensemble feature selection techniques. In *Proceedings of European Conference on Machine Learning (ECML)*, 2008.

[147] Yvan Saeys, Iaki Inza, and Pedro Larraaga. A review of feature selection techniques in bioinformatics. *Bioinformatics*, 23(19):2507–2517, Oct. 2007.

[148] L. K. Saul, K. Q. Weinberger, F. Sha, J. Ham, and D. D. Lee. *Spectral Methods for Dimensionality Reduction*, chapter 16, pages 279–293. MIT Press, 2006.

[149] Frans Schalekamp and Anke van Zuylen. Rank aggregation: Together we're strong. In *Proceedings of the Tenth Workshop on Algorithm Engineering and Experiments (ALENEX)*, 2009.

[150] B. Schölkopf and A. J. Smola. *Learning with Kernels: Support Vector Machines, Regularization, Optimization, and Beyond (Adaptive Computation and Machine Learning)*. MIT Press, 2001.

[151] Christine M.E. Schueller, Andreas Fritz, Eduardo Torres Schumann, Karsten Wenger, Kaj Albermann, George A. Komatsoulis, Peter A. Covitz, Lawrence W. Wright, and Frank Hartel. Towards a comprehensive catalog of gene-disease and gene-drug relationships in cancer. Technical report, National Cancer Institute, 2005.

[152] John P Scott. *Social Network Analysis: A Handbook*. Sage Publications, 2000.

[153] M. W. Seeger. Bayesian inference and optimal design for the sparse linear model. *Journal of Machine Learning Research*, 9:759–813, 2008.

[154] J. C. Shafer, R. Agrawal, and M. Mehta. Sprint: A scalable parallel classifier for data mining. In *International Conference on Very Large Data Bases (VLDB)*, pages 544–555, 1996.

[155] Blake Shaw and Tony Jebara. Structure preserving embedding. In *Proceedings of the 26th International Conference on Machine Learning (ICML 2009)*, 2009.

[156] J. Shi and J. Malik. Normalized cuts and image segmentation. In *IEEE Conf. Computer Vision and Pattern Recognition (CVPR)*, 1997.

[157] J. Shi and J. Malik. Normalized cuts and image segmentation. *IEEE Transactions on Pattern Analysis and Machine Intelligence*, 22(8):888–905, 2000.

[158] M. R. Sikonja and I. Kononenko. Theoretical and empirical analysis of Relief and ReliefF. *Machine Learning*, 53:23–69, 2003.

[159] C. Sima and E. R. Dougherty. What should be expected from feature selection in small-sample settings. *Bioinformatics*, 22:2430–2436, 2006.

[160] Sameer Singh, Jeremy Kubica, Scott Larsen, and Daria Sorokina. Parallel large scale feature selection for logistic regression. In *SIAM Data Mining Conference (SDM)*, 2009.

[161] Sanasam Ranbir Singh, Hema A. Murthy, and Timothy A. Gonsalves. Feature selection for text classification based on Gini coefficient of inequality. In *The Fourth Workshop on Feature Selection in Data Mining*, 2010.

[162] A. J. Smola and I. R. Kondor. Kernels and regularization on graphs. In *Proceedings of the Annual Conference on Computational Learning Theory (COLT)*, 2003.

[163] Marc Snir, Steve Otto, Steven Huss-Lederman, David Walker, and Jack Dongarra. *MPI: The Complete Reference*. MIT Press Cambridge, 1995.

[164] L. Song, A. Smola, A. Gretton, J. Bedo, and K. Borgwardt. Feature selection via dependence maximization. *Journal of Machine Learning Research*, 2007.

[165] L. Song, A. Smola, A. Gretton, K. Borgwardt, and J. Bedo. Supervised feature selection via dependence estimation. In *International Conference on Machine Learning*, 2007.

[166] M. R. Spiegel. *Theory and Problems of Probability and Statistics*. New York: McGraw-Hill, second edition, 1992.

[167] Ingo Steinwart and Andreas Christmann. *Support Vector Machines*. Springer, 2008.

[168] Shireesh Srivastava, Linxia Zhang, Rong Jin, and Christina Chan. A novel method incorporating gene ontology information for unsupervised clustering and feature selection. *PLoS ONE*, 3(12):e3860, 2008.

[169] Chris Stark, Bobby-Joe Breitkreutz, Teresa Reguly, Lorrie Boucher, Ashton Breitkreutz, and Mike Tyers. Biogrid: A general repository for interaction datasets. *Nucleic Acids Research*, 34:535–539, 2006.

[170] Elias M. Stein and Rami Shakarchi. *Fourier Analysis: An Introduction*. Princeton University Press, 2003.

[171] Petre Stoica and Randolph L. Moses. *Introduction to Spectral Analysis*. Prentice Hall, 1997.

[172] Aravind Subramanian, Pablo Tamayo, Vamsi K. Mootha, Sayan Mukherjee, Benjamin L. Ebert, Michael A. Gillette, Amanda Paulovich, Scott L. Pomeroy, Todd R. Golub, Eric S. Lander, and Jill P. Mesirov. Gene set enrichment analysis: A knowledge-based approach for interpreting genome-wide expression profiles. *Proceedings of National Academy of Sciences (PNAS)*, 102:15545–15550, 2005.

[173] Arvind Sujeeth, HyoukJoong Lee, Kevin Brown, Tiark Rompf, Hassan Chafi, Michael Wu, Anand Atreya, Martin Odersky, and Kunle Olukotun. Optiml: An implicitly parallel domain-specific language for machine learning. In *The 28th International Conference on Machine Learning*, 2011.

[174] Marc Sultan, Marcel H. Schulz, Hugues Richard, Alon Magen, Andreas Klingenhoff, Matthias Scherf, Martin Seifert, Tatjana Borodina, Aleksey Soldatov, Dmitri Parkhomchuk, Dominic Schmidt, Sean O'Keeffe, Stefan Haas, Martin Vingron, Hans Lehrach, and Marie-Laure Yaspo. A global view of gene activity and alternative splicing by deep sequencing of the human transcriptome. *Science*, 321:956–960, 2008.

[175] A. Suminoe, A. Matsuzaki, H. Hattori, Y. Koga, E. Ishii, and T. Hara. Expression of matrix metalloproteinase (mmp) and tissue inhibitor of mmp (timp) genes in blasts of infant acute lymphoblastic leukemia with organ involvement. *Leukemia Research*, 10:1437–40, 2007.

[176] Liang Sun, Shuiwang Ji, and Jieping Ye. A least squares formulation for a class of generalized eigenvalue problems in machine learning. In *Proceedings of the 26th International Conference on Machine Learning*, 2009.

[177] Y. Sun, C. F. Babbs, and E. J. Delp. A comparison of feature selection methods for the detection of breast cancers in mammograms: adaptive sequential floating search vs. genetic algorithm. *In Proceedings of the 27th International Conference of IEEE Engineering in Medicine and Biology Society*, 6:6532–6535, 2005.

[178] J.A.K. Suykens and J. Vandewalle. Least squares support vector machine classifiers. *Neural Processing Letters*, 9(3):1370–4621, 1999.

[179] Michael D. Swartz, Robert K. Yu, and Sanjay Shete. Finding factors influencing risk: Comparing Bayesian stochastic search and standard variable selection methods applied to logistic regression models of cases and controls. *Statistics Medicine*, 27(29):6158–6174, Dec. 2008.

[180] D. L. Swets and J. J. Weng. Efficient content-based image retrieval using automatic feature selection. In *IEEE International Symposium on Computer Vision*, pages 85–90, 1995.

[181] T. Boehm, L. Foreni, Y. Kaneko, M. F. Perutz, and T. H. Rabbitts. The rhombotin family of cysteine-rich lim-domain oncogenes: Distinct members are involved in t-cell translocations to human chromosomes 11p15 and 11p13. *Proceedings of National Academy of Sciences (PNAS)*, 88:4367–71, 1991.

[182] J. Tenenbaum, V. de Silva, and J. Langford. A global geometric framework for nonlinear dimensionality reduction. *Science*, 290(5500):2319–2323, 2000.

[183] L. N. Teow, H. Liu, H. T. Ng, and E. Yap. Refining the wrapper approach — smoothed error estimates for feature selection. In *Proceedings of the Nineteenth International Conference on Machine Learning*, pages 626–633, 2002.

[184] S. Tong and D. Koller. Support vector machine active learning with applications to text classification. *Machine Learning Research*, 2:45–66, 2001.

[185] P. Tseng. Convergence of block coordinate descent method for nondifferentiable minimization. *Journal of Optimization Theory and Applications*, 109:474–494, 2001.

[186] P. Tseng and S. Yun. A coordinate gradient descent method for nonsmooth separable minimization. *Mathematical Programming*, 117(1): 387–423, 2009.

[187] V.N. Vapnik. *The Nature of Statistical Learning Theory*. Springer-Verlag, 1995.

[188] U. von Luxburg. A tutorial on spectral clustering. Technical report, Max Planck Institute for Biological Cybernetics, 2007.

[189] Shinichiro Wachi, Ken Yoneda, and Reen Wu. Interactome-transcriptome analysis reveals the high centrality of genes differentially expressed in lung cancer tissues. *Bioinformatics*, 21:4205–4208, 2005.

[190] R. E. Walpole and R. H. Myers. *Probability and Statistics for Engineers and Scientists*. Macmillan, fifth edition, 1993.

[191] K. Q. Weinberger, B. D. Packer, and L. K. Saul. Nonlinear dimensionality reduction by semidefinite programming and kernel matrix factorization. In *Proceedings of the Tenth International Workshop on AI and Statistics (AISTATS-05)*, 2005.

[192] J. Weston, A. Elisseff, B. Schoelkopf, and M. Tipping. Use of the zero norm with linear models and kernel methods. *Journal of Machine Learning Research*, 3:1439–1461, 2003.

[193] Tom White. *Hadoop: The Definitive Guide*. Yahoo Press, 2010.

[194] Kristian Woodsend and Jacek Gondzio. Hybrid mpi/openmp parallel linear support vector machine training. *Journal of Machine Learning Research*, 10:1937–1953, 2009.

[195] Lin Xiao, Jun Sun, and Stephen Boyd. A duality view of spectral methods for dimensionality reduction. In *Proceedings of the 23rd International Conference on Machine Learning*, 2006.

[196] L. Xu and D. Schuurmans. Unsupervised and semi-supervised multiclass support vector machines. In *AAAI-05, The Twentieth National Conference on Artificial Intelligence*, 2005.

[197] Zenglin Xu, Rong Jin, Jieping Ye, Michael R. Lyu, and Irwin King. Discriminative semi-supervised feature selection via manifold regularization. In *IJCAI '09: Proceedings of the 21th International Joint Conference on Artificial Intelligence*, 2009.

[198] Shuicheng Yan, Dong Xu, Benyu Zhang, Hong-Jiang Zhang, Qiang Yang, and Stephen Lin. Graph embedding and extensions: A general framework for dimensionality reduction. *IEEE Transactions on Pattern Analysis and Machine Intelligence (PAMI)*, 29(1):40–51, 2007.

[199] J. Ye. Characterization of a family of algorithms for generalized discriminant analysis on undersampled problems. *Journal of Machine Learning Research*, 6:483–502, 2005.

[200] J. Ye, R. Janardan, and Q. Li. Two-dimensional linear discriminant analysis. In *NIPS*, 2004.

[201] J. Ye, R. Janardan, Q. Li, and H. Park. Feature extraction via generalized uncorrelated linear discriminant analysis. In *Proceedings of ICML*, 2004.

[202] J. Ye and T. Xiong. Null space verus orthogonal linear discriminant analysis. In *Proceedings of ICML*, 2006.

[203] J. Ye, L. Yu, and H. Liu. Sparse linear discriminant analysis. Technical Report Department of Computer Science and Engineering, Arizona State University, 2006.

[204] Jieping Ye. Least squares linear discriminant analysis. In *Proceedings of the 24th International Conference on Machine Learning (ICML'07)*, 2007.

[205] Jieping Ye, Jianhui Chen, Ravi Janardan, and Sudhir Kumar. Developmental stage annotation of drosophila gene expression pattern images via an entire solution path for LDA. *ACM Transactions on Knowledge Discovery from Data, special issue on Bioinformatics*, 2:1–21, 2007.

[206] Jieping Ye, Shuiwang Ji, and Jianhui Chen. Multi-class discriminant kernel learning via convex programming. *Journal of Machine Learning Research*, 9:719–758, 2008.

[207] Jieping Ye and Tao Xiong. Computational and theoretical analysis of null space and orthogonal linear discriminant analysis. *Journal of Machine Learning Research*, 7:1183–1204, 2006.

[208] Jieping Ye and Tao Xiong. SVM versus least squares SVM. In *The Eleventh International Conference on Artificial Intelligence and Statistics*, pages 640–647, 2007.

[209] Hua Yu and Richard Jove. The stats of cancer — New molecular targets come of age. *Nature Reviews Cancer*, 4:97–105, 2004.

[210] L. Yu and H. Liu. Efficient feature selection via analysis of relevance and redundancy. *Journal of Machine Learning Research*, 5(Oct):1205–1224, 2004.

[211] Lei Yu, Chris Ding, and Steven Loscalzo. Stable feature selection via dense feature groups. In *Proceedings of the 14th ACM SIGKDD International Conference on Knowledge Discovery and Data Mining (KDD-08)*, 2008.

[212] Lei Yu and Huan Liu. Efficient feature selection via analysis of relevance and redundancy. *Journal of Machine Learning Research*, 5:1205–1224, 2004.

[213] Guo-Xun Yuan, Kai-Wei Chang, Cho-Jui Hsieh, and Chih-Jen Lin. A comparison of optimization methods and software for large-scale L1-regularized linear classification. *Journal of Machine Learning Research*, 11:3153–3204, 2010.

[214] M. Yuan and Y. Lin. Model selection and estimation in regression with grouped variables. *Journal of the Royal Statistical Society Series B*, 68:49–67, 2006.

[215] Mohammed J. Zaki and Ching-Tien Ho, editors. *Large-Scale Parallel Data Mining*. Springer, 2000.

[216] H. Zhang, J. Ahn, X. Lin, and C. Park. Gene selection using support vector machines with non-convex penalty. *Bioinformatics*, 22:88–95, 2005.

[217] Tong Zhang and Rie Ando. Analysis of spectral kernel design based semi-supervised learning. In *Advances in Neural Information Processing Systems 18*, pages 1601–1608, 2006.

[218] P. Zhao, G. Rocha, and B. Yu. The composite absolute penalties family for grouped and hierarchical variable selection. *Annals of Statistics*, 37:3468–3497, 2009.

[219] Zheng Zhao and Huan Liu. Semi-supervised feature selection via spectral analysis. Technical Report TR-06-022, Computer Science and Engineering, Arizona State University, 2006.

[220] Zheng Zhao and Huan Liu. Searching for interacting features. In *International Joint Conference on AI (IJCAI)*, 2007.

[221] Zheng Zhao and Huan Liu. Semi-supervised feature selection via spectral analysis. In *Proceedings of SIAM International Conference on Data Mining (SDM)*, 2007.

[222] Zheng Zhao and Huan Liu. Spectral feature selection for supervised and unsupervised learning. In *International Conference on Machine Learning (ICML)*, 2007.

[223] Zheng Zhao and Huan Liu. Multi-source feature selection via geometry-dependent covariance analysis. In *Journal of Machine Learning Research, Workshop and Conference Proceedings, Volume 4: New Challenges for Feature Selection in Data Mining and Knowledge Discovery*, pages 36–47, 2008.

[224] Zheng Zhao, Jiangxin Wang, Huan Liu, and Yung Chang. Biological relevance detection via network dynamic analysis. In *Proceedings of 2nd International Conference on Bioinformatics and Computational Biology (BICoB)*, 2010.

[225] Zheng Zhao, Jiangxin Wang, Huan Liu, Jieping Ye, and Yung Chang. Identifying biologically relevant genes via multiple heterogeneous data sources. In *The Fourteenth ACM SIGKDD International Conference on Knowledge Discovery and Data Mining (SIGKDD 2008)*, 2008.

[226] Zheng Zhao, Jiangxin Wang, Shashvata Sharma, Nitin Agarwal, Huan Liu, and Yung Chang. An integrative approach to identifying biologically relevant genes. In *Proceedings of SIAM International Conference on Data Mining (SDM)*, 2010.

[227] Zheng Zhao, Lei Wang, and Huan Liu. Efficient spectral feature selection with minimum redundancy. In *Proceedings of the Twenty-Fourth AAAI Conference on Artificial Intelligence (AAAI)*, 2010.

[228] D. Zhou and C. Burges. Spectral clustering and transductive learning with multiple views. In *Proceedings of the 24th International Conference on Machine Learning*, 2007.

[229] Ji Zhu, Saharon Rosset, Trevor Hastie, and Rob Tibshirani. 1-norm support vector machines. In *Advances in Neural Information Processing Systems 16*, 2003.

[230] Hui Zou, Trevor Hastiey, and Robert Tibshirani. Sparse principal component analysis. Technical report, Department of Statistics, Stanford University, 2004.

Index

Printed and bound by CPI Group (UK) Ltd, Croydon, CR0 4YY

23/10/2024

01777708-0013